W9-BYP-303

PREACHING
THE
NEW COMMON
LECTIONARY

PREACHING
THE
NEW COMMON LECTIONARY

YEAR B

After Pentecost

Commentary by:
Fred B. Craddock
John H. Hayes
Carl R. Holladay
Gene M. Tucker

ABINGDON PRESS
Nashville

Preaching the New Common Lectionary
Year B   After Pentecost

Copyright © 1985 by Abingdon Press
Sixth Printing 1990
All rights reserved.

No part of this work may be reproduced or transmitted in any form or by any means, electronic or mechanical, including photocopying and recording, or by any information storage or retrieval system, except as may be expressly permitted by the 1976 Copyright Act or in writing from the publisher. Requests for permission should be addressed in writing to Abingdon Press, 201 Eighth Avenue South, Nashville, TN 37202.

This book is printed on acid-free paper.

Library of Congress Cataloging in Publication Data

Main entry under title:
  Preaching the new common lectionary. Year B,
  After Pentecost.
  Includes index.
  1. Bible—Homiletical use. 2. Bible—Liturgical
  lessons, English. I. Craddock, Fred B.
  BS534.5.P728   1985   251   84-20532

ISBN 0-687-33847-6

Scripture quotations unless otherwise noted are from the Revised Standard Version of the Bible, copyrighted 1946, 1952, 1971, © 1973, by the Division of Christian Education of the National Council of the Churches of Christ in the U.S.A., and used by permission.

Quotations noted NEB are from The New English Bible. © the Delegates of the Oxford University Press and the Syndics of the Cambridge University Press 1961, 1970. Reprinted by permission.

MANUFACTURED IN THE UNITED STATES OF AMERICA

Contents

---

*Propers 1, 2, and 3 are part of Epiphany.

Christ the King

Special Days

Introduction

It might be helpful to the reader if we make a few remarks about our understanding of our task and what we have sought to accomplish in this volume. The following comments will touch on four topics.

The Scripture in Preaching

There is no substitute for direct exposure to the biblical text, both for the preacher in preparation and for the listener in worship. The Scriptures are therefore not only studied privately but read aloud as an act of worship in and of itself and not solely as prelude to a sermon. The sermon is an interpretation of Scripture in the sense that the preacher seeks to bring the text forward into the present in order to effect a new hearing of the Word. In this sense the text has its future and its fulfillment in preaching. In fact, the Bible itself is the record of the continual rehearing and reinterpreting of its own traditions in new settings and for new generations of believers. New settings and new circumstances are properly as well as inescapably integral to a hearing of God's Word in and through the text. Whatever else may be said to characterize God's Word, it is always appropriate to the hearers. But the desire to be immediately relevant should not abbreviate study of the text or divorce the sermon from the biblical tradition. Such sermons are orphaned, released without memory into the world. It is the task of the preacher and teacher to see that the principle of fidelity to Scripture is not abandoned in the life and worship of the church. The endeavor to understand a text in its historical, literary, and theological contexts does create, to be sure, a sense of distance between the Bible and the congregation. The preacher may grow impatient during this period of feeling a long way from a sermon. But this time of study can be most fruitful. By holding text and parishioners apart for a while, the preacher can hear each more clearly and exegete each more honestly. Then, when the two intersect in the sermon, neither the text nor the congregation is consumed by the other. Because the Bible is an ancient book, it invites the preacher back into its world in order to understand; because the Bible is the church's Scripture, it moves forward into our world and addresses us here and now.

The Lectionary and Preaching

Ever increasing numbers of preachers are using a lectionary as a guide for preaching and worship. The intent of lectionaries is to provide for the church over a given period of time (usually three years) large units of Scripture arranged according to the seasons of the Christian year and selected because they carry the central message of the Bible. Lectionaries are not designed to limit one's message or restrict the freedom of the pulpit. On the contrary, churches that use a lectionary usually hear more Scripture in worship than those that do not. And ministers who preach from the lectionary find themselves stretched into areas of the canon into which they would not have gone had they kept to the path of personal preference. Other values of the lectionary are well known: the readings provide a common ground for discussions in ministerial peer groups; family worship can more easily join public worship through shared readings; ministers and worship committees can work with common biblical texts to prepare services that have movement and integrity; and the lectionary encourages more disciplined study and advance preparation. All these and other values are increased if the different churches share a common lectionary. A common lectionary could conceivably generate a community-wide Christian conversation.

This Book and Preaching

This volume is not designed as a substitute for work with the biblical text; on the contrary, its intent is to encourage such work. Neither is it our desire to relieve the preacher of regular visits to concordances, lexicons, and commentaries; rather it is our hope that the comments on the texts here will be sufficiently germinal to give direction and purpose to those visits to major reference works. Our commentaries are efforts to be faithful to the text and to begin moving the text toward the pulpit. There are no sermons as such here, nor could there be. No one can preach long distance. Only the one who preaches can do an exegesis of the listeners and mix into sermon preparation enough local soil so as to effect an indigenous hearing of the Word. But we hope we have contributed to that end. The reader will also notice that, while each of us has been aware of the other readings for each service, there has been no attempt to offer a collaborated commentary on all texts or a homogenized interpretation as though there were not four texts but one. We have tried to respect the integrity of each biblical passage and remain within the limits of our own areas of knowledge. It is assumed that the season of the year, the needs of the listeners, the preacher's own abilities, as well as the overall unity of the message of the Scriptures will prompt the preacher to find among the four readings the word for the day. Sometimes the four texts will join arm in arm, sometimes they will debate with one another, sometimes one will lead while the others follow, albeit at times reluctantly. Such is the wealth of the biblical witness.

A final word about our comments. The lections from the Psalter have been treated in the same manner as the other readings even though some Protestant churches often omit the reading of the Psalm or replace it with a hymn. We have chosen to regard the Psalm as an equal among the texts, primarily for three reasons. First, there is growing interest in the use of Psalms in public worship, and comments about them may help make that use more informed. Second, the Psalms were a major source for worship and preaching in the early church and they continue to inspire and inform Christian witness today. And third, comments on the Psalms may make this volume helpful to Roman Catholic preachers who have maintained the long tradition of using the Psalms in Christian services.

This Season and Preaching

Pentecost completed the liturgical year which began with Advent, the coming of the Christ into the world, and concludes with Pentecost, the coming of the Holy Spirit to the church.

The Season After Pentecost begins with Trinity Sunday, important for two reasons. First, it reminds the church to set the emphasis on the Holy Spirit at Pentecost within the inclusive doctrine of the Trinity. Second, the proclamation of the Trinity announces the tradition of faith within which the texts of this season will be explicated and heard. This season concludes with the celebration of Christ the King on the Sunday preceding the beginning of Advent.

In some traditions these Sundays between Pentecost and Advent are called "Ordinary Time." During this period there is no concerted movement toward a day of high significance or the clustering of texts with a governing focus as is the case in the seasons from Advent to Pentecost. What this means for the preacher is the opportunity to work with texts that do not possess the thematic unity that characterizes the lections for the remainder of the year. Although the readings for each Sunday are not unhappily joined, an effort has been made to provide continuity of readings from books of both Old and New Testaments. The benefits of this opportunity to develop sustained themes and to deepen one's understanding and appreciation of texts that continue for several weeks are not inconsiderable, both for the preacher and the hearer.

Fred B. Craddock (Gospels)
John H. Hayes (Psalms)
Carl R. Holladay (Epistles)
Gene M. Tucker (Old Testament)

Trinity Sunday

Isaiah 6:1-8; Psalm 29; Romans 8:12-17; John 3:1-17

Isaiah 6:1-8

The New Testament readings for Trinity Sunday continue from Pentecost the emphasis on the Spirit of God and at the same time call attention to the threefold nature of God. Psalm 29, a hymn of praise, celebrates the awesome power of the voice of God in the world; its final verses describing the Lord on his throne are linked directly to Isaiah's vision. Isaiah 6, because of the threefold Sanctus and the fact that God speaks in the first person plural ("Whom shall I send, and who will go for us?") has long been a classical Christian trinitarian text.

Our reading, Isaiah's report of his call to be a prophet, is one of the most familiar in the Old Testament. For that very reason it bears careful reading and study, lest our familiarity lead us and our congregations to miss important aspects of the account. It is a strange, startling, and dramatic sequence of events which unfolds, and stranger still if the remainder of the chapter (verses 9-13) is added to the lection.

The location of the vocation report in the Book of Isaiah is unusual. Those of Jeremiah and Ezekiel are found more logically at the very beginning of the books. Isaiah 6 is preserved with a series of other reports and accounts, mainly concerning the prophet's activities (Isa. 6:1–9:7). Moreover, the reports appear to interrupt a previously established collection of the prophet's speeches, each concluding with the expression, "For all this his anger is not turned away and his hand is stretched out still." (See 5:25; 9:12, 17; 10:4.) This collection began in 5:8 and, following the reports, is resumed in 10:1. These features of the book suggest that the material in Isaiah 6:1–9:7 probably once circulated independently among the prophet's followers before it was combined with the surrounding speeches. Thus the text before us bears the marks of various communities of faith for whom it communicated the Word of God.

The calls of prophets and of other servants of God are very private and individual matters. It is all the more remarkable, therefore, to discover that Isaiah's report of his call has a great many features in common with other Old Testament vocation reports. These include the vocation accounts of Moses (Exod. 3:1–4:17), Gideon (Judg. 6:11-24), Jeremiah (Jer. 1:4-10), and Ezekiel (Ezek. 1–3). In all cases there is a report of an encounter with God, either directly or through a messenger, a commission to do the Lord's will or speak the Lord's word, and a ritual act or sign symbolizing the designated role. In all cases except Ezekiel the one who is called objects to the vocation, and then is given reassurance. The persistence of this feature in vocation reports indicates that the resistance to the call is not linked so much to individual personalities as it is to the experience of standing in the presence of God. It is part of the office, even verifying that one is called by God, to feel unworthy in one way or another.

In its more specific features, Isaiah 6 closely parallels Ezekiel 1–3. Both are reports of visions of the Lord's heavenly throne. Similar also is the scene described by Micaiah ben Imlah in I Kings 22:19-22: "I saw the Lord sitting on his throne, and all the host of heaven standing beside him." Neither Isaiah nor Ezekiel sees God directly, but both have the sense of being on the outskirts of the heavenly throne room and hearing the deliberations going on there. This Old Testament imagery is indebted to ancient Near Eastern traditions concerning the heavenly court. In those polytheistic traditions the court includes the chief god and other deities; in the Old Testament God holds court with his messengers (see also Job 1:6-12).

Isaiah's vocation report begins with a date formula which also sets the mood. "The year that King Uzziah died" would have been about 742 B.C., but that king's death signaled the end of an era of relative independence for Judah. During most of Isaiah's lifetime the nation lived under the threat of Assyrian domination. The prophet was active for some forty years, from the date indicated here until at least 701 B.C.

But the date formula is mainly a preface to the description of the vision of Yahweh as king on a throne (verses 1-4). The fact that his "train" filled the temple indicates that the prophet stands at the entrance to the sacred precincts and that probably the ark was thought of as the symbolic throne. Other aspects of temple worship are the antiphonal hymn of praise sung by the seraphim, and the smoke, probably from offerings, which filled the "house"—that is, the temple. The seraphim which attend the Lord must cover both their "feet" (a euphemism for their nakedness) and their faces because no one can see God directly and live.

Isaiah's response to the scene is a cry of woe (verse 5), similar to a confession of sin and an expression of mourning for both himself and his people. In the presence of the Lord he knows that he is unclean, though by the priestly criteria he would have been judged ritually clean before he approached the temple. In reaction to his confession one of the seraphim performs a ritual of purification combining word and deed. He touches Isaiah's mouth with a coal from the altar and pronounces that his guilt is removed and his sin is forgiven. This ritual parallels those in the vocation reports of both Jeremiah and Ezekiel in that all of them concern the mouth of the prophetic spokesman for God.

The vision report reaches a climax when the prophet overhears the Lord asking the heavenly court whom he shall send, and the prophet steps forward (verse 8). The remainder of the chapter consists of the Lord's terrible commission to the prophet to bring a word of judgment, interrupted only by the prophet's prayer of intercession.

Viewed in the context of other vocation reports, the purpose of this account becomes clear. The authority of prophets to speak frequently was challenged (see Amos 7:10-17), especially if their message was one of judgment. Since prophets in Israel had no "official" standing comparable to that of, for example, priests, their right to speak in the name of the Lord was open to question. The vocation reports were their responses. They were not only entitled to speak but also compelled to because of their calls. In the case of

Isaiah 6, the prophet specifically justifies his harsh message by reporting his vocation.

A great many features of this passage cry out for proclamation. There is first of all the emphasis on the sacred, including its cultic dimensions. In the temple Isaiah experiences the awe-inspiring presence of the Lord, is aware of his uncleanness, and is purified. The holiness of God—the radical difference between divine and human—is a persistent theme in the words of Isaiah. Second, there is the call itself and the prophet's response. God does not address Isaiah directly, but the one purified by the divine messenger is able to hear the call and accept the commission. Third, there are the specific elements of this passage related to Trinity Sunday, the threefold Sanctus and the fact that the Lord speaks in the first person plural. Neither of these is a direct allusion to the Trinity, and there is no doctrine of the Trinity as such in the Bible. Still, there are indications of the experiences that gave rise to the doctrine. God is encountered in different ways, and human language must find means to express the reality of those encounters.

Psalm 29

The theme of the lections for this Sunday are the various forms of the manifestation of God and human responses to that manifestation. Psalm 29 focuses on the revelation of God in the awesome power of the thunderstorm.

Modern scholarship is generally agreed that this psalm probably had an origin outside Israel and was adapted for use in the Israelite cult. The psalm seems to presuppose a polytheistic background: note the reference to the sons of God in verse 1. (See RSV note.) Perhaps the text was once at home in some Phoenician setting as is suggested by the geographical references.

The central theme of the psalm is the voice of the Lord, that is, the thunder that accompanies a severe Mediterranean rainstorm. Seven times this voice is referred to.

No doubt this psalm praises the coming and appearance of God in the first thunderstorm of the autumn rainy season. In Palestine, the summer from late May to early October is completely dry with no rainfall whatever. This summer drought is broken when clouds move in from the Mediterranean (see I Kings 18:41-46). The first rains moisten and soften the ground so that sowing and plowing can take place.

This psalm may be outlined as follows: the glory of God— *Gloria in Excelsis* (verses 1-2), the gathering of the storm (verses 3-4), the shattering onslaught of the storm (verses 5-7), the passing and subsiding of the storm (verses 8-9), and the peace—the *pax in terris*—which follows the storm's passage (verses 10-11).

In the opening prelude, there is a threefold repetition of the phrase, "Ascribe to the Lord." Although it is the heavenly beings that are called on to praise God, no doubt this psalm was sung in the temple worship of Jerusalem by cultic choirs. Thus the earthly worship of humans was joined to the heavenly worship of the angelic beings.

The gathering of the storm depicted in the first strophe (verses 3-4) can be understood in the pattern of a typical Palestinian thunderstorm. The voice of God rumbles over the sea and gradually comes closer becoming more powerful the nearer it approaches.

The second strophe (verses 5-7) depicts the violence of the storm as it moves from the west onto the coastal mountain region ripping at the great cedars of Lebanon. These great trees, symbolic of strength and solidity, are shattered and broken in the manifestation of God's voice. Sirion or Mt. Hermon, whose snowcapped peaks at over 9,000 feet in height towered over and were visible throughout the region, is treated by the storm as if it were a calf or some young wild ox. Before the majesty and might of the Divine, they skip in awe and fear. Lightning that flashes forth like flames of fire accompanies the thunderous voice of God.

The third strophe (verses 8-9) describes the dying away of the storm as it moves into the desert shaking the wilderness, whirling trees, and stripping bare the forest. The ominous presence and power of the Deity in the storm leaves nature battered, bruised, and wounded. Yet in his temple all say, "Glory." The response to the presence of God is here described as a response of pure adoration extolled in worship.

The postlude (verses 10-11) concludes the psalm, first of all, with a confession that Yahweh sits enthroned upon the flood—that is, he reigns over the chaotic waters—and rules as king forever. The violence of the thunderstorm is not seen as the unleashing of the destructive powers of the deep but as the life-giving and hope-restoring rainfall that nurtures the earth and begins a new agricultural year with all its promises and expectations of abundance. Finally the benediction (in verse 11) asks that God give strength and peace to his people.

This psalm, which praises the presence and revelation of God not just in nature but also in one of nature's most dramatic expressions, the storm, delights in the God who displays his rule and his blessing in such momentous fashion.

Romans 8:12-17

In this passage Paul speaks of God whom we address in prayer as "Abba! Father!" (verse 15), Christ as God's own Son (verse 3) with whom we as children of God are fellow heirs (verse 17), and the Spirit of God (verse 14), or alternatively, the "Spirit of Christ" (verse 9). He appears not to draw a sharp distinction between the Spirit of God and the Spirit of Christ, and this reminds us that Paul's language here is triadic rather than Trinitarian. He does not operate with a clearly differentiated view of the Trinity as was the case in later Christian centuries, when elaborate efforts were made to distinguish the three members of the Godhead and to define their respective roles. Even so, we should not conclude that his understanding of the Spirit and its role in the life of the Christian were vague and undefined. Quite the contrary! Our epistolary text today attests the vitality of Paul's understanding of the Spirit. It has served as one of the most illuminating passages in Paul's writings for the way in which it clarifies the role of the Spirit in the moral life.

We should notice the sharp antithesis between "flesh" and "spirit"—a distinction Paul typically makes, indeed insists on (Gal. 5:16-25; 6:8). Earlier, he distinguishes between two opposing outlooks: the outlook of the flesh and the outlook of the Spirit (verses 5-8 NEB). Clearly, these are not only philosophical world views, but moral options, for he speaks of "living according to the flesh" and "living according to the Spirit" (verse 5). For Paul, "flesh" is not synonymous with skin and bone. Neither is it the same as "body." Rather, it stands for that which is "human," "physical," "earthly," or that which has to do with "this world." It stands over against God: in fact, it may be said to exclude God. Its relationship with God is one of hostility and enmity (verse 7). It tends to be self-serving rather than self-giving. Excluding the transcendent, "flesh" is unable to transcend itself. "Spirit," by contrast, points in a different direction. It emanates from God as an eschatological reality mediated to "this age" through Christ. The Spirit is the agent, or source of power, through which God raised Christ from the dead, and as such becomes the empowering source for Christians (verse 11). There is a direct connection between the Spirit and resurrection: the power unleashed by God in Christ's resurrection has been unleashed in this age. This power is essentially life-giving, for as God gave Life to Christ in raising him from the dead, so does God give Life to the Christian through the indwelling Spirit (verse 11).

The Spirit is the supreme eschatological reality ushered into "this age" by the resurrection of Christ. With it comes life and peace; without it, death is inevitable (verse 13). Through it, we can "put to death the deeds of the body" (verse 13), and thereby experience genuine life (cf. Gal. 5:24; Rom. 6:6). Accordingly, it is a force within us, but also external to us, for we can live either "by it" or "against it." As such, it serves as a moral norm by which one can walk and to which one can conform one's behavior. It provides a clear option to walking "according to the flesh" (verse 12). More than this, however, the Spirit is said to exercise dynamic force over the Christian. Not only are we "in the Spirit" in the sense of living within its world, or sphere of influence, but also it is said that the Spirit dwells in us (verse 9). We may be said, then, to be "led by the Spirit" or "moved by the Spirit" (JB; cf. also Gal. 5:18). As a living force indwelling us, the Spirit becomes an active force shaping who we are and what we do.

Specifically, the Spirit enables us to understand our identity as God's children. The metaphor is actually more specific here. The contrast is between Christ as God's own Son (verse 3) who cried, "Abba, Father" (cf. Mark 14:36), and us as "sons of God" (verse 14) who experience resurrected life through the Spirit, and thereby truly become the heirs of life, even as Christ did. Hence, we are fellow heirs with Christ (verse 17). By recalling the Aramaic language of prayer Jesus used in Gethsemane, Paul draws an analogy between Christ's experience of suffering and our own. The thrust of his remarks suggests that he saw the Spirit as the empowering agent of Jesus in the garden: to the degree that Jesus himself was "led by the Spirit of God" he became the Son of God through his complete obedience. Similarly, he did not recoil in fear as a slave, but rather prayed in confidence as a true and obedient Son. Similarly, when we confront moments of severe testing that call our very existence as children of God into question, it is God's, and perhaps even Christ's, own Spirit who jointly confirms what our own inward spirit knows—that we are children of God. The Spirit becomes the very catalyst for genuine and complete filial obedience, bringing about in us the courageous level of "sonship" that it wrought in Christ himself in the garden.

Paul's remarks recall, in many respects, the language of the Gospel reading for today, with its sharp distinction between flesh and Spirit and its emphasis on "birth from above." What the Spirit accomplishes is a change in our status—from being slaves to the flesh and thus debtors to the flesh (cf. II Tim. 1:7) to becoming children of God (cf. 8:23; Gal. 4:6-7; Eph. 1:5; also Deut. 14:1). As such, we share in Christ's own exalted status as an "heir" (cf. Mark 12:7; Heb. 1:2; Rev. 21:7). There is also the sobering reminder, however, that such "sonship" inevitably entails suffering (verse 17; also II Tim. 2:3, 12; I Pet. 4:3; 5:1), even though such suffering will eventually give way to glorification with him (cf. II Cor. 4:10).

John 3:1-17

Our Gospel for today continues the subject central to this season: the Holy Spirit. However, as the text will make clear to us, the subject is also Jesus Christ. But more careful listening to the text reveals that the primary subject is God from whom came both Christ and the Spirit. John 3:1-17 opens and closes with statements about God, reminding us that talk of the Spirit or of Jesus Christ must take place as part of our talk about God.

Because the lection extends to verse 17, the first task of the preacher is to decide how to handle a passage with two textures, like two different fabrics. It is not simply a matter of ascertaining where the quotation marks go (after verse 15 or after verse 21) but determining what to do with verses 16-17 which belong to the theological summary (verses 16-21), which the writer often places after conversations and sign stories (for example, 3:31-36; 5:19-29). One way to look at the text without interfering with its integrity is to regard the conversation with Nicodemus (verses 1-15) as cradled between an introduction (2:23-25) and a summary (3:16-17). The introduction provides a setting not only of time and place (Passover, Jerusalem) but also of general response to Jesus (many believed because of the signs). Nicodemus becomes, then, a particular case of faith based on signs. Following the conversation, the central truth about God, which seems to have escaped Nicodemus, is declared openly: "For God so loved . . . not to condemn . . . might be saved" (verses 16-17).

The conversation unfolds beautifully. Two men, both teachers, meet in private to discuss a subject vital to both, the kingdom of God. They meet "at night" (the Greek word designates *kind* of time, not a point in time or duration of time), alerting the reader to ambiguity and mystery. Through the common Johannine device of double meanings, two quite different views of life in the kingdom are unfolded. By use of a word which may be understood two ways, Jesus calls for birth "from above" which Nicodemus hears as being born "again." At verse 7 the conversation is enlarged into a sermon as is evident by the shift from singular to plural "you." Now the readers are being addressed in what is clearly a post-Easter Christian sermon. Note: Christian baptism and its association with the Holy Spirit (verses 5-8); the plurals "you" (verses 7, 11, 12) and "we" (verse 11); the reference to Christ's ascension as a past event (verse 13); and in John, the giving of the Spirit as a post-ascension event

(7:39). And so a private conversation opens into a presentation of two widely divergent perspectives on life before God. The one seeks sufficient proofs, historical and logical, in order to arrive at faith which is safe, solid, and clearly the conclusion that one has reached on the basis of the evidence admitted into the case. The other insists that life in the kingdom is given by God and is unachieved. Being from above this life is uncontrolled and uncalculated, like the whence and whither of the wind. The shift from succeeding in religion to having eternal life is as radical as being born anew.

Were we to use the language of Paul we would say that the subject here is the grace of God. Jesus Christ is the subject in the sense of his being the revealer of this truth about God. The Holy Spirit is the subject in the sense of its being the active presence of God effecting the radical change of perspective. But the overall affirmation of the text is that God is a life-giving God. This is no new word, as though God had ceased to be a wrathful judge and had now mellowed into forgiving love. The Hebrew Scriptures had declared God's grace in the story of the brazen serpent in Numbers 21:4-9 (verses 14-15). Our text proclaims, then, what has always been true of God, and what is comforting to hear again: God loves the world; God desires that none perish; God gives the Son that all may live; God has acted in Christ not to condemn but to save. To trust in this is to have life anew, life eternal.

Proper 4

Sunday Between May 29 and June 4 Inclusive
(If After Trinity Sunday)

I Samuel 16:1-13; Psalm 20; II Corinthians 4:5-12; Mark 2:23–3:6

I Samuel 16:1-13

Although the Gospel lection contains a reference to David, the Old Testament lesson gives the account of David's anointing as king, and the responsorial psalm is a prayer for the king's success in battle, the texts for the day concern quite different matters. Mark 2:23–3:6 contains sayings of Jesus about sabbath laws, and in II Corinthians 4:5-12 Paul relates the life and death of Jesus to the life and death of the faithful. One should be cautious about forcing the readings to speak with a single voice, or even address the same questions. After all, the lectionary represents to the church at worship a rich and diverse canon of scripture.

This Old Testament lesson begins a series of fourteen selections which survey or recapitulate most of the life of David, and thus a major era in the history of ancient Israel. This initial reading reports how the Lord selected David and had Samuel anoint him to be king, and the final selection (for Proper 17) is the account of David's death and the succession of Solomon to the throne. The continuity of readings suggests the possibility of a series of sermons on David's life. Finally, the theme of kingship will be taken to its eschatological implications on the last day of this season and of the liturgical year (Proper 29, Christ the King).

This passage gives an account of Samuel's final public act and of David's initial appearance in the biblical narrative. The old prophet designated and anointed the youngest son of Jesse to be king. In pre-monarchical times, and even subsequently on occasion in the Northern Kingdom, kings or other leaders were designated and anointed by prophets.

The essential conclusion of this report is that David later became king in accordance with the will of Yahweh and received the power and authority of Yahweh's Spirit: "And the Spirit of the Lord came mightily upon David from that day forward" (verse 13). The biblical tradition means to place that sentence as the heading for the entire life of David.

The setting for the story's plot is stated in verse 1, which presupposes the events in the previous chapter. Though he will continue to reign until his death, Saul has been rejected by Yahweh and is estranged from Samuel. What is to become of the monarchy? Yahweh announces to Samuel that he is to go to Bethlehem and anoint one of Jesse's sons.

As Samuel responds to the word of the Lord and goes to Bethlehem, narrative tension develops (verses 2-5). First, Samuel fears for his life. Saul will kill him if he learns that the prophet has gone to anoint another. Yahweh instructs him to take a heifer along with him and say he is doing his duty, offering a sacrifice. Anointing in the context of a service of sacrifice is not unexpected, but we cannot miss the note of concealment. The action is not to be known publicly. Second, when Samuel arrives in Bethlehem leading the heifer he has to reassure the fearful elders. We can only suppose that they—like Samuel—are afraid of Saul. Then this direction of the narrative is quickly forgotten as the sacrifice is arranged.

The account is drawn out to its resolution. Like Samuel, we were told only that Yahweh has provided one of the sons of Jesse as a king. First one and then another is brought forth and rejected in turn. Yahweh instructs Samuel, obviously impressed with the appearance of Eliab: "Man looks on the outward appearance, but the Lord looks on the heart" (verse 7). When it seems that all the sons have been considered Jesse acknowledges that there is one more, keeping the sheep (verse 11). Probably we are to understand that he was absent in the first place because he was too young to participate in the sacrifice. The description of this youngest son's attractive appearance (verse 12*a*) is surprising considering what is stated in verse 7.

Then comes the climax of the story with Yahweh's revelation that this is the one (verse 12*b*) and Samuel's anointing (verse 13*a*). The final lines (verse 13*b*) give the denouement, the explanation of the meaning and implications of the events. Only here do we finally hear the name of the anointed one, David.

The point of the story is that David came to the throne, not because of ambition or anything he did, but through divine designation. Like Saul before him (I Sam. 9:1–10:16) he was anointed by Samuel, not just in the moment of need but in advance. It is not a story of David at all—he says not a word and does only what he is told—but of the word of the Lord through the prophetic figure of Samuel. The process by which that word is made known is a combination of the prophetic—Yahweh speaks to him—and the priestly—the sacrifice and the pattern of events like election by lot.

Closely connected to the main theme is another, that the Lord makes the least expected choice. Expectations are reversed. The last is indeed made the first, and God's power is to be manifested in weakness.

Psalm 20

This psalm is a fitting reading to accompany the use of I Samuel 16:1-13. The psalm was composed to be used in a liturgy in which the king was the central figure. The liturgy and the ritual were probably carried out prior to the departure of the monarch and his army for battle.

The psalm is comprised of three component parts: an address to the king (verses 1-5), a confession of confidence spoken by the monarch (verses 6-8), and a prayer of intercession on behalf of the king (verse 9).

The appearance of many terms associated with worship make it possible to sense many of the actions as well as the orientation of the ritual in which this psalm was used. The reference to offerings and burnt sacrifices (verse 3) suggest that the king offered these to gain the favor of God. The mention of the "heart's desire," "your plans" (verse 4), and "your petitions" (verse 5) indicate that the king offered prayers to God requesting plans and strategy for the future, hoping to acquire divine blessing.

The address to the king, in verses 1-5, is the community's response to the king, offering him encouragement and well-wishing. It has the quality of indirect intercession. One can imagine the statements formulated as a prayer to God: "O Lord, answer the king in the day of trouble" (see verse 9 which has this prayer form) and so on. One can compare these to the form of certain of our well-wishes which are themselves forms of indirect prayer. "God bless you" when someone sneezes has this characteristic.

The community wishes a number of things for the monarch: an answer and protection from the divine in the day of trouble, help and support from the temple, God's remembrance and favorable regard of the king's offering of worship, and the fruition of the king's plans and desires. Such texts as these clearly indicate that ancient Israel could closely associate human needs and desires with worship and see these as legitimate interests in worship. Prayers and worship focusing on success were common features of worship. Self-interest was certainly not ruled out of Israelite worship. In verse 5, the self-interest of the community becomes the focus and the congregation expresses its hope that it might share in the king's victory and mark off its own territory. In preaching on such texts with their clear self-interest, the minister should not be apologetic about such a position. Instead, it can be emphasized that it may be best to express our wishes and self-interests in a religious context where that context and its theology can perform a moderating, enlightening role. In worship, the self-interest of the participants can be judged by other perspectives than merely the slide rule of success.

The king's responses, in verses 6-8, are expressions of confidence that God will answer and make the king victorious. ("His anointed" refers to the reigning king and could be translated "his [God's] Messiah.") The declaration "now" implies that something had happened in worship which gave the king assurance. It could have been the community's expression of its concerns (verses 1-5) or some sign of the Divine's favor such as a prophetic oracle or a special word from the priest.

The plural first-person pronouns ("we") in verses 7-8 suggest that the king spoke on behalf of the entire community or that the community joined in the statements of assurance. These verses emphasize two things.

1. Hope of success in war is not to be found in chariots and horses but in God. (This, of course, doesn't mean that the ancient Hebrew army marched out to battle unarmed!) Here there is the acknowledgment that divine concerns lie behind human issues.

2. Those who boast of their armaments—horses and chariots—but do not worship God are doomed to failure, whereas those trusting God will be granted success.

The psalm concludes with an intercessory prayer on behalf of the king requesting that he be granted victory in the forthcoming battle (verse 9).

II Corinthians 4:5-12

This epistolary lection begins a cycle of readings from Second Corinthians that extends over the next five weeks. Hence, a few preliminary remarks about this letter are in order.

It should be recalled that Second Corinthians probably comprises at least two, perhaps more, of Paul's letters to the church at Corinth. Chapters 10–13 seem to constitute a separate letter in its own right. With its severely polemical tone, it is best read as Paul's own defense of his apostolic ministry directed against his opponents. Chapters 1–9 form a separate letter and appear to have been written after chapters 10–13; in fact, chapters 8 and 9, which treat the collection of funds for the Jerusalem poor, originally may have been a separate letter, or letters. In any case, the mood and tone of chapters 1–9 are far less stormy, even though we still hear echoes of the controversy concerning Paul's ministry and his apostolic life-style. What unfolds in chapters 1–7, especially in 2:14–6:10, is an elaborate statement of Paul's theology of ministry. The epistolary lections for the first four weeks (II Cor. 4:5-12; 4:13–5:1; 5:6-10, 14-17; 5:18–6:2) derive from this section; the next lection (II Cor. 8:7-15) derives from the section treating the collection; and the final lection (II Cor. 12:1-10) derives from Paul's own defense *(apologia)* of his ministry.

In today's lection, Paul's opening remark, "What we preach is not ourselves" (verse 5), doubtless responds to the charges of his detractors who accused him of self-commendation (II Cor. 3:1). As the letter shows, at issue was what constituted authentic ministry, or, what form of ministry most adequately expressed the heart of the gospel. Was it ministry whose appeal and authority derived essentially from the minister's personal charisma, powerful presence, and strength as demonstrated in rhetorical ability or the ability to perform signs and wonders? Or, was it ministry anchored in human weakness, human frailty, and actual experiences of human suffering, that derived its appeal and authority from its capacity not merely to endure these but to transcend and transform them—to experience strength through suffering, power through weakness, and living through dying?

For Paul, it is the latter. The former way of viewing ministry tends to make the minister a "lord." In verse 5, he may in fact be saying, "For what we preach is not ourselves [as Lord], but Jesus Christ as Lord." Consequently, that form of ministry will tend to be authoritarian and stress rank more than service (cf. II Cor. 1:24). By contrast, Paul's essential role is that of servant (I Cor. 3:5). At the heart of his gospel is the basic Christian confession, "Jesus Christ is Lord" (cf. Rom. 10:9; I Cor. 12:3; Phil. 2:11; also Col. 2:6). Paul is not insisting here that he preaches the gospel apart from his own person, or personality, for preaching inevitably occurs through a human personality. The important question, however, is what message is mediated through the preacher's personality. As verse 6 shows, Paul insists that the ultimate source of revelation for his gospel is the Creator God who said, "Let light shine out of darkness" (cf. Gen. 1:3; Ps. 112:4; Job 37:15; Isa. 9:1-2). Just as God gave light to the universe through the spoken word at creation, so now has God brought light to all humanity through the new creation accomplished in the Christ-event. Just as the face of Moses radiated the brilliant splendor of God's revelation (cf. II Cor. 3:7-13), so now the "face of Christ" radiates the unveiled splendor of God's new revelation.

In verses 7-12, the metaphor shifts. No longer is the gospel seen as dazzling light shining through darkness (cf. I Pet. 2:9; Acts 26:18; Eph. 5:8; I Thess. 5:4-5; II Pet. 1:3), but as a "treasure in earthen vessels" (verse 7; cf. II Cor. 5:1; Lam. 4:2). The image of the clay pot serves to underscore the weakness and fragility of the minister as messenger. The message of the gospel mediated through the messenger is "treasure," to be sure (Matt. 13:44; Eph. 3:8), but it derives its value not from the case that contains it but from its intrinsic worth. Thus, the transcendent power of the gospel is derived from God, not from the minister.

As evidence of this, Paul rehearses in schematic fashion the afflictions he has endured as an apostle (verse 8; also 1:4, 8; 7:5; cf. I Cor. 4:9-13; II Cor. 6:3-10; 11:21-29). In every case, however, he has overcome, for while in his afflictions he was "carrying in [his] body the death of Jesus," precisely through these afflictions the "life of Jesus" manifested itself. He has not been forsaken (cf. Heb. 13:5). He has literally been given up to death in these experiences of human suffering and "dying," and through them he has reenacted the event of the cross itself (cf. II Cor. 1:5; 13:4; Gal. 6:17; I Cor. 15:38). Yet, through them, resurrection has also been at work (Rom. 6:8; 8:17; Phil. 3:10-11). He has experienced living through dying, and in doing so has proclaimed the essence of the gospel of the crucified Christ: through death comes life (cf. Phil. 1:20-21; I Cor. 6:20; II Cor. 6:9). As the message of the crucified Christ has been proclaimed through his own apostolic life-style, those who have heard him preach and seen him live have themselves come to experience life: "So death is at work in us, but life in you" (verse 12).

Mark 2:23–3:6

Today's Gospel lection is a portion of the collection of five conflict stories recorded in Mark 2:1–3:6. This material is called a collection because the stories are joined topically rather than chronologically. This is evident from three characteristics of the section: (1) the stories have other locations in Matthew and Luke; (2) the stories have different settings (at home, 2:1-12; in Levi's house, 2:13-17; no setting given, 2:18-22; in a grain field, 2:23-28; in a synagogue, 3:1-6); and (3) each story has a Markan style introduction and is rounded off at the end. Hence, stories that probably circulated separately are here clustered, perhaps as a kind of arsenal for the early church members who looked to Jesus for both precedent and pronouncement to enable them to handle their own conflicts.

However, it is striking that Mark has placed this section at this point in his Gospel. At the same time that Jesus is drawing huge and favorable crowds in cities, villages, countrysides, and by the sea (1:28, 33, 37, 39, 45), Mark says Jesus is also drawing hostile attention from religious leaders. In fact, the opposition mounts to the point of a conspiracy against his life, according to 3:6 which apparently is intended as the conclusion to the entire section instead of just 3:1-5. And thus as early as 3:6 Jesus' death enters the story, a subject which will dominate Mark's narrative after 8:31.

Our text, 2:23–3:6, records the last two conflicts. The first three concerned charges of blasphemy, eating with sinners and not observing fasts, while both of these concern sabbath regulations. The first occurs in the grain fields (2:23-28). The disciples pluck heads of grain, an act for which the law made provision as long as none of the grain was put in containers and taken home (Deut. 23:25). According to the Pharisees, however, what they did constituted harvesting on the sabbath. Jesus' defense of his followers consisted of citing a precedent from David's career (I Sam. 21:2-7) in which human need took precedence over the law. (Ahimelech and not Abiathar was high priest; some manuscripts of Mark have made the correction by omitting the name, as Matthew and Luke have done.) Verses 27-28 contain two pronouncements (Matt. 12:8 and Luke 6:5 use only the second) for which the story serves as introduction. The pronouncements are different, and it is unlikely that both would have been stated on one occasion. The first (verse 27) is a general principle that law is to serve human life not vice versa. The second (verse 28) is a christological claim made by One far greater than either David or the law.

The second conflict (3:1-5) involves a healing in a synagogue on the sabbath. The pronouncement at the center of this brief account is in the form of a stabbing question which silenced those who lay in wait for Jesus. They were silent because their own law made provision in emergencies to care for both animal and human life (Matt. 12:11; Luke 14:5) on the sabbath. Though the healing he did here might not be classified as an emergency, Jesus is announcing by his act and word, that it is never the wrong day to do good, to heal, to save life. The hostility against Jesus produces one of those odd unions that overriding hatreds sometime create: Pharisees in league with Herodians (8:15; 12:13), religion and politics clutching the same sword.

It requires no great act of imagination to observe how similar are the conflicts that lie in the path of discipleship today. Structures of religious custom and tradition, originally designed to praise God and serve humanity, can become corrupted and cruel. Hence occasions arise in which both human life and tradition cannot be preserved unbroken.

Proper 5

Sunday Between June 5 and 11 Inclusive
(If After Trinity Sunday)

I Samuel 16:14-23; Psalm 57; II Corinthians 4:13–5:1;
Mark 3:20-35

I Samuel 16:14-23

All of today's readings except the Psalm include some explicit reference to the Spirit of God, and they draw attention to the problem of testing the spirits. That is clearest in the New Testament readings. In the Gospel pericope Jesus is accused of casting out demons by the prince of demons, and his response includes the charge concerning the seriousness of blasphemy against the Holy Spirit. In II Corinthians 4:13–5:1 Paul considers the effects on faith of the "spirit of faith." Psalm 57, an individual lament, is linked to the Old Testament reading by its references to musical instruments, not by its superscription which connects it to a subsequent event in David's life.

Our reading begins precisely where last week's lection left off, with another theological interpretation of history. "The Spirit of the Lord departed from Saul" (verse 14), whom Samuel had earlier designated and anointed, but whom the Lord later rejected. At one level, then, these accounts of kings and prophets are like the Book of Acts: they are the history of the Spirit of God with individuals and peoples. The narrator's perspective is thus omniscient, knowing not only everything that happens to all characters, but also the mind of God, revealed through the words and actions of prophetic figures. Consequently the reader shares with the writer secrets not known to most of the participants in the story. The young musician who comes to soothe the spirit of Saul has already been designated by God to succeed him as king.

That the sources and traditions concerning the life of David are diverse and complicated is revealed by comparison of this account with the story of David and Goliath which follows in chapter 17. In I Samuel 16 David was anointed and then entered the service of Saul, even becoming "his armor-bearer" (verse 21). But in the next episode, when the army of Israel is challenged by the Philistine hero Goliath, David appears on the scene as a stranger, still a young shepherd who brings food to his brothers in the army. Neither Saul nor anyone else had ever heard of him. According to I Samuel 17, David comes into Saul's service by virtue of his first heroic act, not by his musical capabilities. Both traditions agree concerning several points, including David's parentage, his youth, the fact that he was a shepherd, and the fact that he was precocious and attractive in significant ways.

While the account of David's introduction into the court of Saul carries forward the theme of the divine will through the Spirit of the Lord by means of the transition of authority from Saul to David, it is also a self-contained and complete narrative. We are presented with a setting, a problem which creates tension, and a resolution to the problem. The setting is the court of Saul, and the problem concerns the king. Not only had the Spirit of the Lord departed from him, but also "an evil spirit from the Lord tormented him" (verse 14). This note introduces the factor that will trouble Saul's remaining years. He becomes a genuinely tragic figure. The resolution to the problem is initiated by the king's servants, who suggest that a skillful musician be brought in to play each time the evil spirit torments him. Saul agrees to the proposal. One of the servants has heard of a young man, a son of Jesse in Bethlehem, who is not only accomplished with the lyre, but also comes highly recommended in all important ways. Saul sends for David, who brings gifts from his father and enters Saul's service. Saul comes to love him greatly, makes him his armor-bearer, and asks Jesse to allow him to remain in the king's service permanently. The story concludes with the observation that the initial problem has been solved. Whenever Saul is possessed, David plays and the evil spirit departs.

The major theme of this story in its context concerns the Spirit of the Lord. The problem arises when the Spirit of the Lord which departed from Saul is given to David. The hiddenness of these facts is stressed in the magnificent recommendation of David to Saul, which concludes with the observation that "the Lord is with him" (verse 18). That ordinarily would have simply meant that he was a person blessed by God, not particularly surprising with all the attributes just listed. However, the readers who know about the designation of David hear that as a reminder.

Within that broader theme of the work of the divine Spirit this account focuses on the "evil spirit." It has always been tempting for commentators to interpret Saul's problem physiologically or emotionally, and it is true that the ancients attributed to evil spirits what we now explain in medical terms. What we know from this account is that Saul was periodically tormented, and the problem will only become worse, leading to the break between Saul and David. Music was known to have an effect on such difficulties.

What we are given is a thoroughly theological interpretation of Saul's illness. It was caused by "an evil spirit from the Lord" (verse 14; verse 15 calls it "an evil spirit from God"). That explanation is likely to jar the modern consciousness— not that there was an evil spirit, but that the evil spirit was from the Lord. Would we be more comfortable if the evil spirit came from Satan or "the prince of demons" (Mark 3:22)? However, the account of Saul's possession is consistent with the view throughout the Old Testament, which refers to "the satan" only a few times, and always as subject to God. The report that Saul's evil spirit came from God is not intended and should not be taken as an explanation of all evil and suffering. It is, in the final analysis, consistent with the perspective in our Gospel reading for the day. All spirits ultimately are subject to God.

Psalm 57

Although fundamentally a lament, this psalm is also a strong statement of confidence and assurance. Verses 7-11 which display the greatest confidence, however, are practically identical with Psalm 108:1-5. The latter psalm, which also contains verses identical with Psalm 60:5-12, seems to be a late composite psalm. Thus the vow in Psalm 57:7-10 appears to have been reused in Psalm 108.

Who may have originally been the speaker in Psalm 57 and have presented a case before God asking for help? The content of 57:9 suggests that the psalm was originally intended for use by a king: only a ruler could be expected to give thanks among the peoples and sing praises among the nations. That is, only a leader would have seen his own salvation as having international consequences.

This psalm has a rather complex structure. There is a twice repeated refrain addressed directly to the Deity (verses 5, 11). The psalm opens with a direct appeal spoken to God (verse 1) which is then followed by a confession of confidence addressed to a human audience (verses 2-3). The description of the distress or trouble, in verses 4 and 6, could have been addressed to God or to a human audience. Finally, the psalm contains a vow addressed to the Deity to be fulfilled in the future and is worded so that there seems little doubt that the requested redemption is a certainty.

The imagery of this psalm suggests that the worshiper's distress is caused by enemies and opponents. The enemies are described in a variety of ways: "storms of destruction" (verse 1), "those who trample" (verse 3), "lions" (verse 4), and hunters (verse 6). The lions are depicted as greedily devouring humans. Their teeth are like spears and arrows and their tongues as sharp swords. These are all metaphors to describe the destructive quality and devouring character of accusation and slander. It is little wonder that the author of Daniel picked up on the imagery of being in the midst of lions to describe a desperate situation (Dan. 6). The consuming and destroying effort of slander and accusation, however, is not something that comes only to a Daniel; often it is a humiliating experience that tests the faith and endurance of the normal, average individual.

Verse 6 which speaks of the opponents as if they were stalking some wild animal—setting nets and digging pits—also depicts them as becoming the victim of their own machinations—they are caught in their own nets and fall into

the pits of their own construction. Such a depiction is based
on the proposition that wickedness is self-destructive, that
plans made against others can rebound against their
perpetrators. Such a way of viewing things assumes that evil
actions create a pattern in which the consequences of evil
engulf the person that sets the pattern into motion: "What
one sows one shall reap." This understanding of retribution
sees the perpetrator as well as the opponent as objectives in
the pattern which evil sets into play. The psalm expresses
confidence that the sower shall reap what has been sown
before its growth destroys the original object.

From the description of the enemies in the psalm, let us
now focus on how the psalmist describes God, the source of
confidence. In verse 1, God is the one who offers the shadow
of his wings under which the seeker can find refuge, safe
while the storms of destruction rage. Verses 2-3 have the
psalmist speak of God as: (1) the one "who fulfills his purpose
for me" (or perhaps "who is good to me"), that is, as one
concerned for the worshiper, and as (2) the one who "will put
to shame those who trample upon me." As so frequently in
the psalms, there is the "double wish" or, in this case, the
"double affirmation" of positive good for the one praying
and of negative consequence for the opponents. God is
depicted as sending down his love and faithfulness as if they
were some angelic messengers from heaven to intervene on
behalf of the supplicant.

The vow of the worshiper, in verses 7-10, exudes optimism
and confidence, as if salvation and redemption were already
present realities. The references to waking suggest that it was
early in the morning when special services were held,
verdicts rendered, oracles proclaimed, and the redemption of
God experienced in worship.

II Corinthians 4:13–5:1

If being "afflicted," "perplexed," "persecuted," and
"struck down" (verses 8-9) are the inescapable lot of Paul's
existence as an apostle, why continue? In today's lection,
Paul explains the basis of his confidence as an apostle.

First, he mentions the "same spirit of faith" as that of the psalmist who wrote, "I believed, and so I spoke" (cf. Ps. 115:1 LXX; 116:10 RSV). Although the Greek version of the psalm differs from that of the Hebrew Bible, it clearly speaks of one who has recovered from severe affliction. As the context of the psalm shows, the psalmist continued to trust in God even though he had been "encompassed by the snares of death" and "suffered distress and anguish" (Ps. 116:3 RSV). In deep trust, he had cried to the Lord, "O Lord, I beseech thee, save my life!" (Ps. 116:4 RSV). His trust had been met with deliverance, and the psalm ends on a note of praise and thanksgiving. In the same spirit of faith, or trust, Paul is able to "speak," both in the sense of proclaiming the gospel and edifying his churches through his teaching. Worth noting here is the strong connection between faith and proclamation: what one speaks, especially what one speaks with conviction, stems directly from the convictions of the heart, what one believes.

At the center of Paul's faith was the conviction that the God who raised the Lord Jesus from the dead would also raise those who shared the Easter faith (cf. I Cor. 6:14; 15:15, 20; Rom. 8:11; II Cor. 13:4). This, for Paul, was a matter of existential knowledge. (Note: "knowing that," verse 14.) The resurrected life that the Lord Jesus had already experienced would eventually be that which all those "in Christ" would experience. Paul thus stresses his own solidarity with his readers: "Will . . . bring us with you into his presence" (verse 14). The work of God through Christ, as well as his own apostolic work, was for their sake. Through the spread of the gospel God's grace would be extended to more people, and as this happened, prayers of thanksgiving to God would also increase to the glory of God (verse 15).

A second basis for confidence is also given in verses 16-18: the eschatological hope and gradual transformation of the one who is in Christ. This obviously derives from his earlier mention of the God who raises the dead (verses 13-15), which leads him to affirm, "So we do not lose heart" (cf. 4:1; also Gal. 6:9; II Thess. 3:13; I Tim. 6:14). Here, Paul distinguishes between the "outer nature" that is wasting away, and the "inner nature" that is being renewed daily (verse 16). It is not clear whether this is a psychological dualism that distinguishes the "inner person" from the "outer person" (cf. Rom. 7:22; Eph. 3:16), or an eschatological dualism that distinguishes the part of us that conforms to "this age" from the part of us that conforms to "the age to come." It may be that both dimensions are in view here. As verses 17-18 show, the contrast is eschatological: this "slight momentary affliction" that we experience now is set over against the incomparable "eternal weight of glory" that we will experience then. Yet, through the Christ-event, God has already begun the process of transformation that will culminate in the Parousia, and in this sense the "form of this world is passing away" (cf. I Cor. 7:31). Therefore, it is possible to distinguish between "the things that are seen" and the "things that are unseen," the former being the world as we know it in its transient state, the latter being the world as it has begun to be transformed by the power of the resurrection, and thus in its "eternal" state.

Certainly, this changed perspective on the world order also alters the way we view our own existence. Our earthly existence is now comparable to that of a tent, the very symbol of transience, for like a tent, our human existence finally folds. In contrast to the earthly tent of our existence, however, God gives us a "house not made with hands" (cf. Mark 14:58; Heb. 8:2; 9:11, 24), "eternal in the heavens."

Mark 3:20-35

Mark will be our Gospel today and for the next six weeks and then we will return to John. Given the broad differences between these two Gospels, the preacher will want to make the transition carefully and help the listeners do the same. In common, however, with the two preceding lessons from John is the subject of the Holy Spirit in today's reading, testifying again not only to its appropriateness for the Pentecost Season but also for any season. The Holy Spirit was the hallmark of early Christianity as portrayed in the major New Testament witnesses. Mark 3:20-35 registers how vital was the activity of the Holy Spirit in the early church and issues a frightening warning to those who attribute that activity to Satan.

In Mark, the geographical context is Jesus' home (3:19*b* RSV). The phrase can also mean "in a house," probably a better rendering since the text says Jesus' family came to the place where he was to get him. Of course, Jesus could have had a home away from his family. The literary context places the event immediately after the appointment of the twelve disciples (3:13-19*a*). Our lection itself is a combination of two stories: Jesus' relation to his family and the scribes' charge that Jesus works in the name of Satan. In Matthew and Luke the charge follows an exorcism (Matt. 12:12; Luke 11:14), and quite naturally so since the accusation has to do with casting out demons. But in Mark the charge by the scribes not only follows the arrival of Jesus' family to seize him (3:21) but is inextricably tied to the family's attempt to take Jesus away. In a pattern typical of Mark, one story (3:22-30) is inserted between two parts of another story (3:20-21, 31-35). Mark divides the account about Jesus' family and sets the accusation about Satanic exorcisms within it. Why?

Mark may have joined the stories because the family's and the scribes' views of Jesus are similar, though differing in seriousness. The family apparently believed the public report that Jesus was insane, beside himself. Jesus was in a pressing crowd in the house and it was impossible even to eat (verses 20-21). The scribes from Jerusalem interpreted Jesus' behavior theologically: he is possessed by Beelzebul, the prince of demons. Beelzebul ("lord of the house") was a Syrian god whose name was mockingly corrupted by some Jews to Beelzebub ("lord of the flies"). Back of the charge was the common assumption that miracles could be performed not only by God but also by evil forces (Exod. 7:11; 8:7; II Thess. 2:9; Rev. 13:13). In Matthew 7:21-23, Jesus attributes the prophesying, exorcisms, and miracles of some persons to the power of evil. In other words, while we ask of the extraordinary, Did it really happen? The scriptures ask, Who did it?

Jesus' response is not only to the scribes but to everyone, as is evident by Mark's familiar "And he called them to him" (verse 23). In a series of brief parabolic statements, Jesus

41

provides a twofold answer: (1) to cast out demons in Satan's name is nonsensical; Satan against Satan would mean the self-destruction of evil, and (2) the real truth is not that evil is self-destructing but that Jesus has entered Satan's house and is overcoming the power of evil. Then comes the pronouncement (verses 28-29) to the effect that forgiveness of sin and blasphemy is broad and embracing, but to attribute the work of the Holy Spirit to Satan, to charge the Spirit of God with evil, to call a blessing a curse is to thwart totally the dynamics of forgiveness. This pronouncement, says Mark, was prompted by the charge that Jesus had an unclean spirit (verse 30). Out of fear of confusing the works of God and Satan, the church has generally been cautious if not totally quiet about what are and what are not the words and deeds of the Holy Spirit. But criteria had to be developed, as the document called *The Didache* testifies, to protect the church against self-appointed, money-hungry evangelists, prophets, and healers.

In verse 31 the account returns to the story of Jesus' family and Jesus' declaration that his true family consists of those who do God's will (verse 35). This dramatic but not isolated scene gives the allegiance of discipleship precedence over family ties (Mark 10:29-30; Luke 9:59-62; 12:51-53; 14:25-26). Some have had to make painful decisions in this matter.

Take one final look at Mark's picture. Outside are the two groups that one would assume should be inside: the family (Mark 6:3), perhaps blinded by familiarity, who do not understand and who believe rumors about Jesus; the scribes from headquarters, experts in Scripture who give theological put-downs to what they do not understand. And inside? A crowd sitting about Jesus, listening for God's will, apparently unaware that they missed lunch.

Proper 6

Sunday Between June 12 and 18 Inclusive (If After Trinity Sunday)

II Samuel 1:1, 17-27; Psalm 46; II Corinthians 5:6-10, 14-17;
Mark 4:26-34

II Samuel 1:1, 17-27

As the lectionary for these next few Sundays leads us through a series of Old Testament readings concerning the life of David, epistolary texts from Second Corinthians, and Gospel lections from Mark, the preaching themes from the various readings do not always coincide. With the exception of the Gospel, which concerns the secret of the kingdom of God, the dominant motif in the readings for this day is death, and our response to it. Second Samuel 1:17-27 is David's lament over the death of Saul and Jonathan. Psalm 46, a hymn to Zion, is a fitting response, beginning as it does with lines that have become a familiar funeral text. Death is also the dark background of Paul's good news in II Corinthians 5:6-10, 14-17 that one who is in Christ is a new creation.

It is important to remind ourselves of the narrative context of the death of Saul and Jonathan and David's dirge. Between the appearance of David in the court of Saul and the death of Israel's first king a great deal has transpired. David has become one of Saul's leading warriors and has developed a very close friendship with Jonathan. Subsequently, however, Saul's illness has caused him to drive David away. Throughout Saul's life Israel has struggled with the Philistines, and it was in a major battle with them that the king and his son lost their lives. But where was David? Remarkably, he and his band of men allied themselves with one of the Philistine kings, Achish of Gath, and engaged in a campaign against the Amalekites.

The report of the battle and the death of Saul and Jonathan is given in I Samuel 31. The part of II Samuel 1 not included in the reading for the day (verses 2-16) reports from David's camp how he heard and responded to the news of the deaths. When the man from Saul's camp reported on Israel's defeat and the death of the king and his son, David's first response included the denial so familiar to us in similar circumstances. "How do you know that Saul and his son Jonathan are dead?" (verse 5). The man reports that he had actually been there, and at the king's insistence had killed the mortally wounded Saul, and then brought the crown and armlet to David. David's next response is mourning, including tearing his clothes, fasting, and weeping. Then, after asking the messenger almost rhetorically how it was that he was not afraid to destroy "the Lord's anointed," David has him killed.

David's lamentation is introduced with the equivalent of a modern footnote, "it is written in the Book of Jashar" (verse 18). Since the only other reference to this book (Josh. 10:13) also introduces poetry, it seems safe to conclude that the Book of Jashar was an ancient collection of songs and poems. Some of these songs and poems were quoted when the history was written, but most of them have been lost. The books of Kings contain a great many "footnotes" such as this, citing "the book of the acts of Solomon" (I Kings 11:41), "the Book of the Chronicles of the Kings of Israel" (I Kings 15:31), and "the Book of the Chronicles of the Kings of Judah" (I Kings 22:45).

Modern scholarship has identified the literary type or genre of a great deal of biblical literature, but this kind of song is one of the few identified by an ancient classification. It is a "lamentation," or dirge (see also Amos 5:1). The situation in which the dirge was used was, of course, the funeral. As a rule such songs were composed according to a standard meter, with alternating lines of three and two accents. The mood, as befits the situation, is somber but dignified.

This lamentation contains no specifically religious expressions at all. There is no prayer, or reference to God. This is consistent with the fact that the funeral in ancient Israel was not a religious occasion; in fact contact with a corpse could render one ritually unclean. Through most of its religious history, ancient Israel considered death the end, a boundary that removed one even from the presence of God.

Perhaps the most valuable contribution such texts can render is to interpret us to ourselves. The situation to which it responds is all too common: death and the accompanying grief. This dirge, like others in the Old Testament, contains many of the expressions that still are necessary at such times.

The elements include:

1. Wailing, moaning, and expressions of the pain of loss. Such notes recur throughout the song: "How are the mighty fallen" (verses 19, 25, 27); "I am distressed for you, my brother Jonathan" (verse 26).

2. A description of the catastrophe (verse 21).

3. Expressions of anger. In this case they are directed both at the Philistines (verse 20) and even at the mountains where Saul and Jonathan died (verse 21).

4. A description of the situation before death, the life with those who died. The song speaks of the great contributions of those who died (verses 22-24) and of the special relationship between the dead one and the bereaved (verse 26).

5. A call for others to mourn or grieve (verse 24).

Mourning and grief will include even more elements, but most of those are always present. What minister visiting a family who has just experienced death has not heard all of those expressions? The strength and value of the Old Testament lamentations, like many of ancient Israel's prayers as well, lie in their realism. One's anguish deserves to be expressed fully and openly.

Psalm 46

Psalm 46 belongs to a group of psalms that extol the greatness of Jerusalem (Zion) and thus may be classified as one of the songs of Zion (see Ps. 137:3). Behind these songs of Zion are two fundamental assumptions which were widespread in the ancient Near East. First of all, a sacred city and a deity were closely associated with each other. While a god might be worshiped anywhere, it was taken for granted that a particular locale was more sacred and special to the deity than any other. For Yahweh, the god of Israel, Jerusalem or Zion was his divinely chosen and especially elected place. Second, sacred sites and cities were frequently associated with the belief in sacred mountains as the dwelling places of the gods—like Mt. Olympus in Greek mythology. Such mountains were often seen as the location of the original paradise, that is, as the site of the Garden of Eden (see Ezek. 28:11-19). Streams that watered the earth were believed to have their origin in this sacred mountain (see Ezek. 47:1; Gen. 2:10-14).

We should imagine Psalm 46 and the other Zion hymns as being sung in the context of a great festival which celebrated Yahweh's choice of Jerusalem and the construction of his temple (his house) on Mt. Zion.

Psalm 46 consists of three stanzas or strophes, verses 1-3, 4-7, and 8-11. The last two strophes have a common refrain: "The Lord of hosts is with us; the God of Jacob is our refuge." The fact that stanza one is a line shorter than the other stanzas would suggest that the same refrain once followed verse 3. The content of these three stanzas may be designated the lord of creation, the lord of history, and the lord of peace.

The first stanza declares God to be a source of strength and refuge and a help in time of trouble. This theme is then expounded in terms of a total disruption in the world of nature or in terms of cosmic conflagration. Verses 2-3 declare that the faithful or the inhabitants of God's city have no reason to fear even if chaos should invade the cosmos—the earth should change, mountains fall into the sea, and the flood waters of the deep roar and foam causing the mountains to tremble. Behind this idea of the threat of chaos and the disarray of creation lies the biblical belief that the world was founded over the waters of chaos. In the flood story, when the world was again returned to its watery state, it was because the foundations of the deep broke forth to inundate the earth (Gen. 7:11). Because of God's special protection, Zion has no need to fear even the powers of chaos itself.

Just as verses 2-3 of this psalm affirm God's protection of Zion against the cosmic threat of chaos, verses 4-6 affirm the stability and security of the city against historical enemies. This section opens with a reference to a river whose streams make glad the city of God. There, of course, was no actual river that flowed in Jerusalem. Here we are dealing with mythological imagery and the idea of the sacred mountain as the source of the waters of the earth. Verses 5-6 declare that the city of God is impregnable. Since God is in her midst, and will help her right early (or "at the turn of the morning"), the city need not fear. Nations may rage and kingdoms come and go but God who is in Zion can utter his voice and the earth will melt.

Verses 8-10 call upon the worshipers to behold the works of Yahweh and thus to find peace and calm. God works desolation in the earth, makes wars cease, breaks the bow, shatters the spear, and consumes the chariots with fire. Although the psalm proclaims these as acts of God already accomplished and thus something one can behold, nonetheless, there is a touch of the unachieved, the eschatological, about these verses that point forward to the future. In worship the people celebrated God's salvation as a reality experienced but not yet fully realized.

Verse 10 contains an oracle of God which calls the people to an acceptance of his rule—an acceptance which can be realized in "stillness." This oracle, spoken by some official in worship, expresses the same call as the prophet Isaiah: "In returning and rest you shall be saved; in quietness and in trust shall be your strength" (Isa. 30:15). God proclaims his rule over the affairs of nations (the historical process) and over the earth (the world of nature).

II Corinthians 5:6-10, 14-17

Today's epistolary reading opens with a word of confident reassurance: "we are always of good courage" (verse 6). Earlier, Paul has insisted that he does not "lose heart," in spite of his apostolic afflictions (II Cor. 4:1, 16). The clear hope of an "eternal weight of glory beyond all comparison" (II Cor. 4:17) does not eliminate the hard realities of earthly existence: "while we are still in this tent, we sigh with anxiety" (II Cor. 5:4). Eventually, our mortal existence will be clothed with a new form of existence, or "swallowed up by life" (II Cor. 5:4). Even now, we have begun to taste this immortal life through the Spirit whom God has given us as a pledge (II Cor. 5:5; cf. II Cor. 1:22; also Rom. 8:23; Gal. 3:14; Eph. 1:14). Mention of the Spirit prompts Paul to reaffirm that his courage is constant.

Christian existence is a dual existence. Those who have already experienced the "age to come," even partially through the earnest of the Spirit, can sharply distinguish between life in the earthly body and life with the Risen Lord (cf. Phil. 1:22-26). Actually, "home" is existence in the earthly body, but preferably the Christian's home is "with the Lord" (Phil. 3:20). Regardless of one's mode of existence, the ultimate aim is to "please the Lord" (cf. Rom. 14:18; Eph. 5:10; Heb. 13:21). What makes it possible to remain confident in spite of this felt distance between earthly existence "in the body" and heavenly existence "with the Lord" is living by faith: "for we walk by faith, not by sight" (verse 7). The life of faith enables Christians to deal with life's optical illusions: things that are visible are transient, while things that are invisible are eternal (II Cor. 4:18). One who walks by sight will obviously focus on the visible, and thereby see only what is temporary, whereas the one who walks by faith will see beyond the visible to what is permanent and eternal. The life of faith, then, by definition transcends bodily existence as it draws its sustaining power from the Risen Lord whom we know but cannot see, except with the eyes of faith.

However much we might wish to be "away from the body and at home with the Lord," we nevertheless become responsible for life in the body. Ultimately, one must account for the "deeds done in the body" at the heavenly tribunal of Christ (cf. Rom. 14:10; Acts 10:42; also Rom. 2:16; II Tim. 4:1; I Pet. 4:5; also Eccles. 12:14).

The second part of today's epistolary lection is prompted by an apologetic concern. Paul remains sensitive to criticisms that he commends himself to his readers and he sometimes behaves as if he is beside himself (verses 11-14). He reassures the Corinthians, however, that it is the "love of Christ," that is, the love that Christ has for him, that controls, or obsesses, him (verse 14). This prompts him to reflect on the work of Christ.

Paul's conviction was that "one has died for all" (verse 14). This doubtless means that Christ has died in behalf of all humanity, rather than in humanity's stead (cf. I Tim. 2:6; also Gal. 1:4; 2:20; Eph. 5:2, 25; Tit. 2:14; also Matt. 20:28 and parallels). The corollary is that "all (Christians) have died." The death of Christ was prototypical in that his self-emptying was complete, and in this sense he died the ultimate death. Similarly, those in Christ have experienced death both to sin and the law (Rom. 6:11; 7:4). Because Christ died for all, those who have gained life through his death may be said to have died to themselves in order to live for the One who died and was raised in their behalf (verse 15).

The effect of Christ's redeeming love on Paul was to alter his perspective completely. Once he had regarded Christ "from a human point of view," or "according to the flesh" *(kata sarka)*. Most likely, this means that prior to his conversion and apostolic call, he had understood Christ in essentially human terms. He had failed to see in the Christ-event the eschatological turning of the ages, and thus for him it was merely an event of "this age." This point of view he held no longer, for he now saw the Christ-event as the triggering event of the New Age. In the Christ-event, God had reordered the universe. The God who brought light out of darkness in the first creation (cf. II Cor. 4:6) had effected a new creation, bringing even more dazzling light to the world through Christ. In the Christ-event, the old age had given way to the New Age.

To be "in Christ" means that one actually becomes a participant in this eschatological process in which the old age gives way to the new. Individually, this means that the one "in Christ" becomes a "new creature" (cf. Gal. 6:15; also Eph. 2:15; Col. 2:10). By experiencing death and resurrection with Christ, one is able to walk "in newness of life" (Rom. 6:4). Corporately, this means that one becomes a participant with God in bringing about reconciliation and peace (verses 18-20).

Mark 4:26-34

All the lections for today register transitions of one type or another: historical, political, theological, or personal. The old comes to an end; something new is beginning. Our Gospel is

49

no exception; Mark presents that something new as the kingdom and he does so in parables about seed.

Mark 4 is devoted entirely to parables, an interpretation of one of them, and Mark's understanding of the role of parables in the ministry of Jesus. The parables found here are obviously a collection and do not represent a single teaching session by Jesus. In fact, it is not only a collection but a selection, a few samples as verses 2, 33-34 make clear. The audiences for this material are two: a large crowd by the sea to whom Jesus speaks in parables (verses 1, 34), and a smaller group of the Twelve and others with them to whom Jesus speaks about the parables (verses 10, 34). Of the many things Jesus taught in parables (verse 2), Mark offers here only three, and they have the common theme of a seed that is sown: the sower (verses 3-8), the seed growing secretly (verses 26-29), and the mustard seed (verses 30-32). Our lection consists of parables two and three and the closing comment about Jesus' use of parables (verses 33-34). We will attend to this closing comment and then look at the two parables.

Mark's statement in verses 33-34 provides his understanding of the parables in Jesus' ministry, making as he does a general principle out of what he described as Jesus' method in verses 10-12. On the basis of what is said in this chapter, several comments on Mark's view of parables can be made.

First, parables are not simple little stories used by Jesus so that everyone within the sound of his voice could understand his teaching. On the contrary, not everyone did understand, even though Jesus' offer was to anyone who had ears to hear (verses 9, 23).

Second, parables are a form of literature which, like poetry, demand a great deal from the listener. They are not obvious to all and sundry, to every casual passerby who may or may not make any personal investment in Jesus or the kingdom. Parables, then, have a revealing/concealing quality, creating their own hearers and non-hearers.

Third, those who do hear are an inner circle, not of superior intelligence but of personal attachment to Jesus. They are "with Jesus." But even for these, understanding is not easy, even with Jesus' further instruction. As the interpretation of the parable of the sower illustrates (verses 14-20), the explanation can be as difficult to grasp as the parable itself. But the point is, understanding is linked to one's relation to Jesus.

Fourth, the use of parables by Jesus is not surprising because Jesus was himself a parable of God. Jesus as the presence of God, as the Son of God, was not obviously so to everyone. He spoke of himself as the lamp and of light and shadow, of the revealed and the hidden (verses 21-25). Only intentional, intense giving of oneself to him and his message is fruitful.

And finally, because the subject matter is the mystery of the kingdom, the listener should expect snatches of insight and partial discoveries rather than mastery of the subject matter.

And what do our two parables say of the kingdom? The parable of the seed growing secretly (verses 26-29), which has no parallel in Matthew or Luke, has been interpreted from two perspectives. If verse 29 is the key, then the parable says now is the time to reap the harvest; this is the end time; all that has gone before was but the growing season. More likely, however, is the interpretation that focuses more upon the growth that takes place totally apart from human effort (the sower sleeps and rises) and from human understanding ("he knows not how"). The seed carries its own future in its bosom and efforts to coerce and force growth are futile. The kingdom of God is exactly that: the kingdom *of God*. The thought both chastens and encourages followers of Jesus.

The parable of the mustard seed (verses 30-32) is clearly a word of encouragement. Let those concerned, frustrated, or even depressed by small beginnings, by the apparent insignificance of the enterprise to which life and resources are committed, take heart. Let the vision of the end ("the greatest of all shrubs") inspire and inform today's effort, knowing all the while that the end as well as the beginning are God's doing and not our own.

51

Proper 7

Sunday Between June 19 and 25 Inclusive (If After Trinity Sunday)

II Samuel 5:1-12; Psalm 48; II Corinthians 5:18–6:2; Mark 4:35-41

II Samuel 5:1-12

The Old Testament reading reports how David became king over all of Israel and how he then captured the city of Jerusalem. As a hymn to Zion, the holy city and its temple, Psalm 48 is a clear and direct response to that reading. Equally important, but not as obvious as a response to the account of David's kingship, is the psalm's emphasis that the Lord is king. Specific links between the epistolary and the Gospel texts, and of either with the Old Testament reading, are difficult to discern.

The account in Second Samuel reports that seven and one half years have passed since the death of Saul and Jonathan. In those years David has become king over Judah in the South (II Sam. 2:11), and Ishbosheth, a son of Saul, has been set up as king in the North by Abner, one of Saul's generals. But Abner has a falling out with Ishbosheth and decides to transfer his loyalty to David, even proposing to the elders of Israel that David should be king of all the tribes (II Sam. 3:17-19). Abner's appearance in the South to make an alliance with David revives the old family feud between Joab, David's general, and Abner. The immediate background of our reading for the day is Joab's murder of Abner and the murder of Ishbosheth by several of his captains. When the murderers carry Ishbosheth's head to David in Hebron, thinking that he will be pleased, David has them executed. As II Samuel 5 begins, then, David is well established in the South and the North is without a leader, either king or general.

Second Samuel 5:1-12 contains four distinct paragraphs. The first (verses 1-3) reports how the representatives of the

Northern tribes took the initiative, came to Hebron, and anointed David. Two steps are described, first the designation by "all the tribes" and then the covenant ceremony with anointing by "all the elders of Israel." The tribes cite the divine promise which is hereby fulfilled: "The Lord said to you, 'You shall be shepherd of my people Israel, and you shall be prince over Israel' " (verse 2). David's authority thus derives from his election by Yahweh and also from the people who acknowledge him and that election. Moreover, David is the one who "made a covenant with them" (verse 3); that is, he submitted himself to the stipulations of the covenant. In ancient Israel, as we shall see later in the life of David, the king does not stand over the law but is subject to the divine law and his obligations to the people. That fact is further underscored here by the note that the covenant was made "before the Lord," that is, in the sanctuary.

The second unit (verses 4-5) is a historical note concerning David's age and the length of his reign. There is no serious reason to doubt the historical reliability of the information. The forty years of his kingship would have been ca. 1000-961 B.C.

The third unit (verses 6-10) reports how David took the city of Jerusalem and made it the capital of the now-united kingdom. The sequence of events is difficult to reconstruct, primarily because the anecdote unfolds as the explanation of a proverbial saying, "The blind and the lame shall not come into the house" (verse 8), that is, into the sanctuary. The original inhabitants of Jerusalem are said to have taunted David, asserting that even the blind and lame could defend the city against him. They could not, and he took the stronghold, apparently by superior tactics. There was no pitched battle, siege, or destruction of the defenses. This action had two far-reaching consequences: (1) the earlier inhabitants were not killed but incorporated into David's state and (2) Jerusalem had not previously belonged to any of the tribes and it was near the border of Judah and Israel. Consequently it was an ideal neutral site to serve as the capital of the new kingdom.

The final paragraph (verses 11-12) notes that David quickly attracted international attention and arranged for Hiram of

Tyre to build him "a house," a palace of some kind. It concludes with the observation that not only had the Lord made David king and exalted the kingdom for the sake of his people Israel, but also that David recognized the activity of God in those events.

When these stories are viewed in their wider biblical context a number of important theological issues and themes for proclamation emerge.

1. The Davidic king, the anointed one or "messiah" of God, and the Holy City, "the city of David," are perpetually linked. With these accounts of David's anointing and the taking of Jerusalem, we are reminded on the one hand that God's activity with human beings occurs in particular and concrete places, and on the other hand that some places are holy, set apart, because they are experienced as special meeting places of human beings with the divine presence.

2. David's kingship evokes reflection on several matters concerning faith and politics. He comes to the throne, we are told, in accordance with the will of the Lord. But the process by which that occurs is recounted with stark realism; it happened in the full light of history. Political intrigue, personal conflicts, murders, and wars all played a part. The ancient Mesopotamian view of the origin of government is radically different. The Sumerian king's list begins, "When kingship first came down from heaven. . . ." Behind these Old Testament accounts of first Saul's and then David's acceptance as king stands a theological controversy: Should the people of God be ruled by a king? Some said, "Yes, it is the will of God." Others said no and for the reason expressed in Psalm 48: "Yahweh is our king." The prevailing Old Testament answer was that the people of God in the world would have a king—a human government—but one whose actions would be subject to God.

Psalm 48

The Old Testament lection for today tells the story of David's capture of Jerusalem. Psalm 48, one of the Zion psalms, provides us with some insight into what the Israelites came to believe about Zion. Thus it represents what one might call biblical Zionism. Like Psalm 46, it proclaims the impregnability of Zion—her protection by God from all her enemies.

Psalm 48, and the other hymns of Zion, were probably used during major festivals and were sung to express the people's faith in Jerusalem and in the God whose temple was there. The last part of this psalm, verses 12-14, seems to presuppose a pilgrim procession circling the city perhaps before entering it for the main festival celebrations.

The following is the structure of the psalm: (1) hymnic praise of Yahweh the God who cares for Mt. Zion (verses 1-3), (2) the divine protection of the sacred mount and the destruction of its enemies (verses 4-8), (3) thanks offered to God for his concern (verses 9-11), and (4) the call to the people to circumambulate the city (verses 12-14).

This psalm has drawn heavily on the mythological thought of the ancient Near East. Mt. Zion is described in terms that greatly exceed any normal description, that is, the sacred mountain is depicted in terms of the ancient concept of a cosmic mountain conceived as the abode and specially defended preserve of the Deity. We will note some of these features throughout the psalm.

Verses 1-3 are a hymn that speaks of God in the third person. In these verses, Zion is described as God's holy mountain, beautiful in elevation, the joy of all the world. Mt. Zion is also spoken of as in the "far north" or in the "recesses of Zaphon." Geographically, of course, Jerusalem was not located in the north of Palestine. This description probably has to be understood in light of Canaanite mythology. In the pre-Israelite religion of Canaan, the god Baal was enthroned and ruled as king on Mount Zaphon. The word *zaphon* in Hebrew came to mean "north" because Mount Zaphon was located north of Palestine in Phoenicia. The imagery of the divine ruling on the mountain of the north has here been applied to the Israelite God and the city of Jerusalem.

The significance and beauty that are assigned to Zion are understood as the consequence of God's presence in the city where his temple or home is. Enthroned in the temple God rules over the world from Jerusalem, the center of the universe, as the great king. Within the city, God's defenses are sure. Such language about Zion is clearly intended to solicit and express feelings of confidence, contentment, and at-home-ness from the worshiper. Zion symbolizes a place of security, a place in which one encounters a special religious dimension, and, as such, Zion is a taste of the world as it was meant to be and someday will be.

Verses 4-8 speak of the enemy kings who assembled to attack Jerusalem only to be seized by panic, terror, and fright. The kings, once they see the sacred mount, become astounded and tremble as if they were women in the throes of childbirth. The reader of this psalm should not seek to find some historical event that gave birth to the psalm. No specific historical event lies behind the description of the assault on Zion; instead, the depiction is dependent on cultic, symbolic imagery. When the community celebrated and proclaimed God's divine protection of the city, the enemies were any and all opponents against God and the Holy City. The reference to the ships of Tarshish in verse 7 clearly does not belong in any realistic presentation of an attack on Jerusalem since the city was miles inland from the sea. Yet such imagery could be used as poetic license to illustrate that Zion is protected from all forms of attack.

Over against the rulers of the world and the enemies of God's people stands the sacred city which God has established to stand forever. Note that each of the first two stanzas has this type of affirmation (in verses 3, 8) to round off the content of each of these sections.

Verses 9-11, which take the form of direct address to the Deity, affirm that it was in worship, "in the midst of thy temple," that the people gave thought to the love of God expressed in his care for Zion. The people confess that the true response to such love was praise, rejoicing, and gladness. One should note the fact that verse 9 focuses on a particular locale—the midst of the temple—while verse 10 affirms that the praise of God has no locale; it extends to the end of the world.

The call to view Zion and march round its fortifications in verses 12-14 can be seen as the call for the people to be a link in the chain of tradition that passes on, from one generation to the next, the truth of God and his care for Zion. Thus the pilgrim worshiper is invited to become a custodian of the lessons of the present for generations yet to come.

II Corinthians 5:18–6:2

"All this is from God." With these words, Paul sounds the theme of the passage. Just before this, he has spoken primarily of the work of Christ (verses 14-17), but now he emphasizes God's role in the work of salvation. Earlier he has stressed the initiative God has taken (II Cor. 2:14, 17; 3:5; 4:1, 6, 14; 5:5), but now he elaborates on this more fully.

God's initiative may be seen in three areas: (1) the work of salvation, (2) the work of Christ, and (3) the work of ministry.

First, God is the primary agent in the work of salvation. The primary initiative in the work of reconciliation was taken by God. A similar point is made in I Corinthians 1:30, "He [God] is the source of your life in Christ Jesus." The Corinthians are what they are solely as the result of an act of God. Being made "the righteousness of God" (5:21) can be seen as nothing else than an expression of the "grace of God" (6:1). Paul quotes Isaiah 49:8 to reinforce this point: "At the acceptable time I have listened to you, and helped you on the day of salvation." The subject, of course, is God who lent an open ear to the prayers of fallen humanity and responded to the call for help.

God's saving work of reconciliation is first said to encompass "us" (5:18), that is, Paul, his colleagues, and doubtless all Christians. But the true scope is cosmic, for it is the world as a whole that is the object of God's reconciling love (5:19). Specifically, God's reconciliation means that God did not count the world's trespasses against them (5:19; cf. also Rom. 4:3-8). Reconciliation means, of course, that a relationship of enmity and hostility has been brought to an end, and in its place stands a relationship of peace and goodwill. Yet, the initiative for bringing an end to the hostility existing between humanity and God lay with God: "all this is from God" (cf. Rom. 11:36; I Cor. 8:6).

Second, God is the chief actor in the work of Christ. The work of Christ is, of course, central, but Paul here stresses that Christ was the agent through whom God achieved reconciliation (5:18-19). This appears to be the sense of verse 19: "God was in Christ reconciling the world to himself." The well-known exegetical problem here is whether this is primarily a christological statement about the incarnation or whether it is primarily a soteriological statement emphasizing the reconciling work of God. If the former, the emphasis will lie on the first part of the verse, "God was in Christ," i.e., incarnate, and reconciliation will be seen as that which was accomplished through the incarnation. If the latter, the emphasis will lie on the statement about reconciliation, and "in Christ" will be taken as parallel to "through Christ" in verse 18. In this case, Christ will be seen as the agent through whom the reconciling work of God was done. Given the way in which Paul's remarks in this passage stress the primacy of God in the work of salvation, the latter interpretation is to be preferred. This same emphasis is seen in 5:21: "For our sake he [God] made him to be sin who knew no sin." It was God, after all, who took the initiative in sending the sinless One "in the likeness of sinful flesh, and for sin" (Rom. 8:3). The sinlessness of the Messiah became a cardinal belief in early Christian thought (cf. John 8:46; Heb. 4:15; 7:26; I Pet. 2:22), and was also a well-documented notion in Jewish thought of the time (cf. Psalms of Solomon 17:40-41; Testament of Judah 24:1; Testament of Levi 18:9).

Third, the work of ministry is ultimately initiated and accomplished by God. The ministry of reconciliation was given by God not only to "us," that is, Paul and his colleagues, but also to all Christians by extension. It should be regarded as a gift of God given by the mercy of God (II Cor. 4:1), as a trust (5:19; also I Cor. 4:1), and consequently ministers are seen here as "ambassadors for Christ," those speaking in Christ's stead (Philem. 9; Eph. 6:20). Called to this ministry of service, ministers quite naturally see themselves as "servants of God" (II Cor. 6:3). The language is quite clear: "God making his appeal through us" (5:20). The person of the messenger simply becomes a vehicle, or conduit, through which the divine message is relayed, so that the appeal the messenger makes is God's own appeal: "Be reconciled to God" (5:20). It is in this sense that we can understand the quite audacious claim that ministers of reconciliation are God's co-workers (6:1; cf. I Cor. 3:9). As those who share in the "new creation in Christ" (5:17), they are participants in the eschatological work of God, and thus with God are able to proclaim, "Behold, now is the acceptable time; behold, now is the day of salvation" (cf. Luke 4:19, 21).

Mark 4:35-41

Today's Gospel lesson records the first of several miracles joined by at least four crossings of the Sea of Galilee (4:35; 5:21; 6:45; 8:13) in the boat which had earlier been prepared for Jesus (3:1) and from which he had taught the crowds in parables (4:1). By means of the sea crossings Mark is able to present the ministry of Jesus as extending to both Jews and Gentiles with equal power to heal and to exorcise demons. This entire section, 4:35–8:21, highlights the power of Jesus and the failure of the disciples to understand who Jesus is.

Jesus' stilling the storm at sea (4:35-41) is clearly an exorcism story. That Jesus is exorcising a storm-demon is evident in the exorcism formula (the rebuke and command to silence) which Jesus used elsewhere in addressing demons (1:25). The story assumes the sea to be the abode of forces hostile to God (Ps. 74:13-14; 89:9-13; 104:5-9; Job 38:8-11) and portrays Jesus as possessing the power of God over those forces (Ps. 65:7; 89:9; Jon. 1:15-16). Our text, then, is a portion of that large portrait of Jesus in Mark 1–8 as the powerful Son of God, able to overcome disease, sin, demons, and death, a sharp contrast to the Jesus of Mark 9–15 who is in prospect and in fact the suffering and crucified Son.

Our text offers us one of those rare stories of Jesus' power being exercised in the presence of and for the benefit of his disciples alone. The boat scene is removed from Jewish crowds on one shore and Gentile crowds on the other (the story in 5:1-20 is an example of a ministry among Gentiles). What we have here is an occasion of Jesus alone with his followers, or in terms of Mark's situation, Jesus directly ministering to and addressing the church. What is being said?

The disciples are on a trip, not of their own choosing but at Jesus' command (verse 35). They are not alone but they act as though they were. The world around them is one enormous storm of wind, wave, and rising water. Jesus is asleep, the picture of quiet confidence in the power of the God who made both land and sea (images and themes here recall Jonah 1: a ship, a storm, and the one person on board who trusts the Creator God is asleep). The activity that changes the situation is framed upon a double reproach. The disciples reproach Jesus (do you not care?) and Jesus reproaches them (why are you afraid?). This double reproach will appear again as the structure for the exchange between Peter and Jesus at Caesarea Philippi (8:27-33). What must not be overlooked here is that the power Jesus exercises over the storm is that of the "Teacher" (verse 38). In Mark this is the title for Jesus not only when he is teaching but when he is casting out demons. Read again 1:21-28 to recall how it is Jesus the teacher who exorcises and Jesus the exorcist who teaches. Undoubtedly Mark is locating Jesus' power in his words, a matter of great importance for a church suffering in a persecuting world. Jesus' word is still present and it is a word of power.

In this as in many stories to follow, the disciples do not understand. Their ignorance is not of the kind that results in poor grades in class; they do not know who Jesus is. So profound and destructive is this ignorance that they eventually will abandon Jesus (14:50). This not knowing Jesus lies at the root of their cowardice and fear. The story is not, as some sermons would have us believe, a simple one with the sequence of storm, fear, and then calm. The fear of the disciples is described as following Jesus' stilling the storm, following Jesus' reproach, "Why are you afraid? Have you no faith?" It is then that Mark says, quite literally, "They feared a great fear" (verse 41). The RSV's "They were filled with awe" is hardly strong enough. The storm is frightening, to be sure, but they are in the presence of a power greater than the storm. They can only turn to one another and ask, "Who then is this, that even wind and sea obey him?" (verse 41). Mark ended the story with this question, confident that even if those first disciples did not know, the church to whom he wrote did. The church knew, but in the storm sometimes it forgot.

Proper 8

Sunday Between June 26 and July 2 Inclusive

II Samuel 6:1-15; Psalm 24; II Corinthians 8:7-15; Mark 5:21-43

II Samuel 6:1-15

With the exception of II Corinthians 8:7-15, which contains Paul's exhortations that the Christian life entails sharing one's possessions with the poor, all the readings touch on the theme of the power of the Holy. Central in the Old Testament lection is the death of Uzzah who touched the ark. Psalm 24 reflects a liturgy for entrance into the sacred precincts of the temple, a liturgy which might have included a procession with the ark. Among the miracle stories in Mark 5:21-43 is the report of the woman who was healed because she touched Jesus' garment, and he sensed that "power had gone forth from him" (verse 30).

Between David's anointing as king over all the tribes and his capture of Jerusalem—considered last week—and today's reading only two matters are reported: (1) he took more wives and concubines, who bore to him a number of children (II Sam. 5:13-16), and (2) David had to deal with a threat from the Philistines, who understandably were disturbed to learn that all Israel had united behind him. Historically, this was of the greatest importance. It was the external threat from the militarily superior Philistines that had moved the tribes to establish a monarchy in the first place. Certainly one of the most significant feats of David's rule is that he succeeded where Saul had failed, finally putting an end to the Philistine threat. Without that accomplishment Israel never could have developed as an independent state.

Second Samuel 6 is the account of how David brought the ark to Jerusalem, thus making it the center of worship as well as the capital. The central figure in the story is the ark itself,

61

not the king. This narrative picks up the account of the movements of the ark where it left off in I Samuel 6:21–7:2, which explains the presence of the ark in Kiriath-jearim. Our chapter is the last of a series of stories about the ark, one of which is the account of its capture by the Philistines, who finally let it go because of its awesome and dangerous power (I Sam. 5–6).

Our reading is a continuous though not quite complete report of the transportation of the ark to its home in Jerusalem. The account is not concluded until 6:19, but in the meantime the story of David's wife Michal the daughter of Saul has begun. She ridiculed David for his public display of exuberance during the procession into Jerusalem, and he put her aside.

The narrative has three distinct parts: it reports (1) how David and his men went to get the ark and began the procession to Jerusalem (verses 1-5), (2) an incident on the way when Uzzah was killed because he touched the ark (verses 6-10), and (3) how the procession to Jerusalem was resumed some three months later (verses 12-15).

From beginning to end the account is replete with liturgical language and ritual activities. Some of these allusions doubtless refer to ancient, pre-monarchical practices, but others must reflect later activities in the temple, such as those reflected in Psalm 24. The mood and rhetorical fullness of the language that characterizes the ark in verse 2*b* reveals it to be a liturgical formula. The processions (verses 5, 12-15), like those on high occasions at the temple, were loud and joyous affairs. Moreover, David clearly performs priestly functions. He offers the sacrifice (verse 13) and wears a priestly garment (verse 14).

For all the descriptions of the ark and the accounts of its exploits, its precise nature and function remain elusive. This much is clear: it was a portable religious shrine, the symbol of the presence of Yahweh. Moreover, its origins almost certainly go back to the time before the Israelite tribes entered Canaan. It is identified variously as, "the ark of Yahweh," "the ark of God," "the ark of the covenant," and "the ark of the testimony." The only detailed description of it (Exod. 25:10-22) comes from the Priestly Document, written long after the ark had disappeared. It would have been a box which contained other sacred objects, and would have been large enough to require several persons—or an ox cart—to carry it. Most likely it symbolized the throne of Yahweh. That certainly is the view of this tradition that speaks of "the ark of God, which is called by the name of the Lord of hosts who sits enthroned on the cherubim" (verse 2).

While this is an easy story to tell it is not an easy one to preach, primarily because of what transpires in its central scene. When the oxen pulling the cart stumbled and the ark was in danger of falling, Uzzah touched it. At this point the Old Testament does not mince words: "God smote him there because he put forth his hand to the ark; and he died" (verse 7). How could those who told and heard this story believe such a thing? The answer lies in the understanding of holiness as terrifying and dangerous. No one could see God and live. In later times, even the name of God was considered so sacred that it could not be uttered out loud.

Obviously, it was possible and necessary for persons to approach the ark and even touch it. How else could it be loaded on the cart? But it must have been believed that one could safely approach it only in certain ritually proper ways. What jars our modern consciousness is that correct movements, postures, and words were more important than one's motives, for clearly Uzzah reached out his hand with the best of intentions.

If we respond in anger at the injustice of Uzzah's death, we are not the first to do so. David himself was both angry and afraid (verses 8-9). This strange story leaves us to ponder the fact that anger and fear are such close cousins. Furthermore, it may stimulate us to pause and reflect on sacredness as distance, on the God who is the radically other.

Psalm 24

The Old Testament reading for this Sunday, II Samuel 6:1-15, tells the story of how David and his supporters brought the ark of the covenant to Jerusalem from its resting place near Kiriath-jearim (see I Sam. 7:2). Psalm 24 was the litany for a cultic ritual in which the ark was carried into the temple during festival celebrations. It celebrates the entrance of God into his holy place.

Of all the psalms, Psalm 24 probably illustrates most clearly the fact that the Psalms were used as the spoken part of cultic rituals. Throughout verses 3-10, the material is comprised of a series of questions and answers probably recited by pilgrims and priests.

The psalm opens (verses 1-2) with a hymnic praise of Yahweh which identifies the God of Israel as the possessor of the world and all that is in it. The ownership of the terrestrial kingdom is his by right of creation. He is the one who anchored the earth in the midst of the seas and established it firmly upon the rivers (or streams) of the deep that ancients believed lay underneath the dry land. (Such a belief is partially based on the presence of springs and wells which suggests that water lies beneath the earth.)

The questions in verse 3 were addressed by the pilgrims to the priests inside the temple as the pilgrims arrived at the gates of the temple. The questions concern the qualifications demanded of those allowed to enter the sacred precincts: "Who shall ascend the hill of the Lord [who can enter the temple precincts]? Who shall stand in his holy place [in the temple in the presence of God]?" The priestly answer in this catechism of admission (verses 4-5) brings together two pairs of ethical qualifications: purity of outward deeds (clean hands) and purity of thought or inward truthfulness (pure heart) followed by purity of religious practice or unadulterated faith (not lifting up the soul to what is vain) and purity in speaking (does not swear deceitfully). These four principles in themselves provide a rather comprehensive perspective of ethical demands and requirements. If such demands as these were made as part of the worship, then one surely cannot condemn ancient worship services of being free from ethical interests and demands.

Verse 6 provides the worshipers' response to the requirements for entrance: "Those are the kind of people we are." Thus they claim the promises of verse 5—blessing and vindication from God.

With verse 7, the focus shifts from humankind and the moral values of living to God himself. The pilgrims or choir outside the sanctuary address the temple gates demanding that they be lifted up so that the King of glory can come in. But how could God enter the sanctuary? No doubt, the ark, the symbol of God's presence, had been carried out of the temple to reenter with the pilgrims on a high holy festival day. The choir or priests within offer a response in the form of a question, "Who is the King of glory?" God is then described as the one strong and mighty, mighty in battle. Perhaps part of the festival involved the proclamation of God's triumph over the forces of evil.

Earlier in the life of the church Psalm 24 became one of the texts associated with Jesus' descent into Hades (hell) and his triumph over the forces of darkness. The influence of this psalm in the gate liturgy of Christ's descent into hell can be seen in the non-canonical *Gospel According to the Hebrews, Gospel of Nicodemus,* and the *Acts of Pilate.* Thus Psalm 24 became a classic text for the harrowing of hell. The gates became those standing against Christ and the church and the Christ became the King of glory.

II Corinthians 8:7-15

Today's epistolary lection should be read in light of chapters 8 and 9, which are devoted to the topic of the collection for the Jerusalem poor. Earlier, Paul gave directions to the Corinthians concerning this relief fund (I Cor. 16:1-2), a project to which he had committed himself early on (Gal. 2:10). His former instructions were primarily matters of protocol on how the funds should be collected within the church. By the time he writes these two chapters, the Corinthians appear to have lost enthusiasm for the project, and Paul's task now is to convince them to make good their earlier intentions (verse 10). As it turns out, these two chapters constitute the most extensive set of remarks in any of his epistles concerning the question of financial stewardship. For this reason, they provide an abundant resource for modern Christians who often need to be challenged to contribute financially to worthwhile projects.

First, a few words about the collection. As we know from various references in the Pauline Letters, this project had vast importance for Paul. It occupied much of his time and attention during his ministry in the Aegean area in the 50s. It was first, and foremost, a charitable gesture toward the poor in Jerusalem, and for this reason alone had merit (cf. Gal. 2:10; Rom. 15:26). But it was more than a relief fund. It also had great symbolic significance in that it served as a concrete expression of solidarity between the Gentile Christians and Jewish Christians. As Paul stresses elsewhere, since the Gentiles had shared in the spiritual legacy of the Jewish Christians, they should express their debt by alleviating the financial needs of the Jerusalem poor (cf. Rom. 15:27; also II Cor. 9:11-14). If successful, this collection could serve as a vivid symbol of the unity of the Jewish and Gentile churches. In addition, there may also have been eschatological significance to this project. As Paul states in Romans 9–11, his hope was that the conversion of the Gentiles would eventually bring about the conversion of all Israel. Once this occurred, the eschaton could be ushered in. The collection appears to have been a central element in his mission strategy and to this degree would have played an important role in his ultimate mission.

In today's epistolary lection, Paul appeals to the Corinthians in several ways to participate in the collection.

First, he adduces the example of the Macedonian churches who had given generously even though they were in no financial position to do so (II Cor. 8:1-5). They had given even beyond their capacity, and in this respect surprised Paul. Yet, the clue to their generosity lay in their prior commitment of their very selves: "first they gave themselves to the Lord" (II Cor. 8:5). He admits quite openly that he tells them about the keenness of the Macedonians in order to put their own love to the test (verse 8).

In appealing to the Corinthians, Paul begins by underscoring their abundance. They excel in everything—"in faith, in utterance, in knowledge, in all earnestness, and in your love for us" (verse 7). He now hopes that their zeal to excel will translate into enthusiastic commitment to "this gracious work also." Earlier, Paul had emphasized how abundantly they had been blessed (I Cor. 1:5). What is striking is the way in which he inventories their pool of resources. All of these things he mentions are spiritual gifts rather than monetary assets, yet Paul insists that they represent a store of abundance out of which the Corinthians can give. As he says later, they have become rich (verse 9; cf. I Cor. 1:5; II Cor. 9:11; also Eph. 3:8). This becomes a salutary reminder that one's possessions are not merely monetary, but that what one has come to enjoy in Christ must be accounted as genuine wealth.

Second, Paul adduces the example of Christ: "though he was rich, yet for your sake he became poor, so that by his poverty you might become rich" (verse 9). Here, of course, he is referring to Christ's exalted status prior to his incarnation (Phil. 2:5-11) which, on any showing, can only be regarded as a position of privilege, indeed wealth. In his self-emptying, however, he relinquished the supreme possession—life with God. As the Gospels make clear, the lot of the historical Jesus was one of modest possessions, if not poverty (Matt. 8:20; Luke 9:58).

The form of this verse is chiastic: Christ, who was rich, became poor, so that we, who are poor, might become rich. Some have suggested that this is a fragment from an early Christian hymn, and it may well be, although it is difficult to prove. By its chiastic pattern, however, the verse does serve to illustrate the paradox of the incarnation (cf. II Cor. 5:21; Rom. 15:3).

Though he does not do so here, Paul might well have appealed to his own example in this respect, for his own apostolic behavior also exemplified a willingness to pauperize himself in order that others might enjoy the riches of the gospel (cf. I Cor. 4:11; 13:3; II Cor. 6:10).

Third, Paul mentions their earlier commitment (verses 10-14). For whatever reason, the Corinthians had earlier committed to the project but had not followed through. Perhaps the controversy with the opponents in the church had preoccupied their attention. Or, they may simply have lost enthusiasm for the project. In any event, Paul stresses that they should give out of what they have and not try to give what they do not have (verse 12). He also stresses that the operative norm should be "equality" (verses 13-14). In this instance, the Jerusalem poor are in need, and the

Corinthians should give out of their abundance to meet their need. In the future, if it turns out that the Corinthians are in need, then from their abundance the Jerusalem church will supply their need. He adduces the example of Israel in the wilderness who, when fed with manna, was equitably served (Exod. 16:18).

Mark 5:21-43

The Gospel lesson for today can best be heard in its dramatic radicality if read in connection with the Old Testament lesson and the psalm. A man touches the ark of the covenant, intending to be helpful, and he falls to the ground dead. The ark is the place of God's presence and therefore is holy. The psalmist raises, then, a very important question, Who can ascend God's holy hill, who can stand in God's holy place? The early Christians did not dismiss the question as solely a Jewish one and glibly declare nothing is sacred. On the contrary, the church addressed the question soberly in both creed and story: in creed by declaring God's coming to us and identifying with us in Christ who was rich but who for our sakes became poor (II Cor. 8:9); in story by telling of Jesus bringing God's healing presence to the diseased, the unclean, the deceased. Our Gospel recalls two such stories.

As stated in the comments last week on Mark 4:35-41, two double crossings of the Sea of Galilee join the stories in 4:35–8:21. Mark says that Jesus ministered without distinction on both the Jewish shore and the Gentile shore of the sea. By this arrangement of the material Mark is declaring that Christ blesses without partiality Jew and Gentile, near and far, clean and unclean. In the immediate context of our lesson, Jesus had crossed the sea (4:35; 5:1) and performed a most extraordinary exorcism in Gentile territory, among swine keepers, no less (5:1-20)! He has now returned to the western shore (verse 21) to Jewish territory, and the two stories that follow are Jewish in context and implication. One has to do with a synagogue ruler (verses 22-24, 35-43) and the other with a woman who was, according to Jewish law (Lev. 15:25-30), unclean by reason of her flow of blood. Both stories also carry symbolically the tradition of Judaism in the number twelve: the woman was ill twelve years (verse 25), the ruler's daughter was twelve years old (verse 42).

We have spent enough time in Mark to recognize in the structure of our text a prominent feature of this Gospel: one story is split (verses 21-24, 35-43) and another is inserted (verses 25-34). We have noticed this trait earlier (1:21-28; 3:20-35) and will have other examples of it later. The question is, What does Mark intend by this? One could see here no more than the style of a good storyteller: the inserted story builds anticipation for the conclusion of the first. Or, one could say that the inserted story is logically necessary to allow time for the condition of the child to worsen and for her to die. But since Mark has elsewhere used this structure to allow stories to interpret one another (as in 1:21-28 and 3:20-35), we may assume this to be the case here.

The stories are alike in their telling. Both involve cases of extreme need: the woman has exhausted all options and all resources and is now desperate; the girl is gravely ill and dies before Jesus arrives. In both, large crowds are on the scene but not privy to what is really happening. As for the disciples they are blind to the one healing and, except for the select three, are absent from the other. In the case of the woman, the disciples are so excited about the big crowd they cannot distinguish between a push and a touch (verses 30-31) and the responses to Jesus' ministry are similar: "fear and trembling" (verse 33) in one, "overcome with amazement" (verse 42) in the other. But the two stories are joined at a deeper level.

Perhaps it would be sufficient to say that Mark, concerned to show the power of the "stronger one" (chapters 1–8), here offers examples of Jesus overcoming sickness and death. That Jesus brought the helping, healing, life-giving presence of God to the human scenes of disease, fear, alienation, and death is good news for a lifetime of witnessing. But the issues are not solely medical nor are the blessings solely private. Social factors are prominent. A girl is dead, and because a corpse defiles, certain taboos are now in place (Lev. 21). A woman has a discharge of blood and therefore is to her family, her friends, her neighbors, and her synagogue, an outcast (Lev. 15:25-30). But the Jesus who ministered among foreigners (verses 1-20) is here among his own people moving across religious and social barriers to offer God's healing and restoring grace. This, says Mark, is not simply the church's belief about Jesus but the warrant, in fact, the mandate, for its own behavior toward all persons.

Proper 9

Sunday Between July 3 and 9 Inclusive

II Samuel 7:1-17; Psalm 89:20-37; II Corinthians 12:1-10;
Mark 6:1-6

II Samuel 7:1-17

The Old Testament lesson contains Nathan's prophecy that the Lord has chosen David and his dynasty to rule over the people of God, and Psalm 89:20-37 is a direct response to it, containing not a prayer but the word of God confirming and affirming that dynasty. The epistolary text is Paul's self-defense—he is a true apostle—and the Gospel lection is the account of the sending of the Twelve. If all the readings share a theme it is the question of the authority and role of those responsible for the people of God. On that question the Old and New Testament texts stand in sharp contrast. In the former God's power is manifest in nothing other than power and glory (though note the divine disclaimer concerning a temple, II Sam. 7:6-7). In the latter God's power "is made perfect in weakness" (II Cor. 12:9), and though he does mighty works, Jesus is a prophet without honor in his own country (Mark 6:4).

Second Samuel 7 is the pivotal chapter in the story of David. It records what for later generations was the most important event in his life, the Lord's covenant with David and with his descendants that they would occupy the throne in Jerusalem "for ever" (verses 13, 16). Its central location is stressed by the first verse, which emphasizes that David is settled into his own "house" in Jerusalem, and the Lord had given him "rest" from his enemies. The promise then comes at the high point of David's life, after he has united the nation, moved the ark to Jerusalem, put an end to external threats (but note II Sam. 8), and before his serious troubles began.

The reading for the day consists of two major parts:

1. Verses 1-3 introduce the event and report David's dialogue with Nathan, who appears here for the first time. The king tells the prophet of his concern for the ark, indicating his intention to build a house for it. While David's words are not phrased as a question, Nathan's response suggests that behind the dialogue lies the practice of consulting prophets or priests for the will of God before a major undertaking, such as going to war or constructing a temple.

2. Verses 4-17 contain, with narrative introduction and conclusion, Nathan's prophecy concerning David and his dynasty. The divine revelation is reported as it came to the prophet in the form of a message for the king.

Nathan's prophecy contains both ancient and later traditions, and is told here from the perspective of later generations who experienced and remembered the monarchy as the incarnation of the grace of God. It is a thoroughly positive view, contrasting, for example, with Samuel's warning as reported in I Samuel 8:10-18. But it is not naïve. Kings, even those elected by God, stray and need divine correction and punishment (verse 14).

Several features of the narrative call for particular remarks.

1. Yahweh's initial response to David's plan (verses 5-7) rejects the idea of a "house" and recalls the history of salvation from the time of the Exodus. While these lines do not go as far as later prophetic critique of the temple cult they do assume that the God of Israel cannot be bound to a single place.

2. The first part of the promise (verses 8-11*a*) concerns only David and the people of Israel. Nothing is said of a dynasty. The Lord has chosen David and made him what he is in order to give the people peace. Whether this has already happened or will come in the future is an open question because it is not certain how the Hebrew tenses of verses 9*b*-11*a* should be read. Most modern translations read them as future, but they could just as well be past or present.

3. What now stands as the heart of the chapter is the prophecy extended to later generations (verses 11*b*-16). It is a play on words. David wanted to build Yahweh a "house" for

the ark, that is a temple, but instead Yahweh promises to make a "house" for David, that is, a dynasty, and one which shall stand forever.

4. Verse 13 stands out as a special note, and one which is in contrast with the view of the temple stated at the outset. Without mentioning his name it indicates that Solomon will be the one to build the temple. That was a historical fact which the tradition could not avoid. First Chronicles 22:7-10 gives a later explanation of the reason Solomon and not David was the one to build the temple.

This passage brings us close to the roots of important aspects of the biblical understanding of a messiah. The word "messiah" comes from the Hebrew word for "anointed one," applied to David and other kings. Its Greek equivalent is "Christ." More particularly, we have here an account of the roots of the New Testament understanding that the Messiah will be a descendant of David. Between the time of David and the time of Jesus, however, a great many transformations took place. The covenant with David (see II Sam. 23:5) was understood early to be a continuation of God's saving history with Israel. Promise to the patriarchs, Exodus, leading in the wilderness, covenant on Mount Sinai, the granting of the land of Canaan—and now David and his dynasty. That faith grew in the southern state of Judah after the division following the death of Solomon, and more and more came to be idealized by both prophets (see Isa. 9, 11) and cultic song. After the end of the state and the monarchy at the hands of the Babylonians, hope for a king in the line of David became more and more an eschatological expectation.

Psalm 89:20-37

In II Samuel 7, we find Nathan telling David that God has promised to establish the house of David as the divinely elected dynasty to rule over Israel for all time. This promise of God or covenant between David and God became the basis for the Old Testament understanding of the king. It was also the seedbed from which soil grew the expectation of a future messiah who would bring salvation to God's people and God's rule on earth.

Psalm 89 is a royal lament in which we find many of the divine promises to the Davidic ruler. This psalm was used when the promises of God and the reality of the eternal covenant were called into question. As such, it is a prayer that God will restore the conditions of the covenant and manifest his divine fidelity to the promises. The contents of the psalm may be outlined as follows: introduction (verses 1-4), hymn of praise (verses 5-18), recitation of the divine-Davidic covenant (verses 19-37), description of the monarch's condition of distress (verses 38-45), and an appeal for help (verses 46-51).

In today's lection, the text focuses on the conditions and promises of the divine covenant with David. As such, the scripture reading may be viewed as a commentary or exposition of the promises delivered to David by the prophet Nathan in II Samuel 7.

Verse 19, not included in the psalm reading, is the introduction to the section on the promises to David. It suggests that the promises to David were spoken in a vision to God's "faithful one" but does not make clear whether the "faithful one" was David himself or Nathan the prophet. The promises, however, are all presented in the first person as spoken by Yahweh himself. The opening divine statement, in verse 19*b*, emphasizes three aspects about David: (1) he is a mighty person (and certainly the Old Testament narratives about David present him as a successful and powerful person), (2) he is one whom God exalted (again the Old Testament text emphasizes that David was Yahweh's favorite whose status depended on divine blessing), and (3) David was a person with common roots whose exalted position was based on divine choice and election (a point emphasized in the story of David's anointing in I Sam. 16:1-13).

Verses 20-29 in today's reading present the promises that relate initially to David; verses 30-37 concern David's posterity, the descendants and successors of David and their relationship to the law and God's punishment for their transgressions of the law.

Verses 20-21 describe the process of David's selection as his "being found" by God. Unlike the situation in other Near Eastern cultures, where the king was regarded as a

74

superhuman if not a god, such texts as this point to the commonness of David before his exaltation by God. A characteristic description of the ruler is that he is God's servant and his role is to be an instrument of the Deity. The anointment, referred to in verse 20*b*, was the act by which the new monarch became the messiah ("the anointed one") in ancient Israel. If verse 21 is a continuation of verse 20 which seems most likely, then anointment could be interpreted as divine assurance of God's continuing presence and support.

The basic promises of God to David or the consequences of the divine covenant are given in verses 22-29. These texts present, in staccato fashion and with a brevity of words, the basic threads interwoven into the royal tapestry that rested so majestically upon the shoulders of every Davidic heir. Among these were the assurance that David would not suffer humiliation at the hand of his enemies (verse 22); that he would prevail over his foes and despisers (verse 23); that God would be true to his commitments and through his name the king would be victorious and acclaimed (verse 24); that the Davidic dominion and rule would be universal extending to the sea and rivers that encircle the habitable world (verse 25); that the king would possess the privilege of addressing God as "Father" and of being the son of the divine (verse 26); that David's reputation would be unexcelled among the kings of the world where he would be treated as first-born and thus heir of twice the portion of any other (verse 27); that God's covenant would be forever established (verse 28); and that the Davidic line would rule forever or as long as the heavens endured (verse 29).

With verse 30, the focus of the psalm shifts to consider how God will respond when the descendants of David do not live according to the laws and commandments of God. This section thus introduces the qualifying conditional aspects related to the Davidic house. Verses 22-29 provide the positive aspects of the relationship ("this is how it is") while verses 30-37, but especially verses 30-33, present the conditions which temper the absolutes of the promises ("however, one must also recognize that . . ."). The "however" of the relationship has God stipulating that when David's children, the members of the dynasty who rule after him, do not remain faithful to the revealed and understood will of God (see the emphasis on the king's relationship to the law in Deut. 17:18-20), then God offers his assurance that their transgressions and iniquities will be severely dealt with—by punishment with rod and scourge.

The concerns of Yahwism for social justice, moral passion, and governmental integrity could not fail but place the monarch under ethical scrutiny. Political wrongdoing, personal immorality, and religious irresponsibility, even or perhaps especially of the monarch, could not be allowed free reign. Royal status was not conceived as guaranteeing royal immunity. The king was to stand beside not above the law.

Nevertheless, in spite of the disciplinary action and punishment that might befall the monarch, God promises that his fidelity to the covenant will never be withdrawn or altered nor will God lie to David. Instead the covenant is presented as lasting forever with a permanence comparable to that of the sun and the moon.

When preaching from this text, the minister of course must take into consideration the fact that verses 19-37 present the Davidic covenant in all its exaggerated claims so that the lament and distress, actually a complaint against God, in verses 38-45, will stand out in stark profile. The Deity is accused of lack of fidelity and a failure to keep his promises.

II Corinthians 12:1-10

In this cycle of readings from Second Corinthians, only this passage stems from the larger section comprising chapters 10–13, Paul's *apologia* of his own apostolic ministry. The tone throughout this section is polemical, as Paul responds directly to the charges made against him by outside opponents who have entered the Corinthian church only to threaten his influence and leadership within the church. From his remarks in this section, it appears that he has been charged with being vacillating and undependable, saying one thing and doing another, behaving one way in their presence and another way when absent (cf. II Cor. 10:1, 10). What emerges from his polemical defense is a rather thorough treatment of his apostolic ministry.

From what we can gather, it looks as if his opponents, who were themselves Christian apostles, or missionaries (II Cor. 11:13), were authenticating their form of ministry by appealing to such things as signs and wonders, visions and revelations, or other such demonstrations of power. In Paul's view, they were "boasting of worldly things," or literally "according to the flesh" (*kata sarka;* II Cor. 11:18). Even though he violently disagrees with this form of authenticating ministry, because of the seriousness of the situation, he concedes to play their game on their turf. He constantly insists that such a line of argument is "foolishness" (II Cor. 11:1, 16-21; 12:11), but he pursues it nevertheless.

In today's epistolary lection, Paul concedes that he is playing the game on their terms: "I must boast," he writes (verse 1), even though it is inappropriate. Given the criteria used by his opponents, he agrees to mention the "visions and revelations of the Lord" that he experienced. From other sources, we know of visions he had experienced (Acts 26:19), as well as revelations he had received from the Lord (Gal. 1:12; 2:2; cf. also I Cor. 14:6, 26; Rom. 2:5; 8:19; I Cor. 1:7; II Thess. 1:7).

He recalls a specific experience of a man in Christ he had known who had been caught up into the third heaven, or Paradise (verses 2-4) fourteen years earlier. Even though he speaks in the third person, there can be little doubt that he is speaking of his own experience. Otherwise, why introduce it here? He does, however, seem to distinguish between the experience of "this man" and that of himself (verse 5), but likely he is merely drawing a distinction between himself as a visionary and himself as a suffering apostle (verse 5). Descriptions of similar experiences are found in literature of the period (cf. I Enoch 39:3-4; II Enoch 7:1; III Baruch 2:2). In this ecstatic state, Paul tells us that he heard unspeakable things: "things that cannot be told, which man may not utter" (verse 4). This is reminiscent of other instances in which a prophetic seer or visionary received sealed revelations (cf. Isa. 8:16; Dan. 12:4; II Enoch 17; Rev. 14:3).

In spite of the many puzzling features of this description, one thing is clear: Paul places little stock in it as an occasion for genuine boasting, or for authenticating his ministry. He is aware, for one thing, that more is often made of such matters than they deserve (verse 6). They also lend themselves to exaggeration.

But Paul does not look to such experiences to authenticate his ministry. Rather, he finds that experiences "from below" rather than experiences "from above" provide the arena in which he has most keenly experienced the power of God. Thus, even though he has had an "abundance of revelations" (verse 7), he has had to contend with "a thorn in the flesh, a messenger of Satan" (verse 7), sent by God to harass him and curb his arrogant spirit. This, of course, is a much contested verse, and explanations for Paul's "thorn in the flesh" have ranged from psychological disorders to physical maladies, such as bad eyesight, stomach problems, and epilepsy. We can never know, nor need we know. We do know that Paul earnestly appealed to the Lord for its removal, only to be told, "My grace is sufficient for you, for my power is made perfect in weakness" (verse 9).

This revelation from the Lord, more than all his other visions and revelations, provided him with the hermeneutical key for interpreting his own experience. What he knew only too well was that "weaknesses, insults, hardships, persecutions, and calamities" (verse 10) were far more frequent and typical of his apostolic life than were visions and revelations. What is more, they placed him in more direct touch with the experience of Christ (Gal. 2:20; 6:17; II Cor. 4:10-11). In this respect, his life was analogous to that of Christ. Indeed, the crucifixion of Christ came to symbolize human suffering experienced in response to a divine calling. It was the cross, after all, that epitomized weakness and impotence; yet, it was precisely through the cross, the symbol of weakness, that God had chosen to exhibit redemptive power. This was the paradox of the cross that formed the center of Paul's preaching (I Cor. 1:18-31). Through the cross, weakness had become the means through which he experienced genuine strength.

Mark 6:1-6

The Gospel for today is a vivid though somewhat sad reminder that the Christian confession of faith is not "I believe in Christ" but "I believe Jesus is the Christ." After all, to believe in a Christ or Messiah, someone who will deliver, bring relief, set a people free is not necessarily a Christian belief. Looking for messiahs is widespread in political as well as religious communities. But the early Christians said, "The Messiah has come and it is Jesus of Nazareth." Mark 6:1-6 is about Jesus of Nazareth. Jesus is in his hometown (1:9), in his home synagogue, where he is identified in a number of ways. The citizens know him as a carpenter, as Mary's son, as sibling to four brothers and several sisters. As sharply as the New Testament states it anywhere, this text presents Jesus in what theologians sometimes call "the scandal of particularity." Just as the Old Testament reading and the Psalms speak of David, just as the Epistle for today speaks of Paul, so Mark portrays Jesus Christ, not as an idea or an image but as a person living under the conditions of time, place, and relationships which all of us know.

Mark's account of Jesus' return to Nazareth and of his break with family, kin, and acquaintances has already been prefigured in 3:21-35 which tells about his unbelieving family who had come to take him away because they heard that he was beside himself. The Nazareth story is not pro-Gentile, anti-Jew in its perspective. The literary setting is the large unit 4:35–8:21 in which Jesus ministers to both Jews and Gentiles. He goes to the synagogue on the sabbath (6:2) as he had on other occasions (1:21, 39). In fact, Mark says that following the rejection at Nazareth, Jesus continued his ministry of teaching in other villages (6:6b), even sending his disciples in teams of two to multiply his work of exorcising, preaching, and healing (6:7-13). Rather than being either Jewish or Gentile in orientation, the story is about a response to Jesus in a community where one might expect acceptance, trust, and discipleship. Jesus himself, while marveling at their unbelief (verse 6), looks on the situation philosophically: that a prophet is received everywhere but at home is a fitting proverb (verse 4). As Mark reports it, the response to Jesus is captured in three words: astonished (verse 2), offended, (verse 3), and disbelieved (verse 6).

But of central importance is the question, To what do the people respond with astonishment, offense, and unbelief? It was not to miracles. In fact, with minor exceptions, Jesus could do no mighty work there (verse 5). This "could not" is softened to "did not" by Matthew 13:58 and omitted altogether by Luke 4:16-30. That which astonishes Jesus' auditors and causes them to speak of his wisdom and power is his teaching (verse 2). In this regard the scene parallels that of 1:21-28 in which Jesus teaches with authority in the synagogue at Capernaum, the people are astonished, and even after Jesus performs an exorcism, the point of amazement is the teaching. Mark is silent here about the content of that teaching, as he is in most references to Jesus teaching. Mark's attention is upon the power and authority of the word of Jesus, the word which exorcizes, heals, and proclaims the Good News of the kingdom. That word was still present and powerful in the church and Mark wanted his readers to live and act in that assurance. Jesus of Nazareth is dead, buried, and raised to God but his word remains.

Our text offers, however, a sober reminder: at the speaking of the word of Christ there is sometimes offense and unbelief. Even Good News may be received and treated as bad news, and perhaps by those who would be expected to be most receptive.

Proper 10

Sunday Between July 10 and 16 Inclusive

II Samuel 7:18-29; Psalm 132:11-18; Ephesians 1:1-10;
Mark 6:7-13

II Samuel 7:18-29

It is one of the characteristics of the new Common Lectionary that the Old Testament lessons for this season, since they provide a semi-continuous story, do not necessarily introduce the themes of those from the New Testament. Still, when they are juxtaposed common issues surface. On the one hand, there is the issue of God's means of leadership for the people of God, and here there is sharp contrast between the Old Testament and the Gospel. Second Samuel 7:18-29 and Psalm 132:18 concern the divine promise of a dynasty to David, with God's power revealed in power and glory. By contrast, in Mark 6:7-13 the Twelve are sent out with all the marks of poverty. On the other hand, there is the common theme of the revelation of the future, evident in the promise of an everlasting Davidic dynasty and in the epistolary text's affirmation that God has made known to us "the mystery of his will . . . as a plan for the fulness of time, to unite all things in him . . ." (Eph. 1:1-10).

The Old Testament lesson for the day continues directly where last week's reading ended. It contains the prayer of David immediately following Nathan's prophecy of an everlasting Davidic dynasty. There is a brief narrative introduction (verse 18*a*) and then the long prayer. That the king "went in and sat before the Lord" doubtless indicates that he entered the tent which housed the ark and sat on the ground.

In terms of both form and style David's prayer is more similar to others in the historical books than to those in the Psalms. (See Judg. 6:13-18; I Sam. 1:11.) It is prose and not poetry, and certainly not structured so as to be sung. The fact that it has few marks of liturgical use, such as different voices—priest, people, prophet—strengthens the impression that it was not used in ancient Israel's worship. It is reported here to emphasize the piety and humility of David, and to strengthen the message of Nathan's prophecy.

The prayer is primarily one of praise of Yahweh and thanksgiving for the promise to the house of David. In the polite formulas of introduction (verses 18b-19) David humbles himself and acknowledges that it is Yahweh who has brought him where he is, and as if that were not enough he has shown him a future in which his descendants will be blessed. The king's reference to his "house" links the prayer to the motif of the preceding verses and uses the word in yet another sense. It had referred to the palace (verses 1-2), to the temple (verses 5-7, 13), and to the dynasty (verses 11, 16, 19). Here it refers to David's ancestral family: there was nothing in that background which would have justified Yahweh's special blessing.

The expressions of praise and thanksgiving are in the narrative mode, reciting what God has done and promised to do. The history of Yahweh's salvation of the people from Egypt is recalled (verse 23), thus emphasizing that the promise to David continues God's history of salvation for Israel. Verse 24 is a narrative form of the heart of the covenant, and thus recalls the events at Mount Sinai. Other expressions of thanksgiving repeat with only minor variations the prophecy of Nathan (verses 25-27, 29).

The prayer also includes the language of petition. David asks that God fulfill the promise and grant his blessing upon the dynasty (verses 25, 28-29). One may take such expressions as David's acceptance, on behalf of all his descendants, of the divine designation.

It is difficult to distinguish between older and later traditions in this material. The prophecy of Nathan itself certainly contains traditions that go back to the earliest generations of the monarchy. But this section, like all the material in the books of Deuteronomy through II Kings, was shaped over the centuries by editors working from the perspective of the Book of Deuteronomy. The final edition comes from the time of the Babylonian Exile (ca. 560 B.C.). Verse 23 contains language that is very similar to that in Deuteronomy 4:7, 34, and thus may be the work of a later editor.

While this entire chapter constantly speaks of David and the everlasting dynasty, they are not in the last analysis the central concern. The fundamental issue concerns the relationship between Yahweh and his people. How was the history of salvation continued, and how will it continue in the future? As noted in the commentary on the first part of this chapter last week, the promise to David represents a major religious change for Israel. Previously Yahweh had cared for the people by freely raising up a charismatic and temporary leader. Now there is a dynasty. God is seen to have made a free choice of that dynasty. In later rituals for the coronation of the Davidic kings (Ps. 2; 89; Isa. 9:1-7) Yahweh will be seen to adopt and crown the successors.

David and the sons of David were human beings, in a genuine sense the incarnation of the will of God for the people of God in human history. Our reflection on the relationship of God to the people of God—whether as families, tribes, a state, or church—as well as our reflection on the kingdom of God can be enriched by reflection on that history.

Psalm 132:11-18

Like the Old Testament reading, a portion of this selection from the psalm focuses on the continuing rule of the family of David. Two features about this continuing rule are stressed: (1) the covenant between David and God is pictured as a sure oath and (2) the promise that David's descendants would rule after him, however, is made conditional on their obedience to the will of Yahweh.

Other aspects of this reading are its emphases upon Zion as the chosen dwelling place of God (verses 12-16) and the promise to bless David (verses 17-18). This bi-polar or double focus on Zion and David is what one finds so frequently in the Old Testament. Sacred city and chosen dynasty are commonly so intricately interwoven as to comprise a single theological tapestry. The reasons for this are based on the fact that David was the conqueror of Jerusalem (Zion) which prior to his day had been no part of Israel or Judah. With the establishment of the political capital there, the Davidic monarch was in a special way the ruler over Jerusalem. This is why the town could be called "the city of David." It was the personal property of the Davidic family by right of conquest.

When Jerusalem was made into the religious capital for the people, this added a new dimension to the city. Zion was understood as the special home of God who "resided" in Jerusalem in a way that was not the case any place else. The special presence of Yahweh in Jerusalem thus supported the claims of the Davidic family. The kings of the line of David were the defenders of Yahweh's city and, at the same time, as the Deity of the city, Yahweh defended David and the rule of his descendants.

The content of Psalm 132 suggests that the psalm was used in a major recurring ritual celebration. Some scholars, however, have argued that the psalm was written for and used on the single occasion when David brought the ark to Jerusalem (II Sam. 6). The differences between this psalm and the account of the bringing of the ark to Jerusalem as well as the reference to David's sons as rulers suggest that the psalm was not composed for that specific occasion. (Note that there is no material in II Sam. 6 similar to David's oath in Ps. 132:1-4.)

The psalm is set up so that the oath of David sworn to God, in verses 3-5 (which has no parallel in any of the narratives about David), is counterbalanced by the oath of God sworn to David, in verses 11*b*-12. The former, however, is not included in this lection. Nonetheless, if one preaches on this psalm reading, the parallel oaths and their stipulations should be noted—the human oath balanced by the divine.

The oath of God to David in verses 11*b*-12 actually has two emphases. There is, first of all, the assurance that one of David's sons would sit on his throne after him. One can understand this affirmation in relationship to Solomon. In fact, such a divine promise to David could be seen as theological justification for the rule of Solomon who usurped the throne from his older brother, Adonijah, under rather shady and questionable circumstances. Second, the eternal rule ("forever") of subsequent Davidic descendants on the throne is promised but is hedged about with a major condition: they must keep the covenant and testimonies of God. There was no blank check made out to the house of David making payable an eternal rule without strings attached. The rights of dominion are tempered by the requirements of discipleship.

In verses 13-16, the emphases of the text focus on the role of Zion and God's special association and attachment to the city. The unique relationship between God and Zion—understood as the consequence of God's election of the city and his habitation in his house (temple) in its environs (verse 13)—is given expression in the form of a direct quote from God (verses 14-16). Such a divine saying must have originated in the form of a prophetic oracle similar to those attributed to Nathan in II Samuel 7.

Zion is described as God's resting place (see II Sam. 7:4-8) and his dwelling. Both verses 13 and 14 speak of God's desiring Zion as if to stress the divine enthusiastic fervor for the place. David's bringing of the ark to Zion (verses 6-7) thus fulfills the yearning and pleasure of God himself. The city (verses 15-16) and the Davidic rulers (verses 17-18) are to be blessed by the Deity who dwells in Zion. The psalm thus stresses not only the blessing bestowed upon David and his descendants but also the blessing of the city and its inhabitants. There is thus no overemphasis on the royal elite in the psalm. The city is promised abundant provisions (food) for its livelihood and bread for its poor. As a consequence or parallel, the priests will be clothed in salvation and the city's saints (inhabitants? cultic ministers?) will shout for joy. Thus the divine promise encompasses both physical and spiritual concerns.

The final two verses of the psalm revert to the theme of the Davidic family although the theme is linked to the material on Zion by the reference to "there" in verse 17. Two images are utilized to speak of the royal descendants: a horn and a lamp. The horn was a symbol of strength and rulership (see Dan. 7:7-8). The lamp is a frequent figure used for the monarch (see II Sam. 21:17), no doubt because of the significance of the lamp in providing light and thus a perspective from which to view life. Finally, the Davidic monarch is promised that his enemies will be humiliated while his own stature and importance, represented by the crown, will only increase in luster. In the international politics of antiquity, a ruler's success was built on the humiliation of others.

Three factors in the psalm may be noted in summary. First of all, the psalm illustrates the central role played by Zion in Israelite life, thus allowing one to appreciate why Jewish hopes and Zionism have always been intertwined. Second, the stress on the obedience of the Davidic rulers as a condition for God's support allowed or reflects an interpretation of history in which the downfall of the state was associated with the disobedience of the ruler (see I Sam. 12:13-15). Third, the stress on the eternal rule of the anointed (= the Messiah) from the house of David fed the expectations of a coming ruler who would reign as the ideal figure, the true Messiah.

Ephesians 1:1-10

This is the first of eight readings from the Letter to the Ephesians. The first two verses are similar in form and content to the introductory salutations in the Pauline Letters. They are remarkable in several respects. First, even though the letter is attributed to the apostle Paul, its authenticity is widely disputed. Many of the themes treated in the letter echo themes found in the undisputed Pauline Letters, but there is a distinct shift in outlook.

Second, the letter is addressed to "the saints who are also faithful in Christ Jesus" (verse 1). In some of the earliest manuscripts the phrase "in Ephesus" is omitted, and this suggests that this letter originally was intended to have a much wider audience. It has been suggested that it served as a cover letter for the Pauline corpus. Certainly, the scope of the letter is general and widely applicable to Christians everywhere.

Verses 3-10 constitute the first part of a magnificent eulogy which, in the original Greek, comprises a single sentence stretching to verse 23. In form, it is a prayer of "blessing," similar to those found in II Corinthians 1:3-7 and I Peter 1:3-9. This prayer sets a lofty tone that is to characterize the letter as a whole. Its mention of "heavenly places" (verse 3) signals the cosmic scope of the letter. As the final verse of today's lection states, it was God's purpose to "unite all things [in Christ], things in heaven and things on earth" (verse 10). Equally broad is the time frame in which the work of God is set. God's redemptive work is said to have begun even "before the foundation of the world" (verse 4), and was achieved in "the fulness of time" (verse 10). One should also note the way in which superlatives are piled on top of one another throughout the prayer. We have here the excess of the language of worship, and the words are intended to elevate the reader to the very heights from which the work of God is seen to have emanated.

The object of blessing is "the God and Father of our Lord Jesus Christ" (verse 3). God deserves to be blessed inasmuch as those in Christ have been blessed with every spiritual blessing in the heavenly places. This stress on believers having access to the "heavenly places" is typical of the letter. Those who have been raised with Christ are envisioned as actually sitting with God in the heavenly places in Christ Jesus (Eph. 2:6). The church becomes the means by which God's manifold wisdom is displayed "to the principalities and powers in the heavenly places" (Eph. 3:10). The Christian struggle is envisioned as a cosmic struggle with principalities and powers "in the heavenly places" (Eph. 6:12).

The mighty acts of God are unfolded.

1. God's work of election is mentioned (verse 4; cf. II Thess. 2:13). Even though Christians may experience God's call in the time and space of their earthly existence, they are reminded here that their salvation actually has primordial origins (cf. John 17:24; I Pet. 1:20). Even then, it was located "in Christ," who quite early on in Christian thinking was seen as a figure who preceded creation (Col. 1:15; Heb. 1:3). The purpose of God's election was to make those chosen "holy and blameless before him" (verse 4; cf. Eph. 5:27; Col. 1:22).

2. God's work of predestination: "he destined us in love to be his sons through Jesus Christ" (verse 5). This recalls a well-established Pauline theme (Rom. 8:29), but occurs elsewhere in the New Testament (I Pet. 1:2). Unfortunately, what should have been taken as a statement of loving reassurance has often been interpreted too narrowly, with far too much emphasis on the individual's fate having been predetermined. As a helpful corrective, the corporate dimension of the passage should be noted. What is being affirmed is not that a certain number of saints have been chosen in advance, but that those who are "sons through Jesus Christ" enjoy a status that was theirs long before they realized it or actualized it.

3. God's grace lavishly bestowed and displayed through Christ. The "glorious grace" of God is praised because it was freely bestowed in Christ, the Beloved (verse 6; cf. Mark 1:11; also Sirach 45:1; 46:13; Isa. 44:2). Through Christ we have redemption (cf. Rom 3:24; 8:23; I Cor. 1:30; Col. 1:14; Eph. 4:30), and this was achieved through the shedding of his blood (Eph. 2:13; Rom. 3:25; Col. 1:20; Heb. 9:22; Rev. 1:5).

4. God's work of revelation (verses 9-10). God's saving work here, as elsewhere, is conceived as a mystery concealed from the beginning of time, but now revealed in its fullness (cf. Rom. 16:25; Eph. 3:3-4, 9; Col. 1:26-27; 2:2; I Pet. 1:20). It is unfolded "in all wisdom and insight" (verse 9; cf. Col. 1:9), and thereby illuminates our own understanding, both of ourselves and God (Eph. 3:18-20). To be sure, the opening up of the mystery did not occur until the "fulness of time" (Gal. 4:4; also Mark 1:15; Col. 1:19; Tobit 14:5). Now, however, in Christ God's intention is manifest: the divine purpose is to bring about the unity of "all things in him," by which is doubtless meant the bringing together of Jews and Gentiles into a "new humanity" (Eph. 2:11-22). In doing so, heaven and earth are seen to become one.

Mark 6:7-13

The preacher will notice that all the lections for today, thought widely divergent in form and context, declare the divine purpose and human achievement within that purpose.

David cannot build God a house but God makes of David's line a house forever. Ephesians declares that the church's work of reconciliation is really God's work, having been established in the divine purpose from the beginning, to unite all creation in Christ Jesus. Within that frame of reference we turn to the Gospel which presents Jesus calling and sending the Twelve to continue his work of exorcising, preaching, and healing.

Mark 6:7-13, the sending out of the Twelve, is the first portion of an account continued in verses 30ff. We have become familiar with the Markan structural trait of inserting a narrative within a narrative, in this case the account of the death of John the Baptist (verses 14-29). The continuation of our text in verses 30-44 will be the Gospel lesson for next Sunday. Mark 6:7-13 has a Matthean parallel in 10:1-42 where it is but a part of a larger unit on instructions and warnings to Christian missionaries. Luke has two parallels, the sending of the Twelve (9:1-6) and the sending of the seventy (10:1-16).

In Mark the mission of the Twelve follows immediately the rejection at Nazareth. This should not be taken, however, as implying a turning away from Israel toward Gentiles. The itinerary of the Twelve, like that of Jesus (6:6*b*), is clearly among villages of Israel, a fact made most explicit by Matthew (10:5-6). "The twelve" in verse 7 serves almost as a title, referring to those persons named in 3:13-19 and appointed to be with Jesus and to be sent out to preach. Mark usually refers to them as "disciples," only once calling them "apostles" (6:30). "The twelve apostles" is in the New Testament primarily a Lukan designation. Apart from Peter, James, and John it is remarkable how little the New Testament tells us of the subsequent histories of these men.

The account of the mission of the Twelve in Mark 6:7-13 unfolds clearly: Jesus calls them to him, gives them authority over demons, and, judging by their activity, sends them to do exactly what he himself has been doing, preaching repentance, casting out demons, and healing (1:14-15; 1:32-39; 3:7-12). They are instructed not to take extra provisions but to depend on the hospitality of those who receive them. Neither are they to move around looking for the most comfortable lodgings but rather they are to stay where they are first received. They are not told to pronounce judgment on the inhospitable and unbelieving but simply to follow the custom of shaking off the dust from the places where they are rejected. Apparently such a witness against the non-receptive will be considered by God in the judgment. In other words, leave them to heaven and move on. Being sent (the verb which gives us the noun "apostle") in teams of two was apparently a common practice among early Christians (Acts 8:14; 15:36-40; I Cor. 9:6). The Twelve perform according to their instructions and the authority given them. Although most frequently presented unfavorably by Mark, the Twelve here are "successful," undoubtedly because they are obedient and because they carry the word and the power of Jesus himself.

Our text is obviously not simply a bit of history about Jesus and the Twelve but a word to Mark's church and subsequently to the church wherever this passage is received as Scripture and as canon. The work of Jesus is to continue and for that purpose the church is called and sent. For that work Jesus grants the word and the power that characterized his own ministry. The church is to go trusting this to be true, never contradicting that trust with the excess baggage of security and wealth that offers the world the image of unbelief, of an institution protecting itself "just in case." There will be rejection and refusal to listen, to be sure, but there will also be those who will welcome both the ministry and the minister. As it was with the Master, so it is with the servant.

Proper 11
Sunday Between July 17 and 23 Inclusive

II Samuel 11:1-15; Psalm 53; Ephesians 2:11-22; Mark 6:30-34

II Samuel 11:1-15

Psalm 53, with its meditation on the universality of corruption, sin, and depravity, is a fitting response to this account of David's sin. Moreover, the psalm, by linking the absence of faith in God to corruption, becomes an interpretation of the cause of such sin. As is so often the case, the Old Testament reading and the psalm can function in the context of worship as confession of sin. Direct links with the New Testament lessons are difficult to discern, though the epistolary text does reflect on the situation under the law.

The account of David's sin is part of what has been called the "Throne Succession Narrative," or "the Court History of David," an ancient source for the latter years of David's reign. Since all the other texts for this season concerning David also come from that source some general comments are called for. The Throne Succession Narrative includes at least II Samuel 9–20 and I Kings 1–2, and probably also some of the material in II Samuel 6–8. It is one of the finest examples of classical Hebrew prose handed down to us. On the basis of the writer's detailed and precise knowledge of the events and the characters in his story, as well as his point of view, scholars have dated the composition to the generation following David, that is, to the time of Solomon. The Deuteronomic editors of the books of Samuel and Kings included the document with little or no modification.

What was the writer's purpose and point of view? Two themes run through the entire work and unify it. On the one hand there is the question of the succession to the throne. Who will follow David? All of the most logical possibilities are considered and eliminated in one way or another. These include the surviving members of Saul's family, a possible union of the families of Saul and David—that is one point of the story of Michal's rejection in II Samuel 6:16-23—and the successive sons of David, including Amnon the eldest and Absalom, apparently next in line. Even the possibility of the dissolution of the kingdom arises. But finally, on his deathbed, David gives his blessing to Solomon. Our narrator had already prepared us for that result by telling us when Solomon was born that "the Lord loved him" (II Sam. 12:24).

On the other hand there is the theme of King David himself, and particularly his decline. The history begins when he is at the peak of his power, having completed his major accomplishments, settled down in Jerusalem, and received the divine promise of an everlasting dynasty. His last years are filled with so much trouble and anguish, both from within his own household and from without, that he is finally only a pale reflection of his former self. Why did the blessing turn to curse? The turning point is reported in our text for the day, the account of his sin with Bathsheba against Uriah the Hittite. Because of this the sword does not depart from his house (II Sam. 12:10).

The author was a historian, though not in the critical modern sense. He did not simply record events but tried to make sense of them, to explain causes and effects, balancing description with interpretation. He has a sensitivity for the characters in the drama and deals in a subtle way with their motivations and feelings. His theology of history is different from that of many of his predecessors and successors. God acts in history, he knows, but more through what we would call secondary causes, in and through human hearts. Direct divine intervention is rarely mentioned, and all the more important when he does report it. The decline of David is Yahweh's punishment, to be sure, but even the reader who did not believe in Yahweh could understand what happened in terms of David's guilt and his character. Solomon came to the throne by divine decree, but the path was a tortuous one through complicated family and political struggles.

The story of David's sin is told with the power of understatement. Even in the introduction which sets the scene (verses 1-2a) the reader is invited to draw some conclusions about David's emotional state. At the time "when kings go forth to battle, David sent Joab. . . ." And one day when the king arose from his afternoon nap he saw a beautiful woman bathing.

We are informed at the outset—and so is David—that Bathsheba is married, so that when she conceives and reports the fact to the king the scene is set for tragedy. We quickly recognize that the major characters in the story are Uriah, David, and—especially in the remainder of chapter 11—Joab the faithful general. Bathsheba does not play a major role in the history until its final scenes (I Kings 1).

The court historian considers it unnecessary to explain David's motives in sending for Uriah. He simply tells the story, and it is one filled with irony. David brings Uriah back to Jerusalem expecting him to spend the night with his wife and thus conceal the adultery. But Uriah's loyalty to the king and his faithfulness to his soldier's vow of sexual abstinence during the battle are his undoing. Even when, on the second night, David gets him drunk (verse 13) he still spends the night on the steps of the palace with the servants. So no alternatives appear to David but to have him killed in battle. The final stroke of irony is that Uriah carries his own death sentence back to Joab (verses 14-15).

It is a story of David's sins against Uriah and consequently against the Lord. The writer attaches no blame to Bathsheba; David was, after all, the king. Given Israel's patriarchal perspective, adultery was a violation against the husband. But the story is not moralistic; we can all recognize how wrong the actions were, and how one violation, as bad as it was, led to another, even worse. Remarkably, in this stark account of human frailty we are able to identify in turn with all the characters. We can recognize how a tired and perhaps middle-aged king succumbs to temptation and goes from adultery to murder, how Bathsheba is a victim, and how Uriah's very loyalties contribute to his death. In this way the Old Testament narrative interprets us to ourselves and helps us understand the human predicament better. Consequently, even if we are not adulterers, murderers, victims, or soldiers trapped by our loyalty, our prayers of confession can be deeper and more realistic.

Psalm 53

The central themes of this psalm are the foolishness of atheism and the universality of wickedness. The psalm offers a portrait of humanity in vivid, but condemnatory, colors. Its selection for reading in association with I Samuel 11 is based on the themes stressed in the psalm. David was depicted in Hebrew tradition as the righteous "man after God's heart," as the one whose wrong deeds were infrequent, and the one whose repentance was swift and from the heart. Nonetheless, the story of his adultery with Bathsheba and his subsequent orders to have her husband Uriah killed represent the most unforgettable tales of evil in the Old Testament. Thus Psalm 53, with its affirmation that all persons are sinners, forms an appropriate interpretative accompaniment to the Samuel account of this evil dimension in David's life.

Psalm 53, which is an almost identical duplicate of Psalm 14, falls into the category of an individual lament. Verses 1-3 are a meditative lament about the universal pervasiveness of godlessness. Verse 4 is a rhetorical question concerning the state of evildoers in the world that is presented as a divine utterance, while verse 5 shifts the focus of thought to the issue of judgment. The concluding verse is a petition for the coming of deliverance.

The psalm opens with a statement that describes the fool as one who in his thought (in his heart) is an atheist. The term "fool" is probably used as a generic term referring to a collective type of human beings. Thus the word should not be interpreted as if it referred to a simpleton or one mentally deficient, lacking intelligence. The "fool" in the psalm is that class of people for whom the Deity does not constitute an important frame of reference in their living. Practical atheism not theoretical or philosophical atheism seems to be under consideration, but one should not overstress the distinction. The issue is the ignoring of God's existence and the consequences that divine existence involves.

The "fools," presumably to whom "they" refers, are described in the second half of verse 1 as corrupt and doing abominable iniquity. The final summarizing affirmation, "there is none that does good," could mean that there is none among the "fools" who does good, or the writer may have incorporated a common generalization descriptive of the whole human race. That sinfulness is a universal characteristic of humankind is an operating assumption of most biblical thought. Ecclesiastes 7:20, for example, declares: "Surely there is not a righteous man on earth who does good and never sins."

Verses 2-3 depict the Deity assessing human activity. God peers down from heaven (see Gen. 11:5) to see if there are any wise persons on earth. The wise are described as those who seek after God (in worship? in study? in the Torah?). Thus the wise person is the opposite of the fool who lives as if God did not exist. Such perspectives on the wise and foolish could provide the structural elements for a sermon.

A rather pessimistic (or perhaps realistic?) evaluation of the human predicament is present in verse 3 which may be understood with verse 4 as a direct pronouncement of the Deity. The unflattering assessment of human life can be seen in the depictions of human nature: fallen away, all alike depraved, none that does good. The NEB translates this verse as: "But all are unfaithful, all are rotten to the core; not one does anything good, no, not even one."

The rhetorical question in verse 4 assumes a negative answer. Two characteristics are used in the verse to describe the evil: lack of understanding and failure to call upon the name of (to worship) God. The evil ones are not people who only damage themselves and disrupt their own lives; they also devour others like one who eats bread. Such a statement suggests that the evil and the foolish in this psalm were not social rejects or failures but rather were what many of the day would have considered successful achievers, pillars of society.

Verse 5 is an enigmatic verse. The state of terror described can be referred to (1) the godless who live in fear of losing what they have achieved and acquired, (2) the fear of some attacking force (see RSV note on 5*b*), or (3) the expected terror to come when God takes action in judgment. The parallel text in Psalm 14:5-6 can be consulted at this point and suggests an assurance that God will look after those whom the evil would devour.

The final verse is a general plea for deliverance/redemption which will alleviate the bad aspects of human existence. The hoped-for redemption is expected to come from Zion (Jerusalem) although its benefits will be known and welcomed by those in the north as well—Jacob and Israel. (This entire verse seems to be an addition so that the psalm could be referred to and used by the entire community.)

Ephesians 2:11-22

By the time this passage was written, Gentiles had won their right to be full-fledged members of the people of God. But it had been a titanic struggle, as the Letters of Paul attest. In fact, this was clearly the most significant controversy faced by the early church in the first few decades of its existence. As the Book of Acts shows, it was not a foregone conclusion that Gentiles would be admitted to the church and enjoy equal status with Jews. Even some of the most prominent Jewish Christians, such as Peter, found it difficult to admit them as equals (cf. Gal. 2:11-21). Eventually, the matter was resolved, largely through the efforts of Paul, and in today's epistolary lection, the author of Ephesians views this struggle in retrospect and interprets it theologically. For him, it is the "mystery of Christ," and he still marvels that "the Gentiles are fellow heirs, members of the same body, and partakers of the promise in Christ Jesus through the gospel" (Eph. 3:6).

First, our passage depicts the changed status of the Gentiles. Their former condition is described in starkly hopeless terms. By the circumcised, they were pejoratively stereotyped as "uncircumcised" (verse 11). This reminds us of how racial and ethnic struggles often degenerate to the level of hurling cliches designed to exclude and belittle. The metaphors chosen are coldly distant: "separated from Christ, alienated from the commonwealth of Israel, strangers to the covenants of promise, having no hope and without God in the world" (verse 12). They, of course, reflect the perspective of those inside, but Jews knew only too well what it meant to be "stangers and sojourners" (Gen. 23:4; I Chron. 29:15; Ps. 39:12; also Heb. 11:13; I Pet. 1:1; 2:11). What we have here is an apt summary of pagan life as viewed through the eyes of Jews who saw themselves as the elect of God (cf. Rom. 1:18-32; I Thess. 4:5). It is the life of the disenfranchised and desolate.

In sharp contrast, their new life in Christ is depicted. In fact, the passage is built on two contrasting phrases: "at one time you were . . . , but now you are" (verses 11, 13, and 19). It has been suggested that this may have been one way in which early Christian sermons were developed. What the Gentiles formerly lacked, they now have come to enjoy: they are now "fellow citizens with the saints and members of the household of God" (verse 19). Here, two metaphors are used: the city and the family. Both of these form the two fundamental social units, and now Gentiles are seen to be full participants in both. In addition, a third metaphor is introduced: the building, or temple, of God (verses 20-22). Actually, the building metaphor is fused with the metaphor of the body, for it is said to "grow" (verse 21). Here, the church is envisioned as the Jewish temple reconstituted, with the apostles and prophets as the foundation (cf. Matt. 16:18; I Cor. 3:9-11; Eph. 3:5; Rev. 21:14), and Christ as the cornerstone (cf. Ps. 118:22-23; Matt. 21:42 and parallels; Acts 4:11; I Pet. 2:4, 6-8). In Christ, the whole building coheres. It is now comprised of both Jews and Gentiles, and the Shekinah, the presence of God, that formerly dwelt in the Most Holy Place of the Jerusalem Temple, is now replaced by the Spirit. This new temple is now the "dwelling place of God" (verse 22; cf. I Pet. 2:5).

A second feature of the passage is the way in which the work of Christ is depicted. The unity of Gentiles and Jews is said to have been achieved "in Christ" (verse 13); that is, Christ has become the meeting place for divided humanity. The shedding of the blood of Christ is seen as the occasion through which those who were "far off" were "brought near" (cf. Col. 1:20; also Acts 2:39). Christ is quite literally said to be "our peace" (cf. Isa. 9:6), since through his reconciling work he "made peace" (verses 14 and 15). In this respect, the fondest prophetic hopes are fulfilled (cf. Isa. 57:19; also 52:7). As the psalmist urged, "Seek peace, and pursue it" (Ps. 34:14), so had Christ blessed the peacemakers (Matt. 5:9). The reconciling work of Christ (II Cor. 5:18-19) placed peace-searching and peace-making on the agenda of every Christian (Mark 9:50; Rom. 12:18; 14:19; II Cor. 13:11; I Thess. 5:13; II Tim. 2:22; Heb. 12:14; James 3:18; I Pet. 3:11).

Our passage states that the unifying work of Christ had been achieved through the abolition of the "dividing wall of hostility," or "the law of commandments and ordinances" (verses 14-15). Regrettably, the Mosaic law became a symbol of exclusiveness, an "iron curtain," as it were, separating Jews and Gentiles (cf. Rom. 3:29-30). Here, the death of Christ is seen as an end to this dividing wall. In a similar vein, Colossians 2:14 asserts that Christ set aside "the bond which stood against us with its legal demands" and "nailed it to the cross" (also II Cor. 3:14). The image of the "dividing wall" is particularly graphic and offers numerous homiletical possibilities, since wall symbolism is universal and since modern people have firmly etched in their minds such images as the Berlin Wall, the Iron Curtain, to say nothing of the many other "no man's land" boundaries separating peoples and nations from one another.

The work of Christ is further defined as creating a "new humanity." In verse 15, we are told that Christ created in himself "one new man." Here, the Body of Christ is seen as a single corporate entity into which both Jews and Gentiles have been fused. They are both "reconciled into one body through the cross" (verse 16), with the result that hostility between them is brought to an end. Here, Jews and Gentiles are viewed as separate humanities who are now fused into a single humanity through the reconciling work of Christ. Christ becomes the sphere in which ethnic and racial distinctions become obliterated, and by extension sexual and social distinctions as well (Gal. 3:26-27). No longer do Jews and Gentiles seek separate ways of access to God, one through the temple and Torah, the other beyond temple and Torah. Now, both Jews and Gentiles "have access in one Spirit to the Father" (verse 18; cf. 3:12; also Heb. 4:16).

What is depicted in today's epistolary lection remains a grand ideal! Although the first-century church resolved the so-called "Jew-Gentile question" in one sense, in another sense it has never been resolved. Issues of inclusiveness and exclusiveness, whether based on race, nation, social status, or gender, still remain unresolved within the people of God. The ideal of a "new humanity" in Christ calls for proclamation, as does the work of peace and reconciliation. Both should be carried out in the hope that eventually hostility will be brought to an end (verse 16).

Mark 6:30-34

The Gospel lection for today is the third and concluding reading from Mark 6. This brief passage joins the Old Testament reading in the portrait of Jesus as shepherd, recalling David, and joins the Epistle reading in presenting Jesus as the one who brings together the scattered and alienated into one flock, one family.

In his customary fashion, Mark inserts a story within a story in chapter 6. Verses 7-13 record Jesus instructing and sending out the Twelve. Verses 30-34 tell of their return, their report to Jesus, and his response. In between is the account of the imprisonment and death of John the Baptist (verses 14-29). This insertion is unusual in its length, considering the brevity of this Gospel, in its location in the middle of an apparently unrelated story, and in the fact that its subject is John, not Jesus. Or is it? It is difficult to believe Mark is here behaving like a distracted preacher who gets carried away from the point by a very dramatic and interesting story. A more reasonable assumption is that Mark is, by his literary device, instructing the reader about Jesus and his disciples. We will return to this point momentarily.

Mark 6:30-34 is an editorial transition, completing verses 7-13 and introducing verses 35-44, the account of feeding the five thousand. Withdrawing from the crowds for privacy is fairly common in Mark (1:35; 4:34; 9:2; 9:28; 13:3), but here it is associated not with a need for prayer or instruction but for rest after the mission. Matthew (14:13) relates this retreat to Jesus' hearing of John's death, while Luke, with no explanation for the action, says Jesus and the disciples withdrew to the city of Bethsaida (9:10). Mark's "lonely place" is unspecified geographically but serves to get the Twelve out of the public traffic which has prevented their having time even to eat (note also 3:20), and sets up the scene for feeding the multitudes who come to the lonely place and are without food (verses 35-36). It is difficult to reconstruct the precise movements of Jesus in Mark 4–8 which speak of ministries on both the eastern (Gentile) and western (Jewish) shores of Galilee with many crossings between, but in 6:32 the boat trip seems to be along the western shore and not across to the other side. The feeding on the eastern shore is recorded in 8:1-10.

In this brief lection, Mark tells us about the Twelve, the crowds, and Jesus. As for the Twelve, the portrait here is favorable, somewhat rare for Mark. According to verse 30, they did what they were sent to do and their work was according to the model of Jesus who was, in addition to preacher and exorcist, a teacher. Teaching is specified when their work is described just as it frequently is when Jesus' ministry is presented. Most noticeably, the Twelve are here called apostles (verse 30). They went on a mission as the Twelve, as the disciples, but when they completed their assignment, they were called apostles. Nowhere else in the Gospel does Mark refer to them by that term. For all the unfavorable attention Mark gives them, he knows that when the shepherd is smitten, the work will fall heavily on the apostles.

The crowds that gather about Jesus are, in Mark's accounts, very large and usually positive about Jesus (verses 31-34; also 1:27-28; 2:2; 3:7-9; 4:1; 5:21; 8:1; 10:1). There is no indication that Mark suspects large crowds of having shallow faith, wrong motives, and herd mentality. Their presence and enthusiasm leave Jesus and the Twelve no time to eat (verse 31); they anticipate Jesus' destination and run on foot from all the towns (verse 33); they arrive ahead of Jesus and wait for him (verse 33); they stay with him until a late hour (verse 35). They are not only drawn to Jesus, but they are driven by their own desperation, being "like sheep without a shepherd" (verse 34; Num. 27:17).

To this wandering and leaderless flock, Jesus is the compassionate shepherd (verse 34). The image was a familiar one for describing the work of priest and prophet and the relation of God to Israel (I Kings 22:17; Jer. 23:1-5; Ezek. 34:1-16). According to Mark's account, the first work of the shepherd was teaching the people (verse 34), and only later did his ministry include feeding them. Transcending both teaching and feeding, however, is the ministry of Jesus' death. The preceding account of John's death (verses 14-29) hangs over this scene as a dark prophecy anticipating 14:27: the shepherd will be smitten and the sheep scattered (Zech. 13:7). But then came the resurrection, and there still continues the gathering of the scattered sheep (14:28; John 10:14-16; 12:32).

Proper 12

Sunday Between July 24 and 30 Inclusive

II Samuel 12:1-14; Psalm 32; Ephesians 3:14-21; John 6:1-15

II Samuel 12:1-14

This passage reports the prophet Nathan's confrontation with David concerning his sin against Uriah, followed by the king's confession. The psalm, an expression of thanksgiving for healing and an affirmation of the value of repentance, responds particularly to David's acknowledgment of his guilt. Each of the New Testament readings has its own point to make. Thus, though Jesus is identified as both prophet and king in the Gospel, it seems wise not to force common concerns upon the readings but to let each text have its own voice.

Nathan's encounter with David is the direct consequence of the king's adultery with Bathsheba and murder of her husband Uriah. The section of the narrative between the readings for this week and last week (II Sam. 11:16-27) reports how David's orders for the death of Uriah were carried out, that David made Bathsheba his wife after her period of mourning was over, and that she bore him a son. In one of his significant interpretive asides, the court historian points out that "the thing that David had done displeased the Lord" (II Sam. 11:27). The reading for the day will show just how displeased the Lord was, and how David responded to that displeasure.

The lesson consists of a dialogue between the prophet and the king, introduced by the briefest narrative framework: "And the Lord sent Nathan to David" (verse 1). Short as it is, the note is not simply incidental; it makes clear at the outset what is confirmed later (verses 7, 11, 13), namely, that Nathan does not speak for himself but for Yahweh. The prophets understood themselves to be messengers of the Lord.

Nathan tells the king a story (verses 1*b*-4) of crass injustice, apparently asking for a royal judgment and possibly intervention. The contrasts are so sharp between the poor man with his single ewe lamb that was almost a part of the family and the greedy rich man that David readily pronounces the death sentence (verses 5-6).

The prophet's reaction (verses 7-12) makes it clear that the story was not the report of an actual event but a parable. Specifically, it is a juridical parable in which the addressee—in this case David—is moved to pronounce judgment upon himself. Isaiah's parable of the vineyard (Isa. 5:1-7) is a close parallel. Such parables consist of a story and its interpretation or application. The interpretation of the parable begins with one of the most memorable Old Testament lines, "You are the man" (verse 7*a*). Though Nathan's speech is not in poetic meter or parallelism, its basic structure is the same as that of the announcements of the prophets of the eighth and following centuries. It includes the messenger formula, "thus says the Lord," at the beginning and as a key transition. The major parts are the indictment or statement of reasons for punishment (verses 7-9) and the announcement of judgment or punishment (verses 10-12).

The statement of reasons for punishment or indictment has two movements. First, Yahweh, through Nathan, reminds David of his gracious care (verses 7-8). He had anointed him king, delivered him from Saul, given him Saul's house and wives—noteworthy given the sin with Bathsheba—and made him king over both Israel and Judah. Furthermore, the Lord was willing to do even more. The recital concerns God's grace toward David himself; there is no mention of the promise of a dynasty (II Sam. 7). Second, the Lord states the indictment (verse 9). David has "despised the word of the Lord" by taking the wife of Uriah as a wife and killing him "with the sword of the Ammonites." At this point there is no mention of the act of adultery.

The announcement of punishment includes the judgments that the sword shall never depart from David's house, that the Lord will raise up evil from his own house, and that

David's wives will be given to another who will lie with them openly. All these things, we shall see as the story unfolds, come to pass.

David's response is a short but full confession of sin (verse 13*a*), whereupon the prophet announces that the sin has been "put away," and the death sentence—which David pronounced upon himself—set aside. Still, there will be punishment; the child of the adulterous union shall die (verse 14).

Encounter with this story generates a wealth of issues for theological and homiletical reflection: (1) in the biblical faith no one, not even the king anointed by God, stands above the law, (2) to act irresponsibly in society, especially against those who have less power, is to "despise the word of the Lord" (verse 9), (3) that election—in this case as king—is a reason for punishment indicates that it entails accountability (see also Amos 3:1-2), and (4) what is the relationship between divine wrath and mercy? The punishment may appear harsh to us, and it is, but to the writer and the original hearers or readers this was also a story of God's mercy. As far as David was concerned, the death penalty, which applied not only to murder but also to adultery (see Deut. 22:22), had been reduced.

Psalm 32

One of the traditional seven penitential psalms, Psalm 32 is a prayer of thanksgiving which was offered by individuals after the forgiveness of sin and the experience of healing. Thus it forms a fitting counterpart to the reading from II Samuel 12:1-14 in which Nathan confronts David with the reality and depth of his sin in the Uriah affair.

Prayers of thanksgiving, like this psalm, were offered in ancient Israelite worship after the passage of trouble and the alleviation of distress. They reflect the people's tendency to look back upon the time of trouble and to celebrate the joy of salvation which had made the trouble a matter of the past (though certainly not something to be lost from memory). This helps explain two factors about thanksgiving psalms: (1) they have the character of a testimonial which bears witness to a prior condition which no longer exists but from which the worshiper has been delivered, and (2) much of the psalm is addressed to a human audience inviting them to participate in the joy and new condition of the redeemed.

The following is the form-critical structure of the psalm: (a) pronouncements of blessedness spoken about or to the one offering thanksgiving, probably spoken by the priest to the worshiper or to the worshiper and the attending congregation (verses 1-2); (b) the description, in the form of a thanksgiving prayer to the Deity, of the condition from which the worshiper was saved (verses 3-5); (c) a prayer to the Deity formulated as an indirect call to prayer by those in attendance (verse 6); (d) the prayer response (verse 7); and (e) instruction by the one offering thanksgiving to those in attendance at the service (verses 8-11).

The two opening verses proclaim the blessed condition or happy estate of the one whose sins have been forgiven. The psalm does not assume the existence of life without sin. It presupposes the existence of sinful persons and proclaims as blessed or happy those whose sin has become a matter of the past. The state of real happiness lies, for the psalmist, not prior to but beyond, on the other side, of sin.

In verses 1-2, and elsewhere (see verse 5), the psalmist uses three different words for sin: (a) transgression (pesha‘) or an act reflecting overt rebellion against God, (b) sin (chattâ'th) or an offense by which one deviates from the correct path or true course, and (c) iniquity ('âwon) or criminal distortion of life without regard for the Deity. The term deceit or slackness (remiyah) also appears in verse 2 and the claim of its absence can probably be seen as referring to the state of honesty which had to prevail when one confessed various sins. Note also that three descriptions are given with regard to the removal of sin: forgiven, covered, not imputed. Such terminological features can provide the bases for structuring a sermon on this psalm.

In the description of the earlier distress, in verses 3-5, the psalmist coordinates four factors: (a) lack of repentance followed by (b) sickness and strain and (c) confession followed by (d) forgiveness. In ancient Israel, acknowledgment and confession of sin, as well as restitution to injured parties, were essential ingredients in the repentance process. From a therapeutic or psychological point of view, one can say that the psalm writer was fully aware of the need for the sinner to tell his/her story as a form of self-identity and self-enlightenment and thus to claim responsibility for wrongdoing. In II Samuel 12:1-14, Nathan tells the "confessional" story with which David then identifies. In ancient Israelite theology, without confession, there was no forgiveness of sin.

The association of sickness and unconfessed sin, noted in verses 3-4, illustrates the close psychosomatic connection between physical and mental health—a connection that is being recognized more and more in contemporary culture. Although the physical consequences are described as the result of unconfessed sins, they are also spoken of as the result of divine action as well ("thy hand was heavy upon me"). This suggests that the understanding of human sentiments and feelings and the understanding of divine actions are closely interrelated.

Verse 5 contains something of the exuberance that comes after long-seething and secret sin is allowed to surface and be exposed to the light of day. The articulation, the coming to expression, of the nagging problem is the first step toward healing. Note that three expressions are used for this unveiling of the suppressed sin—acknowledged, did not hide, will confess. The close connection between confession and forgiveness is affirmed in the recognition that following confession "then thou didst forgive the guilt of my sin."

This section of the psalm (verses 3-5) can be an ideal text for the minister to use in addressing the issues of human sinfulness, confession, and forgiveness. The sentiments and conditions described in the psalm are certainly appropriate for contemporary people. The latter, however, frequently assumes that what one does with wrongdoing is to "stuff" it or keep it under wraps—the exact sentiments seen as so destructive in the psalm.

Verses 6-11 are to be seen in the context of the thanksgiving ritual in which the worshiper calls upon those attending the service (friends, family, associates) to join in the celebration and to learn from the experience which the worshiper has gone through. The forgiven sinner pleads with the others not to be stupid and hardheaded like a mule or a horse which must be controlled with bit and bridle. That is, they are not to be like the worshiper was before his acknowledgment and confession of sin (see verses 3-4).

Ephesians 3:14-21

Today's epistolary lection is a prayer consisting of an opening acclamation of the sovereignty of God (verses 14-15), a set of petitions (verses 16-19), and a doxology (verses 20-21). The prayer actually begins in 3:1, but is interrupted by an extended excursus on the apostle's apostolic ministry to the Gentiles (verses 2-13). In one sense, this prayer is a continuation of the prayer begun earlier in 1:15.

The prayer opens with an acknowledgment of God as Father, before whom the apostle bows his knees in prayer (cf. Luke 11:2; also Phil. 2:10). Just as Yahweh has numbered all the stars of heaven and named them all (Ps. 147:4), so has the Father named every family in heaven and on earth. The English translation obscures the play on words between "Father" *(patēr)* and "family" *(patria)*. Here is the acknowledgment that every "family unit," earthly or heavenly, owes its existence to the paternity of God (cf. Acts 17:28-29; I Cor. 8:6).

The second section of the prayer contains a set of petitions. First, there are two petitions made to the Father on behalf of the readers (verses 16-17*a*). There is first the recognition that all the petitions that follow will be made out of the abundant "riches of his glory" (cf. 1:7; 2:7; 3:8; also Rom. 9:23; 10:12; 11:33; Col. 1:27; Phil. 4:19). Specifically, the Father is asked to grant the readers inner strengthening through his Spirit. Quite often, the Spirit is associated with power *(dunamis),* in fact is seen as the source of divine power (Rom. 8:11; 15:13; I Cor. 2:4). Through Christ, one has access to sources of power that strengthen inner reserves (Eph. 6:10; Col. 1:11). We should also note that this strengthening takes place in the "inner man," that dimension of ourselves where genuine renewal occurs (II Cor. 4:16; also Rom. 7:22; I Pet. 3:4).

In addition to inner strengthening, the Father is asked to bestow the presence of Christ in the hearts of the readers. This, of course, can only occur "through faith." In the Fourth Gospel, the Father and the Son are said to make their home in the hearts of those who love Christ and keep his word (John 14:23). That God would come to dwell within the midst of the people of God was a long-standing hope (Ezek. 37:27), and one that early Christians realized (II Cor. 6:16; Rev. 3:20). The presence of God within him was quite naturally experienced in terms of the presence of Christ.

Following these two petitions for the Father to bestow the gifts of inner power and the presence of Christ on the readers, there occur petitions on behalf of the readers themselves. These, however, are predicated on their "being rooted and grounded in love" (verse 17; cf. Col. 1:23; 2:7). With this proviso, three petitions are made.

First, the apostle prays for them to have the capacity of comprehension (verse 18). This does not occur in isolation, however, for it is a capacity they have in common with "all the saints." It is only as part of the whole people of God that the readers can probe the multiple dimensions of the Christian mystery: its breadth and length and height and depth.

Second, he prays for their capacity to know (verse 19). The object of their knowledge is the "love of Christ which surpasses knowledge." Here, no doubt, he has in mind the love which Christ has for us (II Cor. 8:9).

Third, he prays that through their experience of the surpassing love of Christ they will be filled with all the fullness of God (verse 19*b*).

The prayer concludes with a doxology (verses 20-21). The object of these words of praise is God whose power to transform our inner natures exceeds human expectations (cf. Rom. 16:25; Jude 24; Eph. 1:19). God is often seen to be the source of energy motivating Christian action (Eph. 3:7; Col. 1:29; 2:1; 4:12; I Thess. 2:2). Accordingly, glory, both in the church and in Christ Jesus, is given to God (cf. Rom. 11:36; 16:27; Gal. 1:5; Phil. 4:20; I Tim. 1:17; II Tim. 4:18; Heb. 13:21; I Pet. 4:11; II Pet. 3:18; Jude 25; Rev. 1:6; 4:11; also IV Macc. 18:24).

John 6:1-15

For five consecutive Sundays our Gospel lections will be drawn from John 6. It seems wise, therefore, to take a few minutes to make the shift from Mark to refresh ourselves on the Johannine perspective, and to introduce chapter 6 in particular.

Many commentaries will debate the question of the location of chapter 6 in the overall scheme of the Fourth Gospel. Since chapter 4 concludes with Jesus in Galilee, chapter 5 is set in Jerusalem, chapter 6 has Jesus again in Galilee, and chapter 7 again in Jerusalem, some argue that chapter 6 is mislocated in the Gospel as we now have it. Geography alone would prefer chapters 4, 6, 5, and 7 in that order, having Jesus minister in Galilee and then return to Jerusalem. This is reasonable but it pays more attention to itinerary and chronology than the Gospel does. But more importantly, the Fourth Evangelist apparently wants to highlight the fact that Jesus keeps the Passover as far as possible from Jerusalem, the scene of his rejection at another Passover time. Jesus will die as the Passover lamb in Jerusalem (19:31-37), but now he will observe a Passover meal with the more receptive people in the hill country on the other side of the Sea of Galilee (6:1). For this Evangelist, theology takes precedence over reasonable itineraries. Since this Gospel has no eucharistic last meal in an upper room as do the Synoptics, this narrative is John's theological equivalent of "the last supper."

A second matter important to understanding John 6 is the linking of the feeding, the walking on water, and Peter's confession of faith. Matthew and Mark join the feeding and the walking on water with Peter's confession shortly thereafter (Matt. 14–16; Mark 6–8). Luke omits the walking on water but joins directly the feeding and Peter's confession (9:10-22). Whatever may be the relation of John's Gospel to the Synoptics, at least at this point we have a tradition that had already forged three stories into one narrative prior to the work of the Four Evangelists. Preaching on any one of the three stories should call attention to the whole unit as a witness to Christ.

That the feeding occurs at Passover is important for the writer. At Passover Jesus cleansed the temple and spoke of his death (chapter 2). At Passover Jesus had a meal with his disciples in Jerusalem and spoke of his approaching death (chapter 13). In the account before us, the feeding will not only be told in eucharistic language (verses 11, 23) but it will be followed by a discourse on the life-giving flesh and blood of Jesus (verses 51-59). We have, then, a story that has significance beyond that of Jesus' compassion on hungry crowds. In fact, verses 5-6 make it abundantly clear that Jesus knew what he was going to do, that he would perform a sign providing something qualitatively better than what was expected. The preacher would do well not to reach back into the Synoptics to pick up the "compassion on the hungry" theme. Jesus feeds the people, to be sure, but the reader has already been alerted to look beyond the bread to the Bread. This is no isolated format in John; many of the stories are so developed. Jesus' mother wanted him to provide wine for wedding guests and Jesus performed a revelatory sign beyond the expectation of Mary (chapter 2). Martha and Mary wanted a deceased brother restored and Jesus responded in a way beyond resuscitating a corpse to offering resurrection and life to the world (chapter 11). To preach on John 6:1-15 is to open the door to a ministry of Jesus beyond the immediate wants and expectations of those who seek what he can give.

The crowd, after a good meal, is ready to proclaim Jesus as the successor to Moses who also provided manna in the wilderness (Deut. 18:18). In fact, they want to control and assure their own future by enthroning Jesus as king (verse 15). They do not understand that Jesus' person and place is of God and has nothing to do with their approval or disapproval. There is a big difference between confessing faith in Jesus as Lord and sponsoring Jesus or setting him up as provider. However, we should not be too harsh with these Galileans; it is still easy to praise one who gives much and asks nothing. But Jesus' sermon is yet to come, and one suspects that the enthronement committee will soon be dissolved.

Proper 13

Sunday Between July 31 and August 6 Inclusive

II Samuel 12:15b-24; Psalm 34:11-22; Ephesians 4:1-6; John 6:24-35

II Samuel 12:15*b*-24

At first reading the lessons for the day seem to have little in common, but upon closer inspection similar concerns become visible. The Old Testament lection reports the illness and death of Bathsheba's first son by David and his reactions. Verses 18-22 in particular of Psalm 34 respond with words of comfort to the troubled and bereaved. The remainder of the psalm, like the epistolary reading, contains exhortations to live the proper life of faith, based on trust in God. In some ways the Johannine text confronts the situation described in II Samuel 12:15*b*-24: in the face of death and grief know that Jesus is the bread of life.

With the omission of one line which rounds off the previous reading—"Then Nathan went to his house" (12:15*a*)—our lesson continues where last week's ended. It reports how Nathan's prophecy of punishment begins to be fulfilled and how David behaves under the trying circumstances. The paragraphs in the RSV and most other modern translations properly indicate the two parts of the passage, each of which is essential to the other. First (verses 15*b*-23), there is the account of the child's sickness and death. Second (verses 24-25), there is the report of the birth of a second child, Solomon. Together these paragraphs present a story of divine judgment and grace.

Having heard Nathan's pronouncement of the Lord's judgment we should have been prepared for the opening line, but still it is shocking in its directness: "And the Lord struck the child that Uriah's wife bore to David, and it became

111

sick" (verse 15*b*). The center of attention, however, is David's actions, and they are described with deep insight into the human heart. The king's anguish—doubtless including both grief and guilt—is so great that the servants fear he will harm himself when he hears of the child's death. They are reluctant to tell him the bad news, but when he sees them whispering he knows. Then he surprises the court by cleaning himself up, going to "the house of the Lord" to worship, and asking for food. His explanation of his actions is realistic, but, given his previous behavior, surprising. In effect, he explains, I did what I could while there was hope, but now he is dead, "I shall go to him, but he will not return to me" (verse 23). That line is not a reference to an afterlife; it means only to affirm the inevitability of death. David should know. It is remarkable how often we see him in the posture of grief, standing in the shadow of death.

The rituals which the king followed as he "besought God for the child" (verse 16*a*) are not unusual but are typical features of ceremonies of lament or complaint as reflected in many of the psalms: prayer, prostration of one's self, fasting. The story suggests that David was alone; his officials tried to dissuade him from carrying on so. What we know from other evidence—especially the individual lament psalms—suggests, however, that such services of lamentation and complaint included participants from the family and friends of the supplicant, and usually cultic personnel. David's aim was to move Yahweh to change his mind: "Who knows whether the Lord will be gracious to me, that the child may live?" (verse 22).

Our hearts are drawn to the innocent, nameless child. Like Uriah, he died because of David's sins. But unlike Uriah, the child's death is sacrificial; he dies instead of David, for when the death penalty had been lifted from the king it had been given to the son (12:13-14). Now both David's reactions after the death and the concluding paragraph (verses 24-25) become more understandable. The blow of judgment has fallen, and he is restored to his life with the community, and the future is open once again.

While we may focus on the child's death, the more important point for the narrator is the conclusion. In one of his rare interpretive asides the court historian points out that following Solomon's birth "the Lord loved him" (verse 24). That is a foreshadowing of the future when the son of David and Bathsheba—the widow of a man he murdered—will become king. We are not informed why God was particularly compassionate toward this child. God's grace remains a mystery.

Psalm 34:11-22

Psalm 34 is a thanksgiving psalm intended for use by individuals who had moved through trouble and distress and now enjoyed security on the "redeemed" side of the turmoil. The experience of salvation and redemption is recalled in verses 4-6 which provide a bit of "autobiography" of the worshiper. This psalm, which has a long history of association with communion services in the church because of verse 8, forms an understandable response to the reading of II Samuel 12:15b-24 which reports the death of David's son and the monarch's reaction to that event. As David is pictured moving from great distress of soul to a calmer attitude of acceptance, so this psalm speaks out of a situation in which the person feels and is on top of matters after having undergone trouble.

As we have noted in earlier discussions, one of the major functions of both the thanksgiving rituals and thanksgiving psalms in ancient Israel was the teaching of others through testimonial and admonition. The lection for today, verses 11-22 of Psalm 34, constitutes primarily the admonition section of the psalm. The admonitions with their associated promises and assurances are very similar to the type of material one finds in such a wisdom book as Proverbs. Like the proverbs, the admonitory instructions in the thanksgiving psalms are cast as insightful truths that might be or have been gained from personal experiences. The teaching as in Proverbs is described as the "fear of the Lord" (verse 11).

The rhetorical question in verse 12, which expects the answer "everyone," sets the stage for the instruction that follows. Those who want to live a long life full of good must be willing to commit themselves to the hard-earned lessons of others' experience. The advice that ensues, in verses 14-15, is practical, humanistic, and non-theological: control of the tongue (see Prov. 18:21), avoidance of evil, works that produce good, and the pursuit of peace *(shâlôm)*. All of these are understood as contributing to the length and enjoyment of one's life.

Verses 15-22 of the psalm are much more theological in content and overtly engage in God-talk. Four emphases in these verses are worthy of note and provide perspectives for sermon development. One, however, should be warned that the wisdom answers to life's questions and problems fit a majority but certainly not all cases.

First, God is seen as especially favorably disposed toward the righteous. Such an assurance can be seen as a deduction drawn from long experience with the human condition. Righteousness produces a style of life that is good, long, and full of joy and that has the special protection of God.

Second, the evil and the wicked may expect the opposition of God and their life to end disastrously. In verse 16, it is the face of the Lord that is against evildoers and that will cut off all remembrance of them from the earth, that is, God is said to oversee their death and their disappearance from memory. Almost the same thing is said in verse 21 except here it is the evil itself that will slay the wicked. This double way of saying a thing appears rather frequently in the Old Testament: God is described as taking action to destroy the wicked or wickedness itself is seen as taking its own toll. The first is a theological way of expressing matters; the second is a more humanistic manner of saying things.

Third, God is described as having a special concern for the downtrodden and the calamity-struck. The brokenhearted and those crushed in spirit are the ones God is nearest (verse 18). Another way of making a similar point is to say that the brokenhearted and the crushed in spirit can be more open to God in their lives. Throughout the Old Testament, narrative after narrative shows how God intervenes for the poor and the unpromising and reverses the fate of their lives. Many of the biblical narratives have a Cinderella quality about them.

Finally, this psalm assumes that the righteous in life will not be immune to suffering. Not an absence of suffering is promised but rather compassion and help when suffering comes. Note the following references to the distress of the righteous: "their cry" (verse 15), "cry for help," "their troubles" (verse 17), and "afflictions" (verse 19). What the psalm promises is divine help to see it through.

Ephesians 4:1-6

This passage marks the transition in the Letter to the Ephesians from doctrinal instruction to ethical exhortation. The author "begs" or "beseeches" his readers in the form of an appeal (*parakaleō*, cf. I Cor. 1:10, 16). Specifically, he urges them to follow a particular mode of life appropriate to their calling (cf. I Thess. 2:12; Col. 1:10; Phil. 1:27). "To lead a life" renders the Greek word for "walk," a typical expression of one's form of conduct (cf. Eph. 2:2, 10; 4:17; 5:2, 8, 15). Earlier, the readers were reminded of "the hope to which he has called you" (1:18). Within the New Testament, Christians are commonly spoken of as those who have been called, or elected, by God (I Cor. 1:2; Rom. 1:7; I Thess. 1:4; II Thess. 2:13). Here, the expectation is that the form of one's life should correspond to the elevated calling one has received from God. The appeal has special force, given the author's status as a "prisoner for [the sake of] the Lord" (cf. 3:1; Phil. 1:7, 12-13; Col. 4:18; II Tim. 1:8; 2:9; Philem. 1).

He enjoins the readers to adopt a mode of life characterized by four qualities: lowliness, meekness, patience, and loving forbearance. Paul's own behavior is elsewhere described in these terms (Acts 20:19; I Cor. 13:4-7). Even though they describe the expected behavior of Christians (Phil. 2:1-11; Col. 3:12-13), these qualities of life were also taught in the Old Testament (Isa. 57:15; 66:2; Mic. 6:8). Here, they are seen to be the essential prerequisites to any form of unity and harmony within the church. In Galatians 5:17-23, such qualities are classified as the "fruit of the Spirit," whereas their opposites are said to be "works of the flesh." In a similar vein, the unity that is being sought here is seen as that which derives from the Spirit; the "unity of the Spirit" is the unity which the Spirit gives. Even so, the readers must be "eager to maintain" such unity (cf. Phil. 1:27; Col. 3:14-15). The language suggests that unity is already a given that is to be actualized and "kept," rather than something that they themselves are to bring about. Hence, Christians are urged to "be of one mind" (Phil. 2:2; I Cor. 1:10).

The appeal for unity is buttressed by the statement that there is "one body and one Spirit, just as you were called to the one hope that belongs to your call" (verse 4). There follows what appears to be a primitive confession of faith: "one Lord, one faith, one baptism, one God and Father of us all, who is above all and through all and in all" (verses 5-6).

One body. The Body of Christ is, by definition, unitary, and those who are incorporated into it share a common existence. Earlier, Paul wrote to the Corinthians, "You are the body of Christ" (I Cor. 12:27), insisting that although it has a plurality and diversity of members, it is nevertheless one (I Cor. 12:12, 14-26). In Ephesians, this metaphor is carried further, and the universal church is identified as the Body of Christ (1:23; cf. Rom. 12:5; Col. 3:15). In this "one body" Gentiles and Jews become one (2:16).

One Spirit. To the Corinthians, Paul stressed that the multiplicity of gifts present among them all derived from the same Spirit (I Cor. 12:4, 11). In fact, he insisted that the Spirit was the common administrator of our baptism, and consequently Christians "drink of one Spirit" (I Cor. 12:13). Through a single Spirit we have access to the Father (Eph. 2:18). The "unity of the Spirit" mentioned in verse 3 is predicated on the existence of a single Spirit.

One hope. In God's call, one hope is held out to Christians, and this can be none other than the hope of the resurrection (1:18; cf. I Pet. 1:3; also Col. 1:5, 27).

One Lord. Although unspecified, this can be none other than the Lord Jesus Christ. As the primitive Christian confession preserved in I Corinthians 8:6 states, he is the one "through whom are all things and through whom we exist." It is interesting to notice that, in contrast to this form of the confession, the christological component is listed first here. This article of faith came to be tested severely in the early centuries of the church when Christians were forced to choose between Christ, the one Lord, and the emperor who in the imperial cult was worshiped as lord. Echoes of this are seen especially in Revelation.

One faith. Here, "faith" is used in the sense of the repository of belief shared by all Christians, and more than likely, its essence was the christological confession that Christ had come in the flesh (cf. I John 4:2-3; Jude 3).

One baptism. As noted earlier, through baptism Christians came to drink of the "one Spirit" (I Cor. 12:13), and this initiatory rite enabled them to become clothed with Christ (Gal. 3:26; also Rom. 6:3). It is worth noting that when the Corinthian fellowship began to dissolve, Paul grounded his appeal for unity in their baptismal experience (I Cor. 1:10-17).

One God. Christians inherited from Judaism the cardinal belief in the one God, who was Father of all (cf. Mal. 2:10), and who brooked no rivals (Exod. 20:3; Deut. 6:4; Isa. 44:6-8). Belief in one supreme God—radical monotheism—became an article of their confession (cf. I Tim. 2:5). In the confession preserved in I Corinthians 8:6, Paul says, "For us there is one God, the Father, from whom are all things and for whom we exist." The oneness of God became axiomatic in Paul's thought as he argued for one mode of justification for all humanity, both Jews and Gentiles (Rom. 3:30). Here, God is said to be "above all, through all, and in all." This is an affirmation of God's supremacy over all things as well as an expression of the conviction that God is present in all the affairs of the world, working through them and in them. One textual variant reads that God is "within all of us," in which case the text would be affirming the full presence of God within the church (3:19).

John 6:24-35

Today is the second of five Sundays on which the Gospel lessons are drawn from John 6. In addition to reviewing the introduction to this material in the commentary on last Sunday's Gospel, one might do well to pause here and reflect upon the achievement of the entirety of John 6. Otherwise the preacher could jump in, exhaust in the first sermon the homiletical value of "Jesus as the Bread of Life," and then be left with three Sundays of Gospel readings without further comment. If it is one's intention to have the sermons on these five Sundays focus primarily upon the Gospel readings, then the best counsel for developing those messages is to be found in the way John 6 itself unfolds. The lectionary is very helpful here although the lections from the chapter show how stubbornly the Gospel resists division into smaller units. The lections not only overlap at points in order to sustain the theme from week to week, but also there is one noticeable omission, the episode of Jesus walking on the water (verses 16-21). We need to take a moment to reflect upon this omitted story before continuing the primary theme of the chapter, Jesus as the Bread of God.

As stated last Sunday, the story of Jesus walking on the water had been joined to that of his feeding the crowds prior to the work of the four Evangelists. Paul used the twin images of the water and the food in the wilderness as precursors of baptism and eucharist for the Christians (I Cor. 10:1-5). But even before Paul the two acts were recited in Israel as testimony to the power of God, conquering the sea and giving Israel food in the desert (Ps. 78). By using the name of God in Jesus' word to his fearful disciples ("I am," verse 20), it is clear that the story of Jesus walking on water was understood as a theophany. This complements the word of Jesus to the crowd concerning the feeding: it was not Moses but God who fed Israel the manna (verse 32), the implication being that the bread they had just enjoyed was also from God. Jesus, then, is not properly identified as one like Moses, as the crowd had concluded (verse 14), but was one whose presence was the presence of God. God triumphed over the sea and so did Jesus; God gave food to the people and so did Jesus. It is not enough, then, to say that one like Moses is here; rather one who is in union with God is here. The offense of this claim will soon strike Jesus' auditors.

We return now to the principal story: feeding the multitudes. Phase one or level one of the narrative is the provision of bread and fish for a hungry crowd in the wilderness. At this level the people are not only satisfied but excited about Jesus. They hail him as the new Moses and, in fact, want to enthrone him as king (verses 14-15). We have observed, however, that Jesus has more in mind than a meal,

118

evidenced by the usual Johannine preface to a sign (verses 5-6) and by the eucharistic language (verses 11, 23). The attention given to the bread with the fish disappearing from the story (verses 13, 23) is not only out of eucharistic interest but in anticipation of the discourse on the bread from heaven.

Verses 22-24 set the scene for the second encounter between Jesus and the crowd, this time in Capernaum at the synagogue (verse 59). It is immediately clear that the people are stuck at level one of the event, the free meal. Their question, "When did you come here?" (verse 25) is purely chronological and geographical, but the reader is thinking of the coming of the Son from God for the life of the world. And Jesus charges them with their blind willfulness. They are blind in that they see only food, not a sign of anything more satisfying, more life giving (verses 26-28) than the next meal. They are willful in that they want to "do the works of God" (verse 28); that is, they want to be in charge of their own lives and futures. Their attempt earlier to enthrone Jesus has made this abundantly clear. When told that the work of God is faith in the one God sent (verse 29), they still want to be in charge, even of faith itself. Show *us* a sign, *we* will see, *we* will weigh the evidence, *we* will draw conclusions, and *we* might even decide to believe (verse 30). It is not likely that this, or any audience, can insist upon being in control of their receiving and of their believing and still be open to a message on the bread which is God's gift from heaven.

Even though our lection continues through verse 35 and thus includes the first part of that message, we will wait until next Sunday to give full attention to the discourse on the bread from heaven.

Proper 14

Sunday Between August 7 and 13 Inclusive

*II Samuel 18:1, 5, 9-15; Psalm 143:1-8; Ephesians 4:25–5:2;
John 6:35, 41-51*

II Samuel 18:1, 5, 9-15

The Old Testament reading reports the climactic event in
Absalom's war of rebellion against David. Psalm 143:1-8 is
the prayer of an individual for deliverance from his pursuing
enemies, and as a response could be placed either in the
mouth of David or Absalom. The passage from Ephesians,
with its admonitions concerning gentleness and kindness is
not unlike David's instructions for the treatment of Absalom
(II Sam. 18:5), but its substance is in stark contrast to the
outcome of the narrative.

A great deal has transpired in the life of King David since
last week's lesson, and almost all of it bad. Nathan said that
"the sword shall never depart" from David's house (II Sam.
12:10), and indeed it does not. Following David's successful
campaign against Rabbah (II Sam. 12:26-31), we hear of a
series of troubles among his children: rape, murder, sibling
strife, and the rebellion of one of his sons. Second Samuel 13
reports the rape of Tamar by her half brother Ammon,
David's first born, and then Absalom's calculated murder of
Ammon. Absalom, who was acting to revenge his sister
Tamar then fled fom David's wrath, and subsequently was
allowed to return to Jerusalem (II Sam. 14). Though he was
next in line for the throne, Absalom could not wait, so he
began to plot a rebellion against his father, forcing David to
flee with his faithful followers (II Sam. 15). The report of the
final episode begins in II Samuel 17:24. Absalom pursued
David across the Jordan and the battle is about to begin.

The story of Absalom's death is without a doubt one of the
most dramatic and vivid scenes in the Old Testament. As the

events unfold before our eyes contrasts of character are revealed in such a way that moral issues are posed. The opening verse about David's organization of his troops reminds us of one side of David, the shrewd military tactician. The part of the story omitted from the lection (verses 2-4) extends that point and adds to it David's bravery. He intended to lead the troops, but was dissuaded on the grounds that his loss would mean total defeat. On the other hand, the king's instructions to the commanders to spare Absalom reveal his weakness for his children. It was that very factor which had set into motion the events that led up to Absalom's rebellion, for when David would not deal with Ammon for the rape of Tamar (II Sam. 15:21) Absalom began to take matters into his own hands.

The court historian (see the commentary on II Sam. 11:1-15 for Proper 11, pages 91-94) tells us nothing new about Absalom. The fatal irony is that he was trapped, one might say, by his vanity. Second Samuel 14:25-26, in describing his great beauty, emphasizes that his hair was unusually heavy.

Then there is the unnamed man (verses 10-13), doubtless a soldier, who discovered Absalom and reported to Joab. When the general rebukes him for not killing the rebel his response shows prudence and insight. First he reminds Joab of David's instructions, vowing that he would not disobey for a thousand pieces of silver. Second, he boldly points out what Joab does not deny: if he had killed Absalom the general would have left him to take the consequences alone (verse 13).

The central character in this episode, however, is Joab. Without visible hesitation or regret he strikes down the son of the king. It was not an act of anger or revenge, but a calculated military and political decision, taken at no small personal risk. He acted not for himself but for David and the nation. And lest we dwell simply on his ruthlessness, consider the consequences. Immediately after the death of Absalom, Joab recalls the army (verse 16). The killing was over. As his own troops had reminded David (verse 3), once the head is removed the body dies.

It is a horrible scene, Joab and his bodyguard killing the now helpless pretender to the throne. Behind it stand human love and weakness (David), ambition and rebellion (Absalom), and loyalty (Joab). Was Joab right or wrong? The narrator, who clearly identifies with Joab, offers no simple answers but leaves us to struggle with the ambiguities of moral decisions, and tries to make us aware of the complex causes and motives that put Joab in such a situation.

If we understand the characters we are left with no room for simple self-righteous condemnation of Joab. Nations and peoples have always asked such things of their young men and old soldiers, to kill for the sake of the community.

Psalm 143:1-8

Another of the classical seven penitential psalms, Psalm 143 was composed to be prayed by individuals during times of crisis. The psalm is a true prayer with its entire contents addressed to the Deity. Its references to being pursued, to enemies, and to the need for divine help make it an appropriate responsorial selection for use with the story of David's flight and Absalom's slaughter.

The verses used in the lectionary break the petitionary portion of the psalm in half. The petitions and appeals for help begin in verse 7 and extend throughout the remainder of the text.

The component parts of the psalm selection are *(a)* an address to the Deity with an initial petition (verses 1-2), *(b)* a description of the distress (verse 3-4), *(c)* a statement of confidence in God (verses 5-6), and *(d)* requests for help (verses 7-8).

A special characteristic of the entire psalm is the supplicant's recurring appeal to divine qualities or characteristics as the motivation or basis for redemption. There is no assertion that redemption should come as a consequence or result of the worshiper's righteousness or sinlessness. Note the appeals in the following phrases: "in thy faithfulness," "in thy righteousness," "for thy name's sake," and "in thy steadfast love." The psalmist is willing to leave his/her welfare up to the Divine. "Thou art my God" (verse 10) and

"I am thy servant" (verse 12) is the essence of the psalm's confession.

The nature of the distress being described in the psalm remains a bit uncertain. The most likely suggestion is that the psalm was composed for use by persons who felt themselves falsely accused of some act that they did not commit. In such circumstances, persons could appeal their case to God and undergo a ritual process in the sanctuary during which the priests, acting on behalf of the Deity, reached a decision and handed down a verdict or placed the litigants under a self-imprecation or curse (see Deut. 17:8-13; 19:15-21; I Kings 8:31-32 for references to such rituals).

In the opening address to the Deity (verses 1-2), the worshiper throws himself/herself on the mercy of God appealing for God to act on the basis of his own character rather than on the basis of the worshiper's status. A sense of unworthiness or the fear of the judgment of God in the temple court is allowed to overwhelm the worshiper who can only plead not to be judged. This fear is then undergirded by a sweeping theological truism: "No man living is righteous before thee." Thus the universality of human sinfulness and the incompleteness of every human are affirmed as reflective of the status and condition of the worshiper.

The description of the distress (verses 3-4) mentions the enemy who has made life miserable for the worshiper. Nothing explicit is said about the enemy, perhaps it was the accuser in a court case. At any rate, the psalm describes the state of distress as a state of psychological exhaustion. One might be tempted to see the person as paranoid except for the fact that little interest is shown in the enemy. In preaching and counseling, the minister can learn much from the psalm writers. Note the vivid terminology expressive of a distraught state: "pursued," "crushed," "darkness," "dead," "faints," and "appalled." The cult in ancient Israel did not try to stifle genuine sentiments (as we moderns are so prone to do when we try to convince people nothing is wrong or that they should not feel the way they do). In fact, the psalms and religious worship frequently provided the occasion and even forced the worshipers to go with their feelings, to intensify their emotions, to exaggerate the states of distress and depression, and to give vent to the sense of total fear and fright. Theologically, one can say that such exaggeration was intent on eliciting a divine hearing. Psychologically, one could say that it was the means for therapeutic catharsis. In preaching, the minister should seek ways to imitate the psalmists and thus to legitimate and encourage a temporary abandonment to the emotions or what pop psychology calls "getting in touch with one's feelings."

In spite of all the circumstances depicted in verses 1-4, the psalmist moves to a statement of faith and confidence in verses 5-6. Thus there is a movement in the psalm from the low depicted in the description of the distress to the high found in the statement of confidence. The source of confidence is located neither in the status or achievements of the worshiper, as is so often the case in modern culture, nor in some view about the future (which is always supposed to be getting better!). Instead, confidence is based on a backward look to lessons from the past. It is "the days of old," "all that thou has done," and "what thy hands have wrought" that allow the worshiper not to surrender to the tyranny and terror of the present but to expect and pray for divine aid on the analogy of the past.

The petitions in verses 7-8 request divine aid for the worshiper. The Lord's help and presence are depicted as standing between the worshiper and death. (The pit is a euphemism for the realm of the dead.) The reference to hearing in the morning (verse 8) suggests that the priests proclaimed their verdicts as the decisions of the Deity in conjunction with the dawn of a new day and the rising of the sun. Worshipers involved in such rituals may have spent the night in the temple in a nocturnal vigil (known technically as incubation) awaiting an early morning resolution or word from God. The morning, with its normal connotations of newness and hope, took on special meaning and content in such circumstances.

Ephesians 4:25–5:2

If chapters 1–3 of the Letter to the Ephesians unfold a richly textured theological tapestry, the final four chapters give us concrete instructions about the life of faith. In the early church, as now, there was the constant need for catechesis. New and old Christians needed to be reminded of the ethical implications of their faith. In the preceding verses, the readers, who were former pagans, are called to renounce their former ways (4:17-19). Ethical options are presented to them in terms of "putting off your old nature" and "putting on the new nature" (verses 22-23). What makes this possible is an inward transformation: "be renewed in the spirit of your minds" (verse 23).

Today's lection provides a miscellany of ethical instructions. They deal with everyday, ordinary matters, but they are not trivial. It was typical of early Christian instruction, as it was for Jewish and Greco-Roman ethical instruction as well, to provide catalogs of virtues and vices that delineated profiles of acceptable and unacceptable behavior. Although this passage does not fit neatly this scheme of virtue and vice catalogs, it exhibits the same concern to provide concrete guidelines for behavior appropriate to the Christian calling. Our text is quite matter of fact in insisting that life in Christ requires the "putting away" of certain forms of behavior (cf. Col. 3:8; James 1:21; I Pet. 2:1).

1. *"Putting away falsehood"* (verse 25). In the words of Zechariah 8:16, the text urges that "every one speak the truth with his neighbor." The Decalogue prohibited bearing false witness against a neighbor, especially in a juridical setting (Exod. 20:16). Noteworthy here is the motivation: "for we are members of one another" (cf. Rom. 12:5; I Cor. 12:25; Eph. 5:30). Concern for the community of faith now becomes an operative principle in ethics. No longer is it a matter of an individual making these decisions in isolation, as if only the individual's welfare is affected.

2. *"Be angry but do not sin"* (verses 26-27). Again, this instruction has an Old Testament basis (Ps. 4:4). Jesus insisted that anger was tantamount to murder, since at the bottom of both are active ill will (Matt. 5:22; also I John 3:15). Elsewhere, Christians are cautioned to be "slow to anger" (James 1:19-20). Today's text recognizes that anger can easily make one vulnerable to the wiles of Satan (cf. Eph. 6:11; James 4:7; I Pet. 5:8-9).

3. *"Let the thief no longer steal"* (verse 28). As did the Mosaic law (Exod. 20:15), so did Christian teaching prohibit thievery. Instead, Christians were expected to do "honest work," as did Paul who worked with his own hands (Acts 18:3; 20:34; I Cor. 4:12; I Thess. 2:9; 4:11; II Thess. 3:8). Nor was one to work merely for one's sole benefit, but rather to help the needy (cf. Titus 3:14; I John 3:17).

4. *"Let no evil talk come out of your mouths"* (verse 29). The speech of Christians was expected to be appropriate to the occasion as well as edifying (Col. 3:16; 4:6). Jesus himself had taught that his disciples would be responsible for their words (Matt. 12:37).

5. *"Do not grieve the Holy Spirit"* (verse 30). Once again, the language is borrowed from the Old Testament (Isa. 63:10). Earlier, the readers had been assured that they received the "seal of the Spirit" (1:13-14), and here it is said to last until "the day of redemption" (cf. Rom. 3:24; 8:23; I Cor. 1:30; Col. 1:14). This injunction may be directly related to the previous caution against evil speech, since blasphemy against the Holy Spirit receives such prominent attention in the Gospel tradition (cf. Matt. 12:31-32 and parallels).

6. Verses 31-32 approximate a vice-virtue catalog (cf. Matt. 15:19; Luke 18:11; Rom. 1:29; 13:13; II Cor. 12:20; Gal. 5:19-21; Eph. 5:3-5; Col. 3:5, 8; I Tim. 1:9-10; 6:4-5; II Tim. 3:2-4; Tit. 3:3; I Pet. 4:3; Rev. 9:21; 21:8; 22:15; also IV Macc. 1:26; 2:15). Bitterness, wrath, anger, clamor, and slander—all of which are malicious in their motivation—are to be put away and replaced by kindness, tenderheartedness, and a forgiving spirit (cf. Col. 3:12-13; Matt. 6:14). The latter has a theological motivation: "as God in Christ forgave you" (verse 32).

7. *"Be imitators of God"* (5:1). This injunction has a very important qualifier: "as beloved children." Imitation of God, strictly speaking, is impossible because of the unbridgeable gulf between us and God. Nevertheless, Christians are called on to emulate God *as* children who are the recipients of God's love (cf. Matt. 5:45; I Cor. 11:1; Col. 3:12).

8. *"Walk in love"* (5:2). The Christian "walk" is to be typified by love, since it is predicated on the love Christ had for us in offering himself as a sacrifice to God (cf. I Tim. 2:6;

Gal. 1:4; 2:20; Titus 2:14). His was indeed a "fragrant offering" (cf. Gen. 8:21; Exod. 29:18; Lev. 1:9, 13; Heb. 10:10; Phil. 4:18).

Many of these injunctions, as we have seen, have Old Testament roots, and in this respect Christian ethics owed much to Jewish ethics. Nevertheless, there are some striking features in these instructions, such as the concern for the community of believers as the motivation for honesty, or the relation of these ethical instructions to the work of God, Christ, and the Spirit. They are perhaps most striking for their practicality and concreteness. The preacher should not blithely assume, however, that the Christians to whom he or she speaks have mastered even these seemingly elementary principles of the faith.

John 6:35, 41-51

Against the sober backdrop of violence (II Sam. 18), of sorrow for sin (Ps. 143), and of a call to moral earnestness (Eph. 4–5), the Gospel for today comes as an offer of a gift, an offer of bread from heaven which gives to the recipient life eternal. John 6:35, 41-51 continues a theme begun two Sundays ago.

Without repeating the details from the commentary on John 6 already given, it is enough to recall here that we have referred to the feeding of the multitude as level one of the narrative. On this level the crowd lives, thinks, and acts. Even its talk of God, its immediate embrace of Jesus, its talk of signs and faith is willful, calculating, and self-serving. That the arena of action and conversation is religion instead of money or physical indulgence should not blind us to the fact that the motivational currents here all move toward self-interest. No one in the crowd is talking commitment or discipleship; the entire focus is upon what God through Jesus can do for us. When this Evangelist talks of "the world," nowhere does he deal with the usual popular images of dissipating sin. On the contrary, he uses the world to describe religious practices, places, rituals, traditions, and creeds that are perverted to self-interest. To Jesus' auditors in John 6 bread was bread, not a sign of anything more or better.

The next meal, not new life, was on their minds. Even so, to them Jesus speaks of the true bread from heaven.

Earlier in the Gospel, Jesus had pointed Nicodemus beyond birth to Birth (chapter 3) and the Samaritan woman beyond water to Water (chapter 4). Here he points his listeners beyond the meal of the evening before, beyond even the manna in the wilderness which their ancestors had eaten and died (verses 31, 49), to the true bread which comes down from heaven and gives life to the world (verse 33). The listeners seem to have an appetite for this true bread which gives life (verse 34) until Jesus identifies himself as this bread (verse 35). At this they murmur, able to think of Jesus as being from Nazareth, son of Joseph and Mary, but certainly not from heaven (verses 41-42).

In what sense does the Evangelist want us to understand Jesus as the true bread from heaven? It is too early at this point to be thinking of the eucharistic bread. Jesus as the bread which is consumed (eat my flesh) does not become explicitly the meaning of his reference to himself as bread until verse 51, or at least no earlier than verse 50. That will be level three of the narrative. At level one, bread was bread; at level two the bread is the Word of God (verses 32-50). In other words, Jesus is here the life-giving Logos as in the Prologue (1:1-18), the true bread as in the hymn, "Break Thou the Bread of Life," which was written to precede not the eucharist but the sermon. Notice the references to being *taught* of God, of *hearing* and *learning* from God (verse 45). The Word which reveals God is life-giving. Deuteronomy 8:3 states, "And he humbled you and let you hunger and fed you with manna, which you did not know, nor did your fathers know; that he might make you know that man does not live by bread alone, but that man lives by everything that proceeds out of the mouth of the Lord." Philo of Alexandria, commenting on this verse, had, prior to John's Gospel, identified the manna, which the people did not know, as the Wisdom or Word of God. "Not by bread alone but by every word which proceeds from the mouth of God."

Such an interpretation of Jesus as the life-giving Word from heaven is not only congenial with this Gospel's identification of Jesus as the Word (1:14) but with this Gospel's theological assumption that the fundamental human appetite, the hunger beneath all hungers, is for a word from God. No one has ever seen God (1:18); how then shall we know this God whom to know is life eternal (17:3)? As Philip expressed it, "Lord, show us the Father, and we shall be satisfied" (14:8). The only Son from the bosom of the Father has revealed God (1:18). Jesus, says our writer, not only speaks the word which proceeds from the mouth of God; Jesus *is* that Word, the Bread which is more than bread, the manna which the people do not know.

There is no famine of the Word of God, but at this point in the text the people remain hungry, having refused the Bread.

Proper 15
Sunday Between August 14 and 20 Inclusive

II Samuel 18:24-33; Psalm 102:1-12; Ephesians 5:15-20;
John 6:51-58

II Samuel 18:24-33

All of the readings for this day converge to some extent on a single theme, death and grief. The Old Testament lesson records David's grief over the death of his son Absalom, and the responsorial psalm—an individual lament in the face of death—contains themes that recognize the transitory nature of life. Days pass like smoke (verse 3), like an evening shadow (verse 11), and wither like grass (verse 11). Ephesians 5:15-20 also stresses that one should make the most of one's time. Because the days are evil, time should be spent in praise to God. John 6:51-58 again presents Jesus as the bread which came down from heaven; those who eat of it shall be raised up at the last day (verse 54). However, the Gospel also is a eucharistic text which reminds believers to identify with Jesus in his death.

Second Samuel 18:24-33 is the account of how David received and responded to the news of Absalom's death. Its conclusion contains one of the most poignant cries in all of biblical literature: "O my son Absalom; my son, my son Absalom! Would that I had died instead of you, O Absalom, my son, my son" (verse 33).

The scene transpires in the city where the king anxiously awaited news of the battle between his troops and the hosts of Israel under Absalom. When one considers the discussion back on the battlefield after the death of Absalom (II Sam. 18:19-23) along with our reading, it is striking how much space is given to the account of the messengers. The function of that long interlude in the narrative is to build the tension to its resolution. The reader or hearer can readily sense David's anxiety and impatience as the watchman reports sighting first one and then another messenger (verses 25-26). It is only after the second messenger gives his report that David knows the horrible truth and bursts into grief.

When David hears that there are first one and then a second man running, he knows already that there has been no rout; they are messengers (verses 25, 26). Informed that the leading runner is Ahimaaz he concludes that the news is good (verse 27). Joab would not send a "good man" for the dangerous task of delivering bad news (18:19-20). As soon as he rushes in with what to him is good news, Ahimaaz realizes why Joab had not wanted to send him. David is more concerned about the fate of Absalom than he is about the outcome of the battle. So Ahimaaz pleads ignorance (verse 29). Actually, he lies, for he knew that Absalom was dead. He also knew how David treated the messengers who brought him news of the deaths of those who were close to him (Saul and Jonathan, II Sam. 1:1-15; Ishbosheth, II Sam. 4:5-12).

When the Cushite arrives he gives the same good news, that the Lord has delivered the king from his enemies, and readily answers David's question about Absalom, obviously assuming that David will be pleased with that news as well. The reply is in the form of a curse upon all future enemies: "May the enemies of my lord the king, and all who rise up against you for evil, be like that young man" (verse 32). Then the question of the fate of the messenger with the bad news is forgotten, overshadowed by David's grief.

So once again David is in the posture of grief, under the shadow of the death of another of his children. Seeing him there and hearing his story, we cannot help but be moved to compassion. What parent is there who cannot identify with David's anguish? The court historian is interested in the succession to the throne, but he has told the story in a way that enables us to understand grief and to meditate on our own mortality.

While David's grief is the climax of the story it is not the end. The following paragraph (II Sam. 19:1-8*a*) points out the problem that David's grief created and the way it was resolved. When the troops heard that David was in mourning, they crept quietly back into the city, as if they had lost the battle (verse 3). Once again it was Joab who acted against David's will but in his interest. In a forceful speech (verses 5-7) he reminds the king of his duty. By refusing to recognize the victory, he has shamed those who risked their lives for him. It has become clear to everyone that the life of the rebel son is more valuable to David than are the lives of all his loyal followers. Joab warns the king that his support and with it the kingdom will crumble if he does not act, and quickly. So David pulls himself together and sits in the gate to review the troops (verse 8).

Given the circumstances, we should be able to identify with both Joab and David. The narrator certainly approved of Joab's intervention and viewed it entirely as concern for the king and his people. It leaves us to wrestle with the problems of conflicts between public and private life.

Psalm 102:1-12

This lament, the fifth in the series of seven classical penitential psalms (along with 6, 32, 38, 51, 130, and 143), with its deep sense of the transitoriness of life makes a fitting accompaniment to the reading of II Samuel 18:24-33 which reports David's uncontrolled grief at the death of his son Absalom.

The section chosen for the lectionary reading for this Sunday is only a truncated portion of the psalm, basically only the lament part, although verse 12 is the opening verse of the statement expressing trust and confidence.

The psalm was originally composed, as the title says, for "one afflicted [with sickness], when he is faint and pours out his complaint before the Lord." The original association of the psalm with sickness can be seen in the reference to fever and illness (verses 3-5), a condition that led to isolation and loneliness (verses 6-7), to the taunt of enemies (verse 8), and to complaints and accusations against God as the instigator and source of the trouble (verses 9-11).

The opening cry of the psalm (in verses 1-2) clearly indicates that the one worshiping is in deep trouble, in a day of distress. Prayer, so frequently in the laments, appears reserved for the day of trouble. This approach to human need and the reliance upon worship in the day of trouble suggests a sort of foxhole religion in which the need of the hour is the creator of piety and the cries of the heart become the articulation of address to the Divine. In modern culture, such an attitude toward religion is frequently frowned on primarily because such religious practice appears to be too self-serving. Yet special recourse to the Divine in the depths of distress, and even bargaining with God in such circumstances (see Gen. 28:18-22), is not condemned in the Old Testament. Even in those laments which exhibit this foxhole religion under crisis, many also demonstrate a concern to shape life according to the will and pattern of the Divine. The intensification of religion during times of calamity is certainly normal and akin to the pattern of life with its ups and downs and is probably more healthy than a religion oriented toward success which tries to keep matters on an even keel. Ministers should be willing to explore and affirm special religious fervor in times of great crisis. Like David, we all break in the presence of our personal "Absaloms" and in those moments our appeals to God are natural.

The psalm writer gives full expression, in verses 3-11, to the misery, anguish, and desperation of life. No effort is made to hide the recognition that life is difficult, that life is tough, that life carries in its bosom a burden of shattered dreams, that life moves constantly from abandoned expectation to abandoned expectation. The pain and suffering of life are not camouflaged beneath some insensitive stoic crust. Both the physical and psychological dimensions of trouble are faced clearly.

Verses 3-5 speak of physical agony: days vanishing in smoke, bones smoldering like an unstoked furnace, a heart seared like burned-over grass, pain that eats away the appetite, sounds that are nothing more than articulated groans, and emaciated flesh that leaves nothing between the skin and bones.

The despair of loneliness is the theme of verses 6-7. As if the suffering were not enough, the psalm also describes the sense of aloneness, the sense of isolation that can engulf us all. Three bird images serve to paint the picture—a vulture in the wilderness, an owl in a waste place, a single bird on a housetop. Since birds are accustomed to living in flocks, the solitary one stands as a good example of the isolated soul.

The internal physical and psychological agony are matched by external pressures spoken of in two ways (verse 8). Enemies taunt and then use the worshiper as one whose condition can serve in formulating curses ("may you be as bad off as . . .").

Perhaps the deepest hurt of all comes to expression in verses 9-10. The cause of the person's miseries is conceived as none other than God himself. It is God who in anger and indignation has served up the mourner's food, ashes to be consumed like bread and a cocktail mixed from the drinker's own tears. The Divine thus stands as the author behind the human's chaos and disoriented life. Behind the sickness, the loneliness, the humiliation stands the figure of the Divine.

The honesty reflected in the psalm, the willingness to speak the deep truth of one's strongest feelings, the need even to blame and complain against God are sentiments the minister may find difficult to express in sermons or in the life of the congregation. Yet such intense laments—yes, even exaggeration of the human predicament—can be freeing and liberating and pave the way from plightful petition to jubilant praise.

The ending of this psalm lection juxtaposes two verses that, when so joined and left unharmonized, spark with tension. Verse 11 laments the transitory quality, the shortness and brevity of life—only an evening shadow or withering grass—which is quickly gone. Over against this lot of every human whose life is only a dash between two dates and is full of suffering and woe is God who is "enthroned for ever" and whose name is eternal. One cannot avoid sensing the irony in the psalmist's mind, in the correlation of human finitude and divine infinity. This feeling, probably universally sensed and yet seldom expressed, should not be avoided even if living in its presence brings new and often unnerving dimensions to bear upon one's own existence. In preaching, the minister must be as bold and as challenging as the authors of the Psalms.

Ephesians 5:15-20

The exhortations contained in today's epistolary reading follow numerous injunctions concerning righteous living (5:3-14). In a sense, they serve as a summary of these several ethical admonitions.

Our text opens with a word of caution: "Look carefully then how you walk" (verse 15). The readers are called to exercise discrimination concerning their own behavior. They should not adopt a cavalier attitude about the way they have chosen to walk, as if staying on a straight course is obvious and automatic. Rather, they are called to be deliberate, thoughtful, and self-reflective.

Prudence is such a universal virtue that one does not normally consider it necessary to remind people to behave "not as unwise men but as wise" (verse 15). Yet, virtually every culture and people possess a tradition that embodies the proven wisdom of the ages. Not surprisingly, Jesus frequently draws on the Jewish wisdom tradition as he instructs his disciples about life in the kingdom of God (cf. Matt. 7:24; 10:16; 25:1-12). In fact, one of the most intriguing stories reported in the Gospels is the parable of the unjust steward whose conduct Jesus commended, most likely because he exercised prudence in a time of crisis (cf. Luke 16:1-13).

This advice is rephrased in even more direct terms in verse 17: "Therefore, do not be foolish, but understand what the will of the Lord is." Here, the other side of folly is the ability to be discerning with respect to knowing and doing God's will. This is not a matter of deciphering mysterious hieroglyphics, but rather developing a set of spiritual senses that result from the transformation and renewal of the mind and heart (cf. Rom. 12:2; also Rom. 2:18; Phil. 1:10).

Practically, prudence and discernment will mean that one "makes the most of the time" (verse 16; cf. Col. 4:5). This observation is set within an eschatological framework: "because the days are evil" (cf. Eph. 6:13; Gal. 1:4; also Amos 5:13). The word for "time" here is *kairos* and should perhaps best be rendered "opportunity." NEB: "Use the present opportunity to the full."

Closely connected with the caution against folly is the injunction to avoid getting drunk with wine (verse 18). The Jewish wisdom tradition had long since recognized the folly of drunkenness (Prov. 23:31-35), and Jesus had likewise warned his disciples against "dissipation and drunkenness" (Luke 21:34). Although it is not included in the vice lists earlier in Ephesians (cf. 4:31; 5:3-5), it becomes a stock item in others (cf. Gal. 5:21; I Cor. 6:10).

"Being filled with the Spirit" is offered as an alternative to being filled with wine, or drunkenness. It is not the ecstasy of individual inspiration that is in view here, but the spiritual intoxication that occurs in Christian worship (cf. Col. 3:16; I Cor. 14:15; Acts 16:25). In this setting, one learns that "always and for everything" to give thanks "in the name of our Lord Jesus Christ to God the Father" (Col. 3:16; I Thess. 5:18). Thankfulness, as it turns out, typifies the Christian outlook, since Christians owe their existence to an uncalculated act of loving grace (5:2). Thanksgiving, then, becomes one of the most frequent forms of prayer, as the opening prayers of many of the letters of the New Testament indicate (cf., e.g., I Cor. 1:4-9).

Part of the attraction of this part of the liturgical year is the opportunity it offers the preacher to instruct the church in some of the hard, practical realities of life. Separated from the high liturgical moments such as Christmas and Easter, this period seems fitted for instructions concerning prudence, discernment, and meaningful worship as an alternative to inebriation. These words from Ephesians speak directly to these needs.

John 6:51-58

The lections for today put us in touch with the language with which our biblical ancestors expressed their most profound experiences: grief, remorse, repentance, devotion, love, and joy of life. We who tend to associate all these emotions with "the heart" encounter here the ancient writers' descriptions in terms of bone, breath, flesh, marrow, joints, and stomach. Many of us know how totally the human frame is affected by significant experiences, but we do not express it so fully. The psalmist's sin and remorse reverberate through every bone and sinew (Ps. 102). David's lament over Absalom is total; his whole body joins in a chorus of grief (II Sam. 18–19). Apparently some of the Christians addressed in Ephesus were imbibing wine as a way to get the body to join more fully in the joyous expressions of the Spirit-filled life (Eph. 5). The assumption is that eating and drinking, flesh and bone, are not to be separated from the experiences of soul and spirit. In fact, the New Testament knows no more meaningful act for effecting and witnessing to the relationship of Christians with one another and with Christ than eating together. Whoever has removed eating from the list of profoundly religious acts will have great difficulty with our Gospel for today.

The New Testament is filled with images and analogies which express the close relation of believers with Christ. Paul speaks of one body, of union in his death and resurrection, of Christ in us and of our being in Christ. The Epistle for next Sunday will use the image of husband and wife to portray the mutual love of Christ and the church. The Fourth Gospel gives us many of our most familiar expressions of this relationship: shepherd and sheep, vine and branches, abiding in God's house, Christ abiding in God as we abide in Christ. But in John 6:51-58, language is pressed to the limit to express union and full participation of one life in another: "He who eats my flesh and drinks my blood abides in me and I in him" (verse 56).

If it is the case, as many scholars believe, that this Gospel went through several "editions" in the sense of modifications to meet the theological needs of a changing Christian community, then it is likely that John 6 began with the received tradition of Jesus feeding the multitudes. The story might have been a compassion narrative as it is in Mark 6:34-44 and Matthew 14:13-21. At some point, as is the case with the Synoptics, the story took on eucharistic implications as did most if not all the accounts of Jesus' meals with the disciples. That is, one meal, the last one, affected the way all meals were understood and described. This Evangelist, with his pattern of signs and discourses and in language with double meanings, saw in the event a sign of a greater truth, that Jesus himself is the bread, the word of revelation from God which gives life to the world. We cannot live by bread alone. But the image of Jesus not only providing bread but being the bread was pressed even further, joining it with the common understanding that eating and drinking are the very epitome of intimacy and union. Jesus offers himself as the food and drink. Here, then, is divine self-giving, life for life, and by full participation in Christ's word, his life and his death the believer abides in God. Recall that in this Gospel, "to abide" is the term for expressing unhindered trust that neither wavers nor needs supporting signs for reassurance.

As the writer told us at the outset, this is a Passover story (verse 4). In this Gospel, this means that the death of Jesus is an underlying theme of the narrative. According to John, Jesus did not keep the Passover before his death; he *was* the Passover (19:31-37). He did not eat the Passover meal; he *was* the Passover meal, the food and drink. "He who eats my flesh and drinks my blood has eternal life, and I will raise him up at the last day" (verse 54).

Our language is also pressed to the limit, to find the bold analogy for expressing the continuing relationship of believers with the living Christ.

Proper 16

Sunday Between August 21 and 27 Inclusive

II Samuel 23:1-7; Psalm 67; Ephesians 5:21-33; John 6:55-69

II Samuel 23:1-7

The texts assigned for reading today appear to have little in common, unless it is the broad issue of the way the Spirit of God is made incarnate in human society. The Old Testament lection, the "last words of David," concerns the way God's blessings are extended through the faithful Davidic king. Psalm 67, a song of thanksgiving and a prayer for continued blessings, does not respond to the Davidic themes but to the link between justice and the blessings of nature. The epistolary reading grounds a certain hierarchical organization in the faith that Christ is the head of the church, and the Johannine passage has Peter affirming that Jesus is the "Holy one of God" (John 6:69).

Before turning to II Samuel 23:1-7 itself we should first remind ourselves of its literary context. After the death of Absalom and David's grief (II Sam. 18–19:8a) David's troubles continued. There was an outbreak of sectional strife, reflecting the old tribal organization and the division between Judah and Israel. The occasion appears to be David's return to Jerusalem, and the issue is to determine which tribes will be the first to welcome him (II Sam. 19:9-43). Some of the old tribes revolted under the leadership of "a worthless fellow" (II Sam. 20:1) named Sheba, but once again Joab ended the threat (II Sam. 20). There was a famine, believed to be Yahweh's punishment for Saul's treatment of the Gibeonites, so members of Saul's family were sacrificed to end the danger (II Sam. 21:1-14). There were other wars with the Philistines, and David was judged too old to go into battle

(II Sam. 21:15-22). Immediately before the last words of David stands a hymn of praise (II Sam. 22).

As a theological explanation of the dynasty of David, and the foundation for future messianic expectations, the last words of David are almost as significant as the promise reported in II Samuel 7 (see the commentaries on Proper 9 and Proper 10). The latter comes at the pinnacle of David's career, the former at its end. Both concern the office of the king and the basis for the dynasty in Yahweh's election, and both contain old traditions. Many scholars consider most of II Samuel 23:1-7 to be quite ancient.

The narrative introduction at the beginning ("Now these are the last words of David") recalls the last will and testament of Moses (Deut. 33), the last words of Isaac (Gen. 27:1-2), and the blessing of Jacob (Gen. 49). In ancient Israel, as in most cultures, last words and wills carried great significance. David's "last words" themselves are comprised of a self-introduction in which he claims divine inspiration (verses 1*b*-3*a*), the body of the will concerning the just king and the dynasty (verses 3*b*-5), and concluding remarks about the fate of the godless (verses 6-7).

The self-introduction begins with words of self-praise. David is the one "raised on high," "anointed of God," and the "favorite of the sons of Israel" (verse 1, reading with RSV footnote). What appears at first glance as self-praise is actually praise of God: David is the recipient of God's actions of elevation and anointing. Moreover, this language concerns the office of the king more than the individual. The remainder of the introduction (verses 2-3*a*) is unusual, more appropriate for a prophet than a king. David affirms that it is the "Spirit of the Lord" that speaks through him. On the one hand this reflects the older, pre-monarchical view that Yahweh chose individual leaders by having his spirit fall upon them. On the other hand, the just king was believed to rule through divine guidance (see I Kings 3:5; Isa. 11:2).

The body of the king's will, what David leaves to his successors, is the "everlasting covenant" (verse 5) made by God and reminders of the effects of just and pious rule. Two similes are used to characterize those effects, the morning sun and the rain. The choice of those images is not accidental;

they emphasize the cosmic as well as corporate dimensions of justice. If the king, ruling by divine designation, acts justly and "in the fear of God," then the people as a whole are blessed, and God smiles through nature. If the promise to David in II Samuel 7 links the dynasty to the history of salvation, especially to the exodus traditions, then this text at least implicitly connects the Davidic covenant to creation.

The final words (verses 6-7) are similar to Psalm 1 in that they contrast the fate of the wicked with that of the righteous. Probably they concern those who oppose the divinely ordained king, but it is possible that they could apply also to the king who does not rule justly.

The primary focus of theological and homiletical reflection in this reading will be the question of the relationship between faith and politics. Analogies between the Old Testament situation and the contemporary situation should be drawn cautiously. There are significant differences between a theocratic monarchy, in which the religion and the state are virtually conterminous, and a modern democracy in which there is separation of church and state. Still, who could quarrel with the affirmation of this text, that there is a direct relationship between just rule—also linked with true piety—and the health of the body politic? Moreover, in a democracy every citizen is responsible for just rule.

Psalm 67

Psalm 67 contains both request to receive blessing and thanksgiving for blessing received. Although a psalm expressing community thanks and communal petition, it represents an appropriate responsive reading to II Samuel 23:1-7, "the last words" of David with their emphasis on the royal covenant.

In Psalm 67, verses 1 and 6-7 speak about God, while verses 2-5 directly address God and thus are in prayer form. Verses 3 and 5 are a refrain. Probably different groups of the people or different choirs sang the prayerful requests of verses 2 and 4 and the refrains of verses 3 and 5.

Three elements or emphases in the psalm are of interest and could be developed in preaching. There is, first of all, the benedictory character of the opening verse. In this text, the congregation requests divine favor and blessing. For the "face to shine upon" someone was a way of saying "show favor toward." It is equivalent to our saying, may God "smile" on us. Both in terminology and concern, this opening verse is very similar to the great priestly blessing found in Numbers 6:24-26, truly one of the great texts of the Hebrew Scriptures.

Second, the psalm has a strong universal emphasis. This is expressed in three ways. (1) The request for divine blessing on the Israelite community has, as its rationale, a universal goal. Bless us, it requests, "that thy way may be known upon earth, / thy saving power among all nations." Divine blessing on the worshiping community is thus seen as the means for God to bear witness to himself among other people. (2) The psalm petitions God to let the nations of the world (the Gentiles) join in the praise of him. This envisions others joining the chosen people in the worship of their God but not necessarily their conversion. (3) God is declared ready to be the judge and guide for the nations, a role that he exercises with equity. Such a declaration clearly affirms a universal rule for the Deity.

Finally, the psalm offers thanksgiving for the earth's increase. Verses 6-7 suggest that this psalm may have been used in conjunction with either the spring or the fall harvest seasons. The divine blessing is related, however, not to the worshiping community's own self-enjoyment but as an instrument for the universal acknowledgment and fear of God.

Ephesians 5:21-33

As a way of classifying ethical responsibilities, Christians adopted codes of conduct from Jewish and Greco-Roman moralists. Since these were arranged according to the responsibilities of various members of the household, they are known as "household codes" *(Haustafeln)*. Accordingly, they spell out behavioral guidelines for husbands, wives, parents, children, masters, and slaves (Eph. 5:22–6:9; Col. 3:18–4:1; I Pet. 2:18–3:7). Today's epistolary lection, with its instructions first to wives (verses 22-24), then to husbands (verses 25-33), is the first section of such a household code.

The general rubric for the household code is given in verse 21: "Be subject to one another out of reverence for Christ." Mutual subjection became the earmark of Christian behavior: "through love be servants of one another" (Gal. 5:13; also I Pet. 5:5). The paradox of Christian freedom was that it translated into an ethic of service (I Cor. 9:19). Or, as Luther said, "A Christian is a free lord of all things and subject to nobody. A Christian is an obedient servant in all things and subject to everyone." Such willingness to subject oneself in the service of others arose not merely from humanitarian concerns, but "out of reverence for Christ." Not merely the expectations of Christ, but his example, motivated early Christians to give themselves in service to one another (John 13:1-20).

First, wives are instructed to "be subject to your husbands" (verse 23). The submission of wives to their husbands was the general expectation in early Christian teaching (I Cor. 14:34-35; I Tim. 2:11-12; Tit. 2:5; I Pet. 3:1-6). One basis for this was the perceived hierarchy within the cosmic order: God, Christ, man, and woman (I Cor. 11:3). Thus, here, the husband is said to be "head of the wife as Christ is the head of the church" (verse 23; cf. Eph. 1:22; Col. 1:18; 2:10, 19). The kind of subjection called for here is not unqualified, however. It is "as to the Lord" (verse 22). "Submission within marriage should be of the same type as submission to Christ, voluntary and sincere" (Dahl).

Second, husbands are enjoined to "love your wives" (verse 25). Again, the norm by which the husband-wife relationship is to be measured is that of Christ and the church. The husband's love for his wife is to be as thorough and sacrificial as Christ's love for the church. So defined, marital love calls for the husband to be willing to give himself up for his wife even in death. The sacrifice of Christ becomes the prototype for the Christian husband (cf. Gal. 1:4; 2:20; I Tim. 2:6; Tit. 2:14).

This comparison between the husband's love for his wife and Christ's love for the church prompts the author to reflect more extensively on the theme of the church as the Bride of

Christ (cf. II Cor. 11:2; Rev. 21:2; 22:17; also Ezek. 16:9). The reference to "sanctifying the church" (verse 26) may recall the ancient practice of the bride receiving a nuptial bath prior to being presented to her husband. Underlying this reference is the practice of Christian baptism, which is seen as a lustration leading to the purification from sins (I Cor. 6:11; Tit. 3:5; Heb. 10:22; II Pet. 1:9). The splendid picture of the unblemished Bride recalls Old Testament imagery (cf. Song of Sol. 4:7; Deut. 24:1; cf. Eph. 1:4; Col. 1:22).

A further motivation for the husband to commit his love totally to his wife is given in verse 28, "Husbands should love their wives as their own bodies." This is a specific application of the Old Testament principle that one should love one's neighbor as oneself (Lev. 19:18; cf. Matt. 7:12). Far from being narcissistic in its intent, this instruction calls for even deeper loyalty on the part of the husband. Again, the wife is to be the ultimate concern of the husband as the church is of Christ, and the underlying assumption is that the two are indissolubly joined as one flesh, as the reference to Genesis 2:24 shows (verse 31). Husband and wife are "members of each other" as Christians are of one another (Rom. 12:5; I Cor. 12:25).

The author sees this as a "great mystery" (verse 32). Read one way, Genesis 2:24 speaks of the relationship between a husband and a wife, but read at a deeper level it speaks of Christ and the church. This resembles allegorical exegesis of Genesis as found in other writers of antiquity, such as Philo of Alexandria.

The passage concludes with a summary of the mutual responsibility of husbands and wives have to each other: "let each one of you love his wife as himself, and let the wife see that she respects her husband" (verse 33).

For good reason, this text has established itself as part of the marriage ceremony used in many churches. Marriage is elevated to an extraordinary level when it is seen as an analogy for the relationship Christ has with his bride, the church. Many people find the language of subjection and subordination offensive today, and to the extent that such texts have been used to justify husbands' exploitation of their wives, it should be offensive. But a more careful reading of

144

the passage might reveal that husbands are placed under no less obligation to give themselves mutually to the needs and service of their wives as the wives are to their husbands. The interpretive guide for the entire passage is given at the beginning, "Be subject to one another out of reverence for Christ" (verse 21).

John 6:55-69

Today we conclude John's narrative of the feeding of the multitude and the sermon on bread. Perhaps we should say sermons (plural) because Jesus as the Bread of Heaven is presented along two lines: Jesus is the Bread in the sense of being the Word proceeding from God and the Bread in the sense of the eucharist consumed by the believing community in whom he abides.

The sermon by Jesus in the synagogue at Capernaum (verse 59) is rejected by two groups: the Jews and many Christians. That the former group did not accept Jesus' message is not surprising, given the "Jesus vs. Jews" perspective of most of this Gospel. This viewpoint reflects a time and place in which the writer was much involved in church-synagogue tensions (15:21–16:4). Our responsibility to the text demands, however, that we not assume uncritically that tension and generalize on it but rather examine the grounds for the Jews' rejection of Jesus' sermon.

No doubt one point of offense was the language, "eat my flesh, drink my blood" (verses 51-58). These words not only disturbed those in the audience committed to food laws that forbade eating human flesh and the blood of any living thing, but also many who were numbered among Jesus' disciples. "This is a hard saying; who can listen to it?" (verse 60). Apparently the Johannine church took a position on the eucharist not shared by all Christian groups. It is unrealistic when reading the New Testament to think of only two groups, Jews and Christians. As Judaism contained different groups such as Pharisees, Sadducees, and Essenes so the early church consisted of communities that understood the gospel according to the traditions received, usually finding their identity in an apostle or other outstanding leader. At times this practice became divisive (I Cor. 3). In the verses before us (60-66) one observes the crumbling of a group referred to as "disciples," some leaving because of theological dissent and one by betrayal (verses 64-66). The honesty of the passage in allowing us to see inside the church as well as inside the synagogue should relieve us of prejudging all Jews and idealizing all Christians.

A second stumbling block for the Jewish audience (and possibly some disciples) was Jesus' refusal to accept the crowd's confession of him as the promised one, the one like Moses whom God would raise up (verse 14; Deut. 18:18). Some Christians would be content with that as a confession of faith, a way of saying that Jesus was the promised Messiah. In fact, this was indeed preached in some quarters of the church (Acts 3:22-23). But for this Gospel, such an acknowledgment was not adequate. This is not to say that Jesus rejected outright the designation of "the prophet like Moses," but rather that he is qualitatively more than was expected. Where a Messiah was expected the expectation tended to become defined not by what God would do for the people but by what people wanted from God. "When the Messiah comes" is an expression that may unleash a shopping list of the things we desire. So even the category "Messiah" can become corrupted to the point that a confession that Jesus is the Messiah, that he is the one we have been waiting for, is inappropriate to Jesus' own understanding of himself and his mission. To say this is not to comment solely on Jesus' listeners in the synagogue at Capernaum but on ourselves as well.

John 6 elaborates on a theme running through the entire Gospel: the fundamental offense in the words and work of Jesus is the offense of grace. It is sometimes stated gently: we have life from the Bread which God gives. It is sometimes stated bluntly, so as to offend all our claims of free will and self-determination: no one can come to me unless that person has been drawn of God (verses 37-40, 44, 65). This is truly the hard saying, but the issue is clear. Do we preside over life, demanding that Jesus do as Moses did, calling for signs as proof so we can decide whether or not to believe, electing Jesus king by our acclamation? Or do we accept the gift from

146

heaven? The bread in the wilderness was a gift; the bread as the word from heaven was and is a gift; the bread of the eucharist is a gift. Take, eat, and live.

For all who do not walk away, Simon Peter speaks: "Lord, to whom shall we go? You have the words of eternal life; and we have believed, and have come to know, that you are the Holy One of God" (verses 68-69).

Proper 17

Sunday Between August 28 and September 3 Inclusive

I Kings 2:1-4, 10-12; Psalm 121; Ephesians 6:10-20;
Mark 7:1-8, 14-15, 21-23

I Kings 2:1-4, 10-12

The readings for this day give instructions for leading a proper life before God. First Kings 2:1-4 reports David's charge to Solomon to walk in the ways of the Lord as written in the law of Moses, and the responsorial psalm is a liturgy which assures the Lord's protection to the faithful. The famous passage from Ephesians is a series of admonitions to remain steadfast in the Lord in all ways. The Gospel lesson has Jesus rebuking the Pharisees for substituting human traditions for the "commandment of God" (Mark 7:8) and meditating on the source of all evil thoughts and deeds.

Our Old Testament reading is found in the very last chapter of the Throne Succession Document, the final verse of which is I Kings 2:46b: "So the kingdom was established in the hand of Solomon." As we pointed out in the commentary on II Samuel 11 (see Proper 11), one of the major purposes of that document was to show how Solomon, instead of one of the more logical successors, came to David's throne. First Kings 1 described the final struggle for the succession, with David influenced by Bathsheba and Nathan to have Solomon anointed king. This result had been anticipated at the birth of Solomon when we were told that "the Lord loved him" (II Sam. 12:24).

However, the text assigned for today does not stem from the court historian but from the Deuteronomistic Historian. The books of Deuteronomy, Joshua, Judges, First and Second Samuel, First and Second Kings were edited into their present form by a series of editors whose style and theology were quite similar to that of the Book of Deuteronomy. They relied on a great many sources, both oral and written, including the Throne Succession Document, records or chronicles of the kings, and prophetic traditions, among others. The work was finally completed not long after the last event it describes (II Kings 25:27-30), that is, ca. 560 B.C. during the Babylonian exile.

One major purpose of the history is to explain the disaster of the Exile. The historians have examined the old traditions to discover what went wrong and conclude that the fault was not Yahweh's, but Israel's. The work then—with very few exceptions—is a history of sin.

First Kings 2:1-4 states some of the major themes of the history, including the standard by which sin is recognized. Obedience to the statutes, commandments, ordinances, and testimonies of God are required. Moreover, those requirements are written "in the law of Moses" (verse 3), that is, the laws in the Book of Deuteronomy. By that standard the kings in particular are judged, and virtually all of them are found wanting. Here it is applied not only to Solomon but also to his "sons" (verse 4), and made the condition for the continuation of the dynasty. By the standard of Deuteronomy none of the Northern kings could be approved, since they did not respect the single sanctuary in Jerusalem.

First Kings 2:1-4, then, is one of the important Deuteronomic summaries. Similar material is found in other speeches, especially at key transitions in the history (see Josh. 1, Deut. 31).

The final note concerning the death and burial of David is probably also Deuteronomistic. The expression, "slept with his fathers," is a common euphemism for death. The "city of David" is Jerusalem, during the monarchy the possession not of one of the tribes but of the crown.

The major theological issue of this text—especially when read in connection with Mark 7:1-8, 14-15, 21-23—concerns the law. Our writer clearly identifies what is written in the law of Moses as the law of God, not just "the tradition of men" (Mark 7:8). How are we to distinguish the divine expectations among human traditions? Is it possible to be accountable and responsible to God in some particular form without becoming legalistic and moralistic? One response, with the sayings of Jesus in Mark, is to look to motivations. That perspective is not foreign to Deuteronomy. Perhaps a more troubling problem with the theology of Deuteronomy and the Deuteronomistic Historian is the rather direct connection between obedience and blessing on the one hand and disobedience and suffering on the other. Where does the gospel leave us with that one?

Psalm 121

This psalm forms a part of a collection of psalms put together for use by pilgrims as they made their way to Jerusalem to celebrate the various festivals (note the reference to ascents or pilgrimage in the heading). The psalm has a distinct note of departure about it and thus is fitting for use with the Old Testament reading about David's death, the ultimate departure.

The psalm is clearly human address, without any speech addressed to God. Thus the psalm is not a prayer. A particular feature of the psalm is the change of person between verses 2 and 3. The opening verses are spoken in the first person while the remainder of the psalm is addressed to someone in the second person. The reason for this change of person will become clear in our subsequent discussion.

Before leaving on pilgrimage, the worshipers in a region assembled in a centrally located village in order to travel in a group to Jerusalem. After spending the night in the open air, to avoid any possible contact with uncleanness in the houses, the group moved out under the supervision of a director. The trip to Jerusalem which might take several days was not blessed with any special amenities (like constantly accessible toilet facilities) and like all travel in antiquity was beset with possible hazard and hardship.

Psalm 121 is best understood as a litany of departure recited antiphonally as the pilgrim group departed from the village where they had assembled. Verses 1-2 were sung by the pilgrims and verses 3-8 were sung by those who remained behind, not going on the pilgrimage, or perhaps by the leader/director of the pilgrim group.

Verses 1-2 are to be understood as a confession (the second half of verse 1 should not be translated as a question but as a statement). The worshiper speaks of looking to the hills (of Jerusalem) from whence help comes. That is, one looks to the God of Jerusalem who made heaven and earth.

The affirmation of God as creator of heaven and earth, that is, of everything, may seem so obvious to us and even an innocuous statement. To appreciate fully the impact of such a perspective about the world, one has to realize that for most ancients the world was an arena of conflicting powers and beings. In a polytheistic religion, one god controlled one aspect of life or nature and another some other aspect. Often deities were considered in conflict with one another. Thus, the world was neither a very hospitable nor a very predictable place. One constantly had to worry if the proper gods had been placated. On the other hand, the belief in one god as the creator of the heaven and the earth allowed one to see things as reflective of a single divine will. Such a world view provided a sense of cohesion and security about life.

As the pilgrim faced the dangers of the forthcoming journey to Jerusalem, the confession that the creator God as the source of help was reassuring and confidence-boosting.

Verses 3-8 are a response offering assurance to the individual pilgrim that God will constantly care for and preserve the worshiper. Note the number of statements with imagery concerning travel: the foot stumbling, the guardian constantly awake, a shade along the way, day and night as one was on the road constantly, going out (leaving) and coming in (returning). Both the moon and the sun, referred to in verse 6, were considered deities in the ancient world and could be objects of dread. Since pilgrims traveled by day and slept in the open at night, the sun and moon were constant features of their journey. Travelers feared sunstroke (see II Kings 4:19; Jon. 4:8), and many other disorders such as epilepsy, fever, and lunacy (related to the word lunar or moon) were ascribed to the baneful influence of the moon.

A significant emphasis in this psalm is the constant presence and care of the Deity. God, unlike Baal or other deities (see I Kings 18:29), is described as one who does not sleep or slumber. That is, he is continuously on the job.

In developing sermonic ideas for using this psalm, the minister can easily move from the imagery of an actual pilgrimage reflected in the psalm to the understanding of life itself as pilgrimage.

Ephesians 6:10-20

In this final lection from Ephesians, we are urged to "be strong in the Lord and in the strength of his might" (verse 10). This was the apostle's prayer (3:16). The source of lasting strength is located "in the Lord" who has been exalted to a position of heavenly dominion "far above all rule and authority and power and dominion" (1:21). Such empowering strength is his to give.

The Christian "walk" has been the topic of discussion, especially in chapters 4–6. This final exhortation is realistic in the way it envisions life in Christ as a serious struggle, comparable to waging warfare. The imagery is bold and powerful. The Christian is portrayed as putting on the gear of warfare worn by soldiers. The image of the soldier was commonplace in antiquity so that the metaphor used here had immediate impact. But, the images are not drawn merely from everyday experience. They are already firmly entrenched in the Old Testament, where Yahweh is similarly clothed (Isa. 59:16-17; esp. Wisd. of Sol. 5:17-23). Closely associated with this is the image of Yahweh as the Divine Warrior (cf. Isa. 13, 34; also Ezek. 7). Given this background, we are to take quite literally the injunction: "put on the whole armor of God" (verse 11; also verse 13). We are asked to put on the very armor God wears!

The apostle insists that Christians are not engaged in a conflict between themselves and other human beings: "we are not contending against flesh and blood" (verse 12). This does not mean, however, that ours is simply a psychological battle fought within ourselves, in the recesses of our own minds. It is rather "against the principalities, against the powers, against the world rulers of this present darkness, against the spiritual hosts of wickedness in the heavenly places" (verse 12; cf. Eph. 1:21; 2:2; 3:10; Rom. 8:38; I Cor. 15:24; Col. 1:13, 16; 2:10, 15; I Pet. 3:22; Heb. 2:5; II Pet. 2:10).

The contest is one in which superhuman forces are pitted against one another (cf. Rom. 13:12; II Cor. 6:7; 10:4). The earth is viewed as the arena in which the contest is carried out, but the conflict actually engages cosmic forces, seen here as under the dominion of Satan himself (cf. Eph. 4:14, 27; I Pet. 5:8-9; James 4:7).

We recognize this as the imagery of Jewish apocalyptic, but this should not obscure the central truth that the conflict between Good and Evil in every age, ours included, involves forces that surpass our own human understanding and limitations. Whether we choose to depict the powers of Good and Evil this way, our text reminds us that questions of morality should not be reduced to the level of human transaction, with good and evil serving simply as the sum total of individual actions. Today's text recognizes that the Christian soldier may finally emerge as victor, but not without serious struggle. This alone should caution us against adopting a naive optimism toward critical issues facing us.

What is striking about the individual pieces of armor is that they symbolize qualities of God, not ordinary human virtues: truth, righteousness, peace, faith, salvation, the Word of God. This in itself is suggestive, for it reminds us that it is not within our human capacity to equip ourselves for a battle of such magnitude. It is rather a matter of embodying within ourselves those theological realities and attributes that God uses to achieve the divine purpose within the world.

Some comments on the individual pieces of equipment may be helpful. "Girding your loins with truth" recalls the image of the Messiah who is girded with righteousness and faithfulness (Isa. 11:5; cf. also Exod. 12:11; I Kings 18:46; Nah. 2:1; Luke 12:35; I Pet. 1:13). The "breastplate of righteousness," as noted earlier, recalls God's own character (Isa. 59:17; Wisd. of Sol. 5:18; cf. also I Thess. 5:8). Feet shod "with the equipment of the gospel of peace" recalls the image of the courier bearing the good tidings of peace (Isa. 52:7; Nah. 1:15). This is a salutary reminder that even in waging war metaphorically, the Christian's central message is "the good news of peace" (Acts 10:36; also Luke 2:14; Eph. 2:17). The "shield of faith" enables one to deflect Satan's fiery darts (cf. Wisd. of Sol. 5:19, 21; I Thess. 5:8). The "helmet of salvation," again, recalls the description of Yahweh (Isa. 59:17; also I Thess. 5:8). The only offensive weapon included is the "sword of the Spirit," identified as the Word of God, suggesting the image of words being sharp and penetrating in their effect (Isa. 49:2; Hos. 6:5; Heb. 4:12).

The final section of the passage includes an exhortation to "pray at all times in the Spirit" (cf. Matt. 26:41 and parallels; Col. 4:2; Jude 20), combined with a call for alert perseverance (Mark 13:33; Luke 21:36). Finally, the Apostle enlists the prayers of the readers on his behalf (Rom. 15:30; Col. 4:3; I Thess. 5:25; II Thess. 3:1; Heb. 13:18). His desire is to speak boldly the mystery of the gospel of Christ (cf. Luke 21:15; Col. 4:3; also Acts 4:13, 29, 31; 28:31). As a prisoner (3:1; 4:1), he regards himself as an "ambassador in chains" (cf. II Cor. 5:20), hoping to be able to speak boldly, or in a manner appropriate to the message and task.

It may be that some find the militaristic images used in this passage unsuitable to the message of the gospel. But they are just that—images. What should be noticed is that the "weapons of warfare" depicted here are those things that bring about justice and peace—righteousness, truth, and salvation. Christians are challenged by these words to be vigilant in their struggle to bring about peace and justice. In the words of Betty Williams Perkins, winner of the 1977 Nobel Peace Prize for her work in Northern Ireland, "Without peace there is no justice; without justice, there is no peace." Our text reminds us that neither of these happens automatically, or even naturally, but occur as the result of active and aggressive "fighting" in their behalf. When such warfare is done "in the Lord," it attests the "strength of God's might."

Mark 7:1-8, 14-15, 21-23

We return to Mark for the Gospel lesson and, with the exception of three Sundays, will continue with Mark until the end of Pentecost and the beginning of Advent. The portion of Mark to which we return is the large block of material beginning at 4:1 which presents Jesus as extremely popular as a teacher and healer, traveling with his disciples to both sides of the Sea of Galilee ministering to both Jews and Gentiles. This same body of material portrays the Twelve as continuing in their inability to understand Jesus, the climax coming at 8:31 with Jesus' introduction of his coming passion into his instruction of the disciples.

That today's reading consists of three pieces out of a larger unit (7:1-23) may create some suspicion of editorial violation of Mark in the pursuit of a theme or doctrine. Closer examination, however, reveals that this is not the case. We have had several occasions earlier to notice that a structural characteristic of this Gospel is the writer's insertion of material within material. Within 7:1-23 are at least two insertions by the writer. Verses 3-4 explain to the reader the ritual cleansing practices of Judaism. We can only assume that Mark here is explaining to the Christians of a Gentile background practices with which they were not familiar. Verses 9-13 focus on the practice of Corban as an example of permitting a tradition (oral law) to set aside a command of God as fundamental as honoring one's father and mother. This Corban discussion, which does not necessarily refer to the cleansing practices being argued, probably was brought from another context to serve the writer's point here.

Another characteristic of Mark's structure is the division of a narrative into portions addressed to different audiences. Usually this consists of Jesus speaking to the crowd and then explaining his words to the disciples in private (4:1-12; 9:14-29; 10:1-10; 13:1-8). Our reading fits that pattern. In fact, attention to audiences explains what seems at first a fragmented lection: the Pharisees and scribes are addressed in verses 1-8; the crowd in verses 14-15; the disciples in verses 21-23. At the center of the entire narrative is the pronouncement by Jesus: "There is nothing outside a man which by going into him can defile him; but the things which come out of a man are what defile him" (verse 15).

In form, then, our text is very similar to other pronouncement stories in Mark, such as the one recorded in 3:23-28. First, there is a charge against Jesus' disciples. That it is the disciples who are criticized and Jesus who comes to their defense reflects the condition of the early church facing accusations from the synagogue that Christians violate tradition and misinterpret Scripture. A common defense by the church was to present Jesus' response to such charges. Second, there is the countercharge, and in this case, an illustration supporting the countercharge. Third, Jesus makes the pronouncement, and again explains the pronouncement to the Twelve.

And what issue is at stake here? Jesus' statement that it is not what one puts in the stomach but what proceeds from the heart that determines defilement or cleanliness was not a new or unique criticism of Jewish rituals. Judaism had strong prophetic voices and movements of self-criticism. Many Jews would agree with Jesus and the early church on the matter. But Mark, by having Jesus address confused disciples, was able to have Jesus address two groups in the church. Converts from a Gentile background needed to have both an answer for Jewish critics of church practices and a defense against being lured into legalism and ritualism. The other group consisted of Jewish Christians who probably never totally lost the tug toward their past with its rich traditions, authoritative voices, and familiar rituals. After all, none of us ever outgrows the need to hear Jesus confirm anew that the path of discipleship is liberating and life-giving. Old habits tend to live long past the convictions that gave them birth.

Proper 18
Sunday Between September 4 and 10 Inclusive

Ecclesiasticus 5:8-15 or *Proverbs 2:1-8; Psalm 119:129-136; James 1:17-27; Mark 7:31-37*

Ecclesiasticus 5:8-15

Both Old Testament lessons are wisdom texts with sound advice for those who are or who would be wise. The selection from Psalm 119, a meditation on the law of the Lord, is similar to wisdom literature, though it is in the form of a prayer. James 1:17-27 likewise is concerned with the law and contains admonitions to live the proper life, including some that are quite similar to those in Ecclesiasticus 5:8-15. Both recommend that a person be quick to hear and slow to speak. Mark 7:31-37 is a miracle story that reports how the power of God was manifest in Jesus. But the issue of human speech is also a focus of attention, for Jesus healed a man of deafness and a speech impediment. Moreover, the more he charged the crowd to keep quiet about the healing "the more zealously they proclaimed it" (verse 36).

The book of Ecclesiasticus is also known by the name of its author, Jesus ben Sirach. The book was written about 180 B.C. by a teacher who seems to have conducted an academy (see Ecclus. 51:23) for the study of the Law. It was written in Hebrew, but, except for some fragments found among the Dead Sea Scrolls, no copies in the original language exist. Fortunately, however, the book was translated into Greek by Ben Sirach's grandson.

The topic of the book is wisdom in all of its aspects, divine and human. It comes from the Lord (1:1), and human beings seek it, though finally it is beyond their reach. God gives it to all, but no one completely comprehends it. Wisdom is both a divine attribute and a human capacity; indeed, it is many human capacities, ranging from the wisdom that is like the fear of the Lord to practical knowledge for survival and prosperity.

The book is not a carefully organized treatise. One finds collections of sayings on similar topics, somewhat extended discourses, and almost casual movement from one theme to another.

Ecclesiasticus 5:8-15 is a series of admonitions and prohibitions which, like the other material in the immediate context, are in the form of second person address, as if a teacher or parent were addressing a student or young person. Some of the instructions (5:8, 14, 15–6:1) are followed by motive clauses—introduced by "for"—which explain why the advice should be followed.

The themes of the instructions are various. Verse 8 recommends not depending on dishonest wealth. That it will not benefit one in the "day of calamity" expresses the view of the wisdom teachers that those who are wise and honest will prosper but those who are dishonest will come to ruin. Verses 9 and 10 approach the matter of consistent and steadfast behavior first negatively and then positively. Do not be easily swayed, but be consistent.

Verses 11-14 pick up and elaborate on a particular aspect of the advice in verses 9-10, proper use of the tongue. Listen quickly, answer slowly (verse 11). Answer your neighbor if you have something worth saying, otherwise keep quiet (verse 12). The tongue is a dangerous instrument, bringing both glory and dishonor (verse 13). Verse 14 addresses a particularly dangerous use of the tongue, slander, and similar uses of speech that harm others. The final saying begins in 5:15 and continues through 6:1. One who acts wrongly or becomes an enemy instead of a friend is a "double-tongued sinner" whose bad name brings shame and reproach.

There are no specifically religious or theological notes in this passage. There is a concern for proper behavior, for justice, and respect for the rights of others. Even that, however, as far as these admonitions go, is based on self-interest (5:14–6:1). All of this is sound advice, but does it go far enough? The broader context of the book reminds us that wisdom and the capacity for right behavior are gifts of God, and those gifts should ultimately lead one to the Giver.

Proverbs 2:1-8

The book of Proverbs is a collection of wisdom materials with two distinct parts. Chapters 1–9 contain wisdom instructions and speeches by wisdom personified as a woman; chapters 10–31 consist for the most part of individual proverbs and other kinds of wisdom sayings, sometimes organized into collections, but often appearing in almost random order. The first part is distinctly more theological and abstract than the sayings in the second part. After a superscription (1:1) and an introduction (1:2-7), chapters 1–9 contain some twelve instructions or speeches. Our reading for the day is part of the second instruction (2:1-22).

While chapter 2 is not a full alphabetic acrostic—a poem in which each line or series of lines begins with a successive letter of the alphabet—it has some alphabetic characteristics. Verses 1-11 all begin with aleph, the first letter of the Hebrew alphabet, and verses 12-22 begin with lamedh, the twelfth or first letter in the second half of the alphabet. Moreover, there are twenty-two verses, each with two neatly balanced parallel lines, corresponding to the number of Hebrew letters. The poem is thus a carefully crafted literary piece.

That the entire chapter is an instruction is indicated by its opening, "my son," a conventional formula from the wisdom schools. The speaker is the teacher and the "son" the student. The poem is unlike most such speeches in that it does not use the imperative form or commands and prohibitions in direct address. Instead it is structured as an enlarged conditional sentence. Verses 1-4 state the conditions and verses 5-22 the consequences. It thus has a hortatory and persuasive rather than an authoritarian style. The teacher intends to show the student the values of following a certain direction.

Several facets of a single condition, seeking wisdom, are expressed in three "if" sentences (verses 1-4). The first condition (verse 1) is listening to the teacher. To "treasure up" his commandments means to memorize them: listen and learn and, implicitly, not question what is given to him. Attending to wisdom and understanding is equated with listening to the teacher, that is, to the voice of tradition, experience, and insight (verse 2). The second condition is that one asks for insight and understanding (verse 3), and the third is that one seeks it as a most rare and valuable possession.

Our reading includes only the first of the consequences of following the conditions (verses 5-8), but certainly the most comprehensive. One who seeks wisdom "will understand the fear of the Lord and find the knowledge of God" (verse 5). Verses 6-8 explain why that is so. Yahweh gives wisdom, knowledge, and understanding, storing it up for "the upright," taking care of justice, and protecting the faithful.

The poem is a theological meditation on wisdom. Its theme is the relationship between piety and insight, the knowledge of God and wisdom. Behind it stands a problem for Israel's sages, and perhaps even a theological debate, to which the motto of Proverbs gives an answer: "The fear of the Lord is the beginning of knowledge" (1:7*a*). The wisdom schools revered that insight and understanding which could be gained by drawing conclusions from human observation. If not rationalistic it was amenable to reason and to the human senses. Further, the accumulated knowledge could be passed on from generation to generation. What does such "wisdom" have to do with divine revelation, especially of the law? The issue is not entirely unlike conflicts in our time between science and religion, between "secular humanism" and faith. It was later wisdom, represented in Proverbs 1–9, which concluded that in the last analysis there was no conflict between wisdom and faith. Wisdom and understanding begin with true piety. That view was based on a sense of the order and predictability of the world as God's creation.

Proverbs 2:1-8 is distinctive in that it reverses the well-known conclusion that the fear of the Lord is the beginning of knowledge. The one who seeks wisdom, insight, and understanding comes to know true piety—"the fear of the Lord"—and gains "the knowledge of God" (verse 5). That is because Yahweh is the one who gives wisdom. Implicitly, then, on the path of wisdom one discovers God through God's gift, wisdom. The diligent pursuit of wisdom is not out of self-interest, but in order to know God. In effect, then, the text is a commentary on the command to "love God with all your mind" (Matt. 22:37; Mark 12:30; Luke 10:27; compare Deut. 6:5).

Another distinctive characteristic of this passage is its appropriation of motifs more at home in prophetic literature. The God who gives wisdom also establishes justice (verse 8). The next consequence of seeking wisdom is that one understands "righteousness and justice" (verse 9).

Psalm 119:129-136

Psalm 119 is a psalm eulogizing the "law" of God. Three surface features of the psalm are noteworthy. (1) It is by far the longest psalm in the Psalter consisting of twenty-two stanzas with eight lines to a stanza. (2) The psalm is alphabetic in structure. That is, all eight lines in the first stanza begin with the first letter of the Hebrew alphabet, the second eight with the second letter, and so on through the twenty-two letters of the alphabet. The extended character of this alphabetic structure, with its eight lines for each letter, is without parallel in the Old Testament. The nearest counterpart is chapter three of Lamentations. The pattern and intricacy of this alphabetic form cannot be reproduced in English. Even our simplest ABC books are quite silly with certain letters. (Try an eight-line poem with all the lines beginning with x, y, or z!) (3) Throughout the psalm, there is the constant repetition of eight terms used to speak of God's revelation and will. In the RSV translation these appear as words, promise, testimonies, commandments, law, ordinances, precepts, and statutes (see verses 57-64 where they all appear in the same stanza). Apparently all of these terms are to be understood as synonymous ways of talking about the complete revelation of God's will. They are used throughout the psalm and are interwoven into its fabric to produce a tapestry design that proclaims devotion to and love for the law.

Three features of the theology of the psalm should be noted. (1) The psalmist assumes that there is a divine will which lies behind everything that exists. This divine will expresses itself in a divine order for the whole of existence. The life of a culture and the lives of individuals in the culture should be governed and in tune with the divine order. (2) This divine order and will have been or can be made known in the form of law and statutes. The purpose of these embodiments and expressions of the divine will and order is to serve as directions and as standards for living. They are aids for understanding the divine order of the cosmos and for bringing human life into line with divine order. (3) These expressions of divine order—the Torah or law as well as what the other terms denote—are accepted as cherished possessions to be loved, studied, meditated upon, thought about, and above all lived according to. In this, one finds fulfillment, happiness, security, enlightenment, and counsel.

Many of the general features of the psalm can be seen in the lection selected for today—verses 129-136 in which all the lines open with the letter *p*. Note the appearance of the terms: "testimonies, words, commandments, promise, precepts, statutes, and law" in these verses. The entire section has the form of a prayer to God.

The text may be analyzed in order to stress three factors.

1. There is, first of all, the positive assessment of the "law" or God's revelation. It is wonderful or wondrous, that is, marvelous in what it contains (verse 129; see Ps. 119:18). When God's words become known or reveal themselves, they give light to illuminate the way. They are so enlightening that even the simple-minded or those with simple faith can find understanding (verse 130). Thus the law is not presented as a burden to be borne or an obligation to be fulfilled but as a wondrous gift which brings benefits in its wake.

2. The person's disposition toward the law is presented as one of expectant longing. "I pant" and "I long for" are strong expressions of expectation (verse 131). This sense of expectation may be illustrated by the statement of Job that in former times the people waited for his counsel "as for the rain; and they opened their mouths as for the spring rain" (Job 29:23). The psalmist here suggests this "thirsty waiting" as his attitude before the commandments. The desire for the

commandments is equivalent to desiring God's presence itself, "Turn to me and be gracious" (verse 132), or to experiencing the constant consoling support of the divine, "Keep steady my steps" (verse 133).

3. The service of God and the goal of life are found in following the law. In this text, the person prays that certain conditions will not prevent observance of the law. (*a*) There is, first, the possibility that one's personal iniquity—moral worthlessness or antagonism toward God—will lead to an incapacity for obedience (verse 133). (*b*) Human oppression—bondage to another—is seen as something from which one needs to be redeemed in order to be obedient. Oppression here does not necessarily refer to enforced bondage but simply to commitments and obligations to another which hinder and stifle the opportunities for obedience (verse 134). (*c*) Finally, the blessing of God which is reflected in the expression "thy face shine upon thy servant" makes possible the hearing and keeping of the law (verse 135). Negatively, the same idea can be expressed by saying that without God's blessing, that is, without the normal benefits of life, obedience becomes more difficult. If one's time is spent fighting chaos in one's personal life or struggling to feed oneself and family, then little energy is left for the law and its contemplation.

The lection closes with a statement of the sorrow that comes from experiencing the world as a place where the law is not kept. The psalmist speaks of weeping streams or canals of tears—weeping brought on by the heartbreak of watching people live in a fashion uncommensurate with their own best interest.

To preach from texts like Psalm 119 which extol and praise the law, the Christian minister needs to avoid one old pitfall—the (misunderstood) Pauline view of the law as serving only a negative function—and at the same time attempt to create one new perspective—that of appreciating, even loving, the law. To be avoided is the view that the law is a burdensome imposition of a deadening code which stifles freedom and life. Over against this, one can emphasize the values of seeing the world as an ordered place in which law serves as an ordering principle. At the same time, the listeners should be made aware of the pleasures of a good conscience and the legitimate satisfaction that can come from pleasing duty for duty's sake or, to put it psychologically, from doing what is ultimately for the doer's benefit. Living in a house built by law may be no less pleasurable or fulfilling than living in a house where freedom has torn down all walls.

James 1:17-27

Today begins a series of four lections taken from the Letter of James. According to tradition, the letter is attributed to James, the brother of the Lord, but this is doubtful. It is remarkable how little explicit Christian teaching it contains. For example, it contains only two references to Jesus (1:1; 2:1). Old Testament figures and examples are much more decisive in informing the author. The letter bears many similarities to the Jewish wisdom tradition, and with some qualification could be thought of as a Christian wisdom book. In the next four weeks, the readings from James are juxtaposed with Old Testament readings from the Jewish wisdom writings and both sets of readings may be profitably explored for their similarity in outlook and approach to the religious life.

Like the Jewish wisdom writings, James defies outlining. Often, sayings are clustered in a topical arrangement, but just as often they may be scattered. For this reason, today's lection will be treated in terms of recurrent themes rather than verse-by-verse.

The lection opens with a theological assertion: God as the source of every good gift. This in itself is worth noting since wisdom literature in general, and the Letter of James in particular, are often pilloried as being practical in their outlook but with no deep theological underpinnings. Yet, here God is said to be the "Father of lights," probably a reference to God's creation of the heavenly lights (Gen. 1:14-18; also Ps. 136:7). In other texts, God is actually identified with light (I John 1:5; cf. I Pet. 2:9). The qualifying phrase is difficult: "with whom there is no variation or shadow due to change" (RSV). Other translations may be consulted with profit, but the fundamental assertion appears to be one of God's invariability (cf. Heb. 1:12; Ps. 102:27).

God is not only the source of "every good endowment," but of Christian existence as well (verse 18). We have been brought into being by a divine begetting (I Pet. 1:23; John 3:3, 5), accomplished through the creative power of the "word of truth" (Eph. 1:13; Col. 1:5-6; II Tim. 2:5; Ps. 119:43). With its power to engender life, it is a "living Word" (Heb. 4:12), not a human word but that of God (I Thess. 2:13; also 1:6; Acts 8:14; 17:11). Later, in verse 21, it is said to be an "implanted word, which is able to save your souls" (cf. Luke 8:11). Meekness is a precondition for such reception (cf. Sir. 3:17). The planting metaphor is extended in the description of us as "a kind of first fruits of his creatures" (Rev. 14:4; also Rom. 16:5).

Having established that God is the source of all that we have and are, the author now turns to practical religion.

One theme that emerges has to do with the emotion of anger and the attendant forms of speech: "Let every man be quick to hear, slow to speak, slow to anger" (verse 19). This advice echoes Sirach 5:11, "Be quick to hear, and be deliberate in answering" (cf. Eccles. 5:1-2). The Jewish wisdom tradition also knew the advantage of thoughtful speech (Prov. 15:1-2; Sir. 5:12-13), as well as recognizing that anger usually causes us to say things we later regret. Consequently, wisdom dictated that anger should be curbed (Eccles. 7:9). Later in the passage (verse 26), bridling the tongue is seen as a prerequisite to being religious (Ps. 34:13). This theme receives even fuller treatment later in the letter (3:1-12).

A second theme concerns "hearing and doing" (verses 22-25). The book of James is especially well known for the way in which its emphasis on "faith that works" (2:14-26) provides a counterpoint to the Pauline emphasis on faith alone (Rom. 1:17). The author first notices that there is a distinction between "hearing the word" and "doing it," but this is not his unique observation (cf. Matt. 7:21-27; 21:29; Luke 6:46; Rom. 2:13; I John 3:18). His illustration of the man looking in the mirror suggests that "hearing" is a deliberate act that requires concentration and memory. Consequently, "looking into the perfect law of liberty" (verse 25) requires careful attention and perseverance before appropriate action results. The author seems to have had experience with the self-styled religious person who hears but does not allow the "commandment of the Lord to enlighten the eyes" (Ps. 19:8).

A third, closely related, theme concerns "religion that is pure and undefiled" (verse 27). This is actually an extension of the second theme since it illustrates in concrete terms what is involved in a "religion that does." Singled out for attention here is care for orphans and widows (cf. Exod. 22:21-24; Ps. 10:10, 18). This teaching echoes the sentiments of Jesus' teaching concerning practical discipleship (Matt. 25:31-46). The insistence of this text is that "keeping oneself unstained from the world" (verse 27) occurs as a result of practical acts of Christian charity rather than from ritual purification (cf. II Pet. 3:14).

If one wishes to preach about practical Christianity, one could do worse than begin with this lection from the book of James. To begin with, today's lection illustrates that Christian practice begins with the fundamental recognition of God as the source of every gift, including our own Christian birthright. But then it moves on to the practical plane of Christian living, insisting that the truly "implanted word" received with meekness will produce disciples who are long on obedience and short on words.

Mark 7:31-37

Mark 7:31-37 is one of the few miracle stories offered by Mark with almost no comment (1:30-31 and 8:22-26 are of the same type). The absence of interpretation is both a delight and a challenge to the reader. Why did the writer choose to tell this story from among the many available?

The story itself is not unusual in its format, conforming in general to other miracle stories and in particular to the one recorded in the next chapter (8:22-26). Frequently in Mark persons with special needs are "brought to Jesus" (2:3; 7:32; 8:22; 9:20; 10:13). The methods of healing attributed to Jesus were common to healers and practitioners of magic arts. In the case before us, the deaf mute is taken aside for privacy, the afflicted parts are touched, spittle is applied, the healer looks heavenward, groans, and gives the healing command. Keeping the power word *Ephphatha* in the original Aramaic (cf. also 5:41) not only keeps the sense of mystery but may also reflect the church's practice of preserving traditional healing formulas. Following the healing, Jesus again calls for secrecy, the charge to secrecy is disobeyed by the zealous preaching of the witnesses, and the account closes with a general expression of astonishment.

If Mark offers any commentary at all on this miracle it is in verse 37b: "He even makes the deaf hear and the dumb speak." This description of the ministry of Jesus very likely was intended to recall Isaiah's grand vision of Zion's future in the day of salvation: the blind see, the deaf hear, the mute speak, and the lame leap for joy (35:5-6). But beyond this story's witness to the end time and the presence of God's kingdom, is Mark saying anything else?

In addition to the usual interpretive method of adding commentary to a saying or an action of Jesus, Mark also interprets by the location of a narrative. Where an event occurs geographically and where it is placed within the Gospel are both forms of interpretation and deserve the reader's careful attention.

Geographically, the healing of the deaf mute occurs in Gentile territory. The preceding story, the exorcism of a demon from the daughter of a Syrophoenician woman (7:24-30) took place in the region of Tyre and Sidon. From there Mark describes a most improbable itinerary by Jesus. For example, he says Jesus went from Tyre to Sidon to the Sea of Galilee "in the midst of" (translated "through" RSV) the Decapolis (verse 31). Sidon is north of Tyre and the Sea of Galilee does not lie in the midst of Decapolis. Whatever may have been Mark's knowledge of the country or whatever his sources, there is no doubt about his intention: Jesus made a wide ranging journey in Gentile territory and healed, exorcized, taught, and preached there (5:1-20; 6:53-56; 7:24-30; 7:31-37). The message and blessing of Jesus Christ were being taken to geographical and ethnic limits. Apparently the Christian community Mark addressed needed to know that, or be reminded of it. In no way could the ministry of Jesus be interpreted as support for a church that observed national, racial, or ethnic boundaries. And if Mark's church was indeed open to all persons, they needed to know that their practice was authorized by Jesus himself.

The literary context for the story of the healing of the deaf mute also serves an interpretive purpose. In the cycle of stories in chapters 6–7 Jesus feeds, exorcizes demons, and heals, with great receptions at the fringes of his country but with criticism by Jewish leaders and with misunderstanding by his disciples. The signs of the kingdom are there for those who would perceive and believe. The crowds applaud, the critics continue in hardened opposition. But what of Jesus' disciples, where are they? Not with the applauding crowd, not with the hounding critics. Have they seen and heard enough to be ready for the next word from Jesus: the Son of man must suffer, be rejected, and be killed? If Jesus' own followers miss the point, who shall continue his work?

Proper 19

Sunday Between September 11 and 17 Inclusive

Proverbs 22:1-2, 8-9; Psalm 125; James 2:1-5, 8-10, 14-17; Mark 8:27-38

Proverbs 22:1-2, 8-9

If one wishes to connect the texts for the day in terms of a common theme, such a theme would be the relation of the rich to the poor. Riches, the wealthy and the poor, and the blessings of sharing one's bread with the poor occupy the loosely connected sayings in the Old Testament reading. The discourse in James on faith without works argues that it is contrary to the "royal law, according to the scripture" to show partiality to the wealthy, that God has chosen the poor in the world to be rich in faith and heirs of the kingdom. These concerns may be taken as instances of the call of Jesus in Mark to deny oneself, to find one's life by losing it.

With the exception of the concluding poem on the ideal wife, Proverbs 10–31 is a large collection of short wisdom sayings. There is little systematic organization in the collection, though some sayings are grouped according to content and others according to form or simply linked by catchwords. Most are quite brief, consisting of a single two-part sentence.

There is no way to determine the date and authorship of the individual sayings. The attribution of the book as a whole and of the collection in Proverbs 10:1–22:16 is based on the tradition of Solomon's legendary wisdom. The final form of the book is relatively late, reflecting the literary activity of the wisdom teachers such as ben Sirah (Ecclus. 51:23). But in the collections old and new sayings appear side by side. Some of the forms of the proverbs and doubtless many of the individual sayings come from folk wisdom; others may have been composed by teachers as they reflected on the meaning of life and sought the most apt and memorable way of expressing their conclusions.

The sayings come in various forms and styles and serve different ends. They are different from the formal instructions, such as the ones in Proverbs 1–9 (see the commentary on last week's lesson). Some simply draw a conclusion from experience and state it as a general truth. The purpose is to make sense of reality, especially of human relationships. Others express a value judgment about some aspect of experience and indicate directions for conduct: "He who loves pleasure will be a poor man; he who loves wine and oil will not be rich" (Prov. 21:17). Typical themes of such sayings are the differences between wisdom and foolishness, the values of hard work, and the merits of prudent behavior. Still other sayings go a step farther and give explicit directions for conduct in the form of commands, prohibitions, exhortations, or admonitions: "Do not rob the poor, because he is poor, or crush the afflicted at the gate" (Prov. 22:22). While they are similar to the Old Testament laws their force is different since their authority rests not upon divine revelation but on the persuasiveness of the directions themselves.

Proverbs 22:1 is a saying of the second type. It states a value based on experience and leaves it to the hearer to draw the obvious conclusions about conduct. Reputation ("a good name") and goodwill ("favor") are better than wealth. Consequently, one should act at all times with integrity. There is no real connection between verses 1 and 2 beyond the catchwords "riches"/"the rich." Verse 2 is a simple statement of "fact." It does not inculcate a value or suggest a course of action, though a certain value may be taken for granted. It is to be observed and described, but not fully comprehended, that society consists of both rich and poor, and Yahweh obviously made them all. The social order rests in creation. It is a conclusion that generates further reflection, including our own. Does this saying simply recognize and approve of the status quo? Or does the affirmation that all are created by the Lord suggest equality? Whatever the intention of the saying itself, we certainly can use the theological interpretation of human life as we analyze our society and consider courses of action.

Verse 8 is a statement of "fact," but it is presented in such a way that a course of action is commended to the hearer. The one who acts unjustly will suffer; his deeds will bring him retribution. (Read the second half of the verse with NEB: "and the end of his work will be the rod.") This proverb states the view, frequently encountered in wisdom literature and elsewhere in the Old Testament, that the unrighteous suffer and the righteous prosper. Expression of that perspective is not only moralism, to encourage proper behavior, it is also confirmed by experience. Those who sow the wind do in fact often reap the whirlwind (Hos. 8:7). But, as the books of Job and Ecclesiastes point out, it is a limited view. The righteous do indeed suffer, and the race is not always to the swift, bread to the wise, or riches to the intelligent, "but time and chance happen to them all" (Eccles. 9:11).

Verse 9 clearly states and inculcates a value, generosity to the poor. It should not be taken as the positive side of what was stated in the previous verse. Blessing does not come as a reward to the one who looks kindly upon others ("has a bountiful eye") and shares bread with the poor. Generosity and concern for others is its own reward in that with it comes peace of heart.

Psalm 125

This psalm falls in two parts. The first, in verses 1-3, consists of statements and description of confidence. The second, in verses 4-5, consists of a prayer for the blessing of those who are good and a declaration that evildoers will be led away.

Two motives are given for the expressions of confidence. First of all, "those who trust in the Lord" have the same type of security and divine protection as the city of Zion, the site of the temple. Zion is described as immovable, abiding forever. A basic tenet of Hebrew thought about Zion asserted that it was unconquerable and inviolable (see Pss. 46, 48, 76). The eternal durability of Zion was associated, in later Judaism, with the idea of the navel or center of the universe. The sacred rock over which the temple was constructed was considered to mark the navel of the world and thus the meeting place of the heavenly world and the underworld.

The security of the faithful ones is declared assured since God is round about his people like the mountains which encircle Zion (verse 2). Among the mountains encircling Jerusalem are Mount Scopus and the Mount of Olives, both of which are higher in elevation than the mountain spur on which Jerusalem was built.

Verse 3 is difficult to interpret. The text seems to promise that foreign oppressors or evil rulers ("the scepter of wickedness") will not rule over the holy land ("the land allotted to the righteous"). That they won't is to ensure that the righteous will not depart from the proper path, that is, local citizens won't become collaborators with the foreign power. Throughout much of Israel's history, the land was ruled by outsiders and the local citizens were constantly tempted to cooperate with the occupying troops or even to give up their ancestral ways and religious practices, that is, to cease being Jewish.

Verse 4 is an intercessory prayer that God will do good to those who are good and who are upright in their hearts, in other words, those who are loyal to God externally ("those who are good") and internally ("upright in their hearts").

Verse 5 is not a prayer but a declaration that those who turn aside—the apostates, the unfaithful, the renegades—will be led away—into exile.

The psalm thus begins with a description of those who trust in God—they are firmly anchored and immovable—and concludes with a description of those who in their crookedness act corruptly—they are not fixed but insecure and their future is to be moved away.

James 2:1-5, 8-10, 14-17

In spite of their seeming unrelatedness, all three texts from today's epistolary lection reflect a common theme: proper treatment of the poor.

In the first passage, which should rightly extend through verse 7, is a graphic scene depicting a rich man receiving deferential treatment in finding a seat in the synagogue while a poor man is politely given standing room only, or seated on the floor. It is a scene we all know, and likely have experienced in one form or another. The author's sympathy is with the poor man, as seen in the remarks that follow (verses 5-7). We are reminded that God's choice lies with the poor who turn out to be "rich in faith" and the real "heirs of the kingdom." By contrast, the author has little use for the rich who, in his experience, turn out to be those who oppress the poor, take them to court, and blaspheme the "honorable name," probably Christian.

This unequivocal sympathy with the poor and judgment against the rich is reminiscent of the first Lukan beatitude and woe: "Blessed are the poor; Woe to the rich" (Luke 6:20, 24). In fact, it fits well with the overall depiction of the rich and poor in Luke-Acts. Indeed, earlier (1:9), the "lowly brother" is enjoined to "boast in his exaltation," while the rich is ordered to boast in his humiliation. Although the author's viewpoint is not grounded in the prophetic tradition, it could well have been, for his protest against the rich's treatment of the poor echoes the sentiments of the Old Testament prophets (cf. Amos 4:1; 5:10-13; 8:4-6).

That such discrimination against the poor actually occurred in the early church, even within worship settings, is seen in I Corinthians 11:17-22. A close reading of the text suggests that distinctions based on socio-economic status were being made within the fellowship, and Paul sharply condemns those who "humiliate those who have nothing" (verse 22), literally, the "have-nots." This fits with his remarks that some were eating and drinking to excess while others were going hungry.

The scene in the book of James is depicted to make a single point: Christians are to show no partiality (verse 1). It is this theme that connects the first passage with the second (verses 8-10). Here, "loving one's neighbor as oneself" (Lev. 19:18; Matt. 22:39; Rom. 13:9; Gal. 5:14) is set over against showing partiality, which is treated as a grave offense. In fact, to show partiality is an offense liable to conviction under the Mosaic law, although there it cuts both ways: "You shall do no injustice in judgment; you shall not be partial to the poor or

173

defer to the great, but in righteousness shall you judge your neighbor" (Lev. 19:13; also cf. Exod. 23:3; Deut. 1:17; Sir. 7:6). The text recognizes that some readers will regard this as a relatively trivial matter, and thus it emphasizes that infraction of a single point of the law, however minor it may seem, renders one guilty of breaking the whole law (cf. Matt. 5:19; Gal. 5:3).

No attempt is made in our text to defend the principle of impartiality by appealing to God's impartial nature. But this is certainly an axiomatic principle in Scripture, and one well worth noting in this connection (cf. Acts 10:34; Rom. 2:11; Gal. 2:6; Eph. 6:9; Col. 3:25; I Pet. 1:17; also II Chron. 19:7; Sir. 35:12-13).

The third part of today's lection (verses 14-17) treats the well-known theme of "faith without works." The text ends climactically with the emphatic assertion: "So faith by itself, if it has no works, is dead" (verse 17). This principle may be profitably contrasted with the Pauline doctrine of justification by faith, but given the juxtaposition of this text with the other selections from the chapter, it will be more to the point to notice that the central example has to do with the proper care of the poor. Thus, to the hungry and ill clad, a warm greeting and a hollow prayer will not do. "What does it profit?" The point echoes the teaching of Jesus concerning the hungry and poor (Matt. 25:35-36), and also relates to a similar problem in the Johannine community (I John 3:17).

None of these texts spells out a well-developed social ethic, nor do they spell out an undeveloped social ethic. Insofar as this is done at all in the New Testament, it is done best by Luke-Acts. Rather, what we have here is direct, hard-hitting teaching about the evil and seriousness of discrimination and, by extension, neglect of the poor. We are told that deference toward the rich and denigration of the poor are unacceptable behavior for those who "hold the faith of our Lord Jesus Christ, the Lord of glory" (verse 1); that partiality in these matters is a grievous wrong; and, finally, that the needs of the poor and hungry are not met by proclaiming that we have faith, or even by proclaiming the faith. Rather they are met by the simple gesture of giving a cup of cold water.

This, according to the book of James, constitutes genuine faith.

Mark 8:27-38

Because Mark 8:27-38 is a turning point in the Gospel in that Jesus introduces his coming passion to his disciples and begins to move toward Jerusalem, we need to take a moment to back away and see this text in perspective. It is part of a larger body of material beginning at 8:27 and ending at 10:45. This larger unit is bracketed by stories of healing the blind (8:22-26; 10:46-52). The governing theme is Jesus' predictions of his passion (8:31; 9:31; 10:32-34) and the disciples' total inability to understand or to accept what Jesus said. As Jesus moves toward his destination, the recurring phrase "on the way" gives unity to the narrative (8:27; 9:33; 10:17; 10:32).

Our lection consists of three parts: the confession of Peter (verses 27-30), Jesus' prediction of his passion (verses 31-33), and the instructions to the crowd about discipleship (verses 34-38). Verses 31-33 govern the whole and give the passage its critical importance. The exchanges between Jesus and Peter give to 27-30 and 31-33 a kind of unity, a narrative consisting of three brief episodes. All three episodes focus on who Jesus is.

The first consists of Jesus' inquiry about public opinion and the disciples' response (verses 27-28). The several expressions of the Galileans' views of Jesus all say one thing: they think of Jesus as the forerunner of the Messiah. Jesus' announcement of the approaching kingdom and his words and deeds of power have heightened anticipation but have not persuaded them that he is the fulfillment of that anticipation. They have, as we all have, an image of the coming Messiah, but Jesus does not fit it. After all, it is easier to believe a Messiah *will* come than to believe one *has* come. Messiah as future keeps one's image intact and makes no demands; Messiah as present calls for an altered image and demands an altered self.

The second episode consists of another view of Jesus, followed by a sharp rebuke and charge to silence (verses 29-30). Simon Peter makes it clear that the disciples differ with the crowds in their view of Jesus. You are not the forerunner of the Messiah, says Peter; you *are* the Messiah. One is tempted here to slip over into Matthew and hear Jesus bless Simon for this confession (Matt. 16:17), but in Mark Jesus neither approves nor disapproves; he only charges them to silence. Remember that for Mark, Jesus cannot properly be understood prior to the passion. Until the cross redefines "Messiah" it cannot properly be applied to Jesus. After the cross and resurrection, the disciples can proclaim it (9:9).

The third episode offers yet another view of Jesus, followed by an exchange of rebukes (verses 31-33). Jesus presents himself as the suffering, rejected, crucified, and risen Son of man. Peter's rebuke is a dramatic expression of the disciples' resistance to such an impossible image of a Christ. Jesus' counter rebuke means that Jesus recognizes in Peter the voice of Satan, the adversary of God. The language of rebuke is the same used to silence demons in the exorcism stories, and so these two friends verbalize the clash of good and evil. The wrong thinking of Peter is no less crippling than the other diseases encountered by Jesus. Let the preacher ponder what it means for the locus of satanic power to be in the heart of a disciple and friend who seeks to save life not lose it, to defend Jesus not oppose him. Is there a route to the kingdom which bypasses Golgotha?

Verses 34-38 are editorially joined to the preceding narrative. This is evident in Mark's having the multitudes join the disciples even though the scene is far north from the places of Jesus' ministry and it is clearly a private meeting between Jesus and the Twelve. The editorial hand is even more evident in that the words to the crowd not only indicate that the crowd knew what Jesus had said to the Twelve about his own passion but also assume that they knew that the form of his death was crucifixion. Jesus had not mentioned the cross. This post-passion material is appropriate at this point, however, because the call to self-denial and cross-bearing belongs with Jesus' description of his own fate. And the path of self-denial is not for the Twelve alone; it is for all who would follow. The five sayings of Jesus in these verses have probably been gathered from other contexts since each has its own integrity and meaning. When joined in one place, however, and placed in the shadow of Jesus' words about his own passion, the terms of discipleship are made inescapably clear.

Proper 20
Sunday Between September 18 and 24 Inclusive

Job 28:20-28; Psalm 27:1-6; James 3:13-18; Mark 9:30-37

Job 28:20-28

The Old Testament and the epistolary readings form a particularly good match in that both concern the divine source of wisdom and its effects in the world. If one receives wisdom it is through revelation, "from above" (James 3:17). The reading from Mark is a stimulating contrast. The disciples are caricatures of ignorance who cannot comprehend what Jesus tells them, are afraid to ask for an explanation, and become preoccupied with "jealousy and selfish ambition" (James 3:14).

Any individual passage in the Book of Job must be viewed in its literary context lest it be seriously misunderstood. It makes a major difference whether particular lines are spoken by Job, by one of his friends, or by God. The book as a whole consists of a narrative prologue (1:1–2:13) and epilogue (42:7-17) which bracket a lengthy poem. The poem is structured as a series of dialogues between Job, his three friends, the young upstart Elihu, and God. The poet has taken a traditional story as the starting point for consideration of the problem of the suffering of the righteous. The book is wisdom literature, but it calls into question some of the fundamental beliefs of conventional wisdom.

Though Job 28 is presented in the book as part of Job's last speech to his three friends, it is quite distinctive, unlike the others in form and style. It probably was added after the book was completed. It is not a response to questions posed, or a reflection on the problem of the righteous sufferer, but a hymnic poem in praise of wisdom. In terms of its location after the speeches and its insistence on the inaccessibility of wisdom it is a rebuke of the "wisdom" offered by the friends, and perhaps even of Job's search for wisdom.

The poem as a whole is a magnificent composition in three parts plus a somewhat surprising conclusion in verse 28. (1) Verses 1-11 comment on human technological skill (wisdom), especially the capacity to search for and find precious things such as gold, iron, and copper. A short interlude about the path that even the birds and beasts do not know (verses 7-8) begins to make it clear that the search for what is precious actually is the pursuit of wisdom. (2) Verses 12-22 then emphasize that human beings, for all they know, cannot find the way to wisdom; it is incomparable and inaccessible. (3) There is, however, One who knows the way to wisdom, and that One is God (verses 23-27). God, who created all things, established wisdom as the principle by which creation is ordered.

In the body of the poem wisdom is not a human characteristic, or an extension of the Deity, as in Proverbs 8. In contrast to Lady Wisdom who according to Proverbs 8 calls people to her, wisdom here "is hid from the eyes of all living" (verse 21). This wisdom came into existence at the time of creation, and only God is transcendent over it.

The fundamental point of the chapter, then, is that the wisdom which human beings seek, the principle by which all things are ordered, or the key which will explain the world, is known only to God. It is above all a reminder of the difference between humanity—indeed, all creatures—and God. We do not know and cannot know the answers to all things; to think otherwise is arrogance and a form of idolatry. Moreover, the poem implies, if human beings cannot comprehend the mysterious order then they cannot control the created world.

Verse 28 functions as the conclusion to the poem, but it seems clear that the lines were added by a later editor. "Wisdom" here has quite a different meaning; it is a human capacity or potential. Moreover, it is not inaccessible but—at least in a certain form—genuinely possible: "The fear of the Lord, that is wisdom." The saying is a form of the motto of Proverbs (1:7), but it goes further. The fear of the Lord—obedience, commitment, awe, genuine piety—is not just the beginning of knowledge, it is wisdom itself. It is also

179

different from Proverbs 2:1-8 (see the commentary on the Old Testament reading for Proper 18), which sees the pursuit of wisdom as the path that leads to the fear of the Lord.

This final verse, though disagreeing with the poem about the possibility of wisdom, may be taken as a legitimate interpretation of it. Granted, the wisdom by which Yahweh ordered the world cannot be attained, what are we to do? We are to be faithful, obedient, and in awe of the Lord of that wisdom. The perspective is not without its moral dimensions as well, for that faithfulness is the same as departing from evil.

Psalm 27:1-6

Psalm 27 is divided between two Sundays in the lectionary. The division is made between verses 6 and 7 where there is a change in the mood and sentiments of the psalm. In spite of this shift in tone from a statement of confidence (verses 1-6) to a petitionary prayer for aid (verses 7-12), the psalm nonetheless is a unity and should be seen and interpreted as such. The unity of the psalm can be seen in the following outline: (*a*) an affirmation of confidence addressed by the worshiper (the king?) to a human audience prior to the offering of sacrifices (verses 1-6), (*b*) a petitionary prayer addressed to God probably in conjunction with the offering of sacrifice (verses 7-12), (*c*) a confessional statement by the worshiper to a human audience perhaps to the cultic personnel in charge of the ritual (verse 13; note the confessional counterpart in verse 10), and (*d*) the response of the cultic official to the worshiper (verse 14). All of these components fit together nicely as the component parts in a worship service.

This particular lection is concerned only with the opening statements of confidence or the song of trust in verses 1-6. These verses, while constituting a unity, must be seen as two stanzas. The first, verses 1-3, is an affirmation of confidence, of trust, of confession, of certitude. In spite of the speaker's assertion of his confidence in God's support, spoken to his peers, perhaps by the king to his subjects, a sense of fear and insecurity permeates the material. This is only natural for if fear and fright are not real then neither are confidence and trust. The vocabulary of opposition—evildoers, adversaries, foes, a host, war—is balanced by descriptive assertions about God—my light, my salvation, the stronghold of my life. The speaker's confidence lies not in personal character traits like courage and fortitude but in the assurance of divine support and aid. The sense of confidence is not equivalent to arrogance, as is even clearer when the psalm turns to petition in verse 7. The affirmations of confidence are like islands situated in the sea of life's terrors—safe but always threatened.

The psalmist's opponents are described in metaphorical fashion, as is common in the psalms. The goal of the evildoers in the second line of verse 2 is described as "to devour my flesh." This may refer to slander (so the RSV) or be terminology borrowed from the way one would speak of wild animals and thus denote the enemies as beasts. Adversaries and foes are general terms but verse 3 utilizes military terminology. If this psalm were originally written for the use of the king, then the situation of distress could have been a potential military engagement. At any rate, the speaker is certain of overcoming fear as well as his opposition.

In the second stanza, verses 4-6, the emphasis shifts to focus on expectations associated with entry into the temple. The temple is seen as the source of refuge from the enemy and of communion with the Deity.

Verse 4, with its reference to dwelling in the house of the Lord (= the temple) forever, unless this is to be taken entirely metaphorically, could suggest that the psalm was used by some temple functionary or official. Probably this would not mean a priest since priests did not live in the temple precincts. The priests at the Jerusalem temple served only during the major festival celebrations and for two additional weeks in the year on a rotation basis. It is not impossible that the person speaking was guilty of manslaughter and was seeking the security of asylum in the sanctuary (see Exod. 21:12-14).

The single-minded desire of the psalmist—"that I may dwell in the house of the Lord all the days of my life"—had two goals in mind. The first was to behold the beauty of God and the second was to inquire in his temple (verse 4). The expression "to behold the beauty of the Lord" may have its roots in the ancient practice of carrying statues of the gods in parades so the worshipers could see the deities unveiled. Probably in this text it means to experience the gracious presence of God or to experience the Divine in a state of worshipful ecstasy. "To inquire in the temple" would imply that the worshiper wished either to receive a response from God or to contemplate (note the word's connection with the term "temple") the Divine in an atmosphere of religious intensity.

The consequences of his appearance in the temple are described as twofold. (1) God will protect him from his enemies (verse 5). Three images are employed to convey this expectation: being hidden in a shelter (the word refers to the special booth lived in at the festival of tabernacles), being concealed under the cover of a tent, and being placed on a high rock. The first two images draw on the idea of gaining the asylum and protection from a host while in his company. (2) The worshiper eventually expects to be victorious over the enemy and to celebrate his success with sacrifices of joy, which would involve feasting and celebrating, and singing before the Lord.

In summary, Psalm 27:1-6 expresses the sentiments of confidence and reliance in God of a person who knows enmity and fear but who is willing to see the future in the light of trust in the Divine.

James 3:13-18

Whereas today's Old Testament reading from Job 28:20-28 insists on the inscrutability of wisdom as an exclusive property of God, the New Testament reading from the book of James envisions the possibility that wisdom and understanding can become visibly embodied in the conduct of the righteous. When our text asks, "Who is wise and understanding among you?" (verse 13), the question is not rhetorical. In keeping with the positive evaluation of good works made earlier (2:18), our text points to one's "good life" as the concrete manifestation of the "meekness of wisdom."

This emphasis on public good deeds is also found in the Jewish wisdom tradition (Sir. 3:17). Elsewhere they become an occasion for acceptability among the people of God (I Pet. 2:12).

Our text distinguishes between two types of wisdom: that which does not come down "from above" (verses 14-16), and that which is "from above" (verse 17). The former is designated as "earthly, unspiritual, and devilish" (verse 15). Here, the possibility is allowed that wisdom may be sabotaged by evil forces and desires (cf. Jude 19), and corrupted by persons whose outlook and motives are selfish. The language here—"unspiritual"—recalls that of Paul in I Corinthians 2:14, when he speaks of the "unspiritual" man as being unable to discern spiritual realities.

In particular, what undermines wisdom, according to today's text, are "jealousy and selfish ambition" (verses 14 and 16). Elsewhere, jealousy and strife are regarded as expressions of immature faith (I Cor. 3:3; cf. II Cor. 12:20), works of the flesh (Gal. 5:20), and evil works to be put away (Eph. 4:31). These are also linked with arrogance: "do not boast and be false to the truth" (verse 14). Paul is especially insistent that boasting that does not glorify the Lord is impermissible (I Cor. 1:31; also 3:20).

It may be that these comments about wisdom and understanding should be seen in light of the opening verses of chapter 3, where the topic concerns the proper qualifications of teachers. If so, today's text is stressing the importance of proper conduct for one who aspires to teach, the "wise and understanding," and disallows those qualities that undermine effective teaching, such as boasting, selfish ambition, and being false to the truth.

Against this negative portrait can be seen the positive side: "wisdom from above" (verses 17-18). It is said to be "pure, peaceable, gentle, open to reason, full of mercy and good fruits, without uncertainty or insincerity." Wisdom of this kind is seen to be a gift from God (1:5; also Prov. 2:3-6). The description of wisdom here is a veritable catalog of qualifications for the effective, and memorable, teacher. It could profitably be explored in a sermon, or any other setting, where the characteristics of the model teacher are being discussed. This portrait concludes with a reference to the "harvest of righteousness" that is "sown in peace by those who make peace" (verse 18). When wisdom comes to be embodied in those who exhibit these characteristics, then righteousness can be extended in the earth (cf. Prov. 3:9; 11:30; Amos 6:2; Gal. 5:22; Phil. 1:11; Heb. 12:11). And if the "wisdom from above" excludes boasting, jealousy, and selfish ambition, peace will be sown (Prov. 10:10; Heb. 12:14; also Matt. 5:9).

In many ways, this description of the one who embodies heavenly wisdom is summarized in Isaiah 32:8, "He who is noble devises noble things, and by noble things he stands."

Mark 9:30-37

Last week we introduced Mark 8:27–10:45 as the block of material to which our Gospel lections for six Sundays belong; now we can proceed directly to our text, Mark 9:30-37.

Jesus and the Twelve are not only passing through Galilee (verse 30); they are "on the way" (verses 33-34). This phrase in Mark refers to the way of Jesus, culminating in the cross, and to the path of discipleship defined by Jesus' own life of service and death. Jesus is seeking privacy because he is instructing the Twelve about his passion. Such time alone with his disciples characterizes this section of Mark, but is not confined to it (4:10; 7:17). A common description of this privacy is with the expression "when he was in the house" (verse 33; 7:17); that is, out of the public arena.

We have already noted that Mark 8:27–10:45 is dominated by three predictions of the passion. At each of these three points Mark has the same threefold cluster of material. First, Jesus predicts his suffering, rejection, death, and resurrection (8:31; 9:31; 10:33-34). Second, the disciples respond with misunderstanding, confusion, and an inability to accept his message (8:32; 9:32-34; 10:35-41). Third, Jesus gives instruction on discipleship (8:34-38; 9:35-37; 10:42-45). Our Gospel for today is the second of these clusters of prediction-response-instruction.

184

As to the prediction, it is worth noticing that the primary attention is given to suffering and death and not to the resurrection. This is true in all three predictions even though the wording varies. The resurrection is stated in all three, to be sure, but one has but to read the predictions to understand where the accent is placed. This emphasis upon the cross and its attending abuses and humiliation is appropriate to the entire Gospel which moves to its climax at the crucifixion. The resurrection is reported in 16:1-8 by the empty tomb with a young man in a white robe, but there is no appearance of the risen Christ. By this attention to the cross Mark is not only defining the nature of Jesus' messiahship but also describing the terms of following Jesus "on the way."

The response of the Twelve is stated as one of misunderstanding and fear (verse 32). But their problem is deeper, for when Jesus was teaching them about his approaching death they were involved in a discussion on who was the greatest (verses 33-34). Their obsession with position and power rendered them incapable of comprehending, much less of accepting, Jesus' word about himself. Understanding is a matter not only of intelligence but also of character. But we should be careful about using this and other texts to berate the disciples. A church that offers three glorious services on Easter but none on Good Friday may be in the same camp, claiming the promises of resurrection but avoiding the demands of the cross.

Notice with what deliberate intent Jesus follows their response with instruction on discipleship: "And he sat down and called the twelve; and he said to them" (verse 35). The instruction itself (verse 35) is an aphorism preserved in different forms in different contexts (Mark 10:43-44; Matt. 20:26-27; 23:11; Luke 9:48; 22:26). No teaching of Jesus more frequently or more directly addresses the love of position and prestige that has never ceased to infect the church's leadership, from then until now. As though his point were not clear enough, Jesus elaborates, adding vividness to his words by holding a child in his arms. The child is the classic image of the powerless, those without claim and without capacity to reward or repay. And yet the disciple of Jesus attends to even these, welcoming them, serving them (verses 36-37). To serve the least is to find one's reason not in the return of such service, but in the understanding that this is the life of the kingdom, the life which God has affirmed by the resurrection of Jesus, servant of us all.

Proper 21

Sunday Between September 25 and October 1 Inclusive

Job 42:1-6; Psalm 27:7-14; James 4:13-17; 5:7-11; Mark 9:38-50

Job 42:1-6

This Old Testament reading introduces themes which Psalm 27 and James 4:13-17; 5:7-11 carry forward. Following Yahweh's appearance in the whirlwind Job acknowledges his human limitations and prostrates himself. The psalm reiterates Job's earlier plea that God hear him out and affirms trust in God's goodness. The passage from James cites Job as an example of steadfastness, but the allusion is to texts such as Job 1:21-22 and 2:10 rather than to our reading. What James and Job have in common is rather the acknowledgment that human beings cannot know all that God knows.

Job 42:1-6 confronts us in a direct way with the complicated problem of the meaning of the book as a whole. (See the commentary on the Old Testament reading for last week for a discussion of the book as a whole.) Do we now have, after all the dialogues and speeches, the poet's final word on the issue of the suffering of the righteous? These are the last of the poetic lines, they have the ring of finality, and it is a good literary principle that "the last shall be first," that is, the most important point is the last one.

The tone and content of Job's final speech are quite different from his others, and the issue of the differences cannot be resolved by treating this passage as a secondary addition. It is essential to the book. The problem is that Job seems to acknowledge that he was wrong; he even "repents" of what he said. Does that mean we can now forget everything that has transpired earlier? By no means.

The book resists simple formulations of its meaning. Does one find the poet's perspective expressed in Job's speeches (and if so which ones), in the Yahweh speeches, or in the words of the friends? All are presented with equal poetic power, and there is something to be said even for the insensitive advice of the friends, who in the face of real pain offer conventional theology.

Throughout the book Job insists upon his innocence, questions the conventional answers, and angrily demands that God vindicate him and give him some answers. In the end when God does grant him his wish for a direct encounter, Job's charges are not addressed directly. Yahweh does not vindicate Job, and he raises even more questions, demonstrating that knowledge of the order of the cosmos is beyond human ken or control.

Then Job in genuine humility acknowledges his finitude and the limits of his wisdom. What has brought about the change? Above all, it is the fact that he has experienced the divine revelation, God in the whirlwind. Given the turmoil of the book, that imagery makes good sense. He now stands in awe before God. Does the encounter with God convince him that there is order and meaning, and purpose, even if he cannot fully comprehend them?

Job's repentance (verse 6) does not mean that he regrets what he said. It indicates that his perspective is now changed, moved in another direction. What he confesses as wrong is his attempt to know what only God can know. Moreover, in the verse which follows our reading (42:7), the poet has God approve of what Job said all along, in contrast to the friends. Job told the truth, he was innocent, and even his angry insistence on a hearing was "right."

Job's final speech is an affirmation of trust in the power and wisdom of God and a recognition of human limitations. Set into the context of the book, three further observations are called for: (1) if one comes to such a point of faith it is through the struggle, including the struggle with God; (2) Job was right to be angry, to quarrel with God, and to challenge the conventional theological formulations; the God of Job expects honest prayers and is not destroyed by our questions or our anger; and (3) these final words of Job may in the last analysis be all we can say in the face of innocent suffering, to stand in humble acknowledgment that God can do all things, and that we can never fully comprehend God's purposes. Still, such words might very well be wrong as one's immediate response to persons in suffering—righteous or otherwise. To do so could place one in the posture of Job's friends, who offered theology when friendship was called for.

Psalm 27:7-14

In this portion of Psalm 27, the worshiper addresses the Deity directly (verses 7-12). In the early portion of the psalm, the speaker addressed a human audience. The person-to-person address, in verses 1-6, is characterized by confidence and reliance. In fact, it might be said to contain a slight air of braggadocio. The address to the Deity is radically different. It is a lament pleading with the Deity for support and for his presence.

The lament opens with a request for a hearing and for a favorable response from the Deity (verse 7). The psalmist reminds God that he is now doing what has been the divine invitation, namely seeking the face of God (verse 8). "To seek the face of" could here refer not only to worship but also to a direct appeal to the Deity which would result in a divine decision communicated to the worshiper, probably through the cultic personnel in charge of the ritual. "To turn one's face from" or "to hide one's face" was to give a negative response. (See the priestly benediction in Num. 6:24-26 where "to make the face shine" is an expression of favor.)

The same request as found in verses 7-9*a*, but expressed in different words, appears in verse 9*bc*. Here the request is formulated in terms of the impact on the worshiper: "Turn not thy servant away . . . cast me not off, forsake me not." Whereas the worshiper had earlier bragged of having the presence of God which made him confident even though beset by an army, he now pleads not to experience the absence of God, not to be forced to endure the divine forsakenness.

Verse 10 is an interesting verse. Its reference to the Lord in the third person seems to disrupt the prayer that is expressed directly to God in verses 7-9 and in verses 11-12. The verse could be seen as a confessional statement made by the worshiper in the midst of a service but addressed to the cultic leader assuring the human audience that his faith is still strong and that solid confidence still lays beneath the surface fear of being abandoned. The reference to having been forsaken by both parents can be understood in various ways (see Job 19:13-14; Ps. 38:11): (*a*) it may have been merely a metaphorical expression intending to indicate how all alone and isolated one felt, (*b*) the person could have been an abandoned child, perhaps one given to the temple (see verse 4), and (*c*) as one considered guilty, the person may have been deserted even by his own kith and kin. As such, he would have been abandoned even by those—the family— whose support should endure regardless of the conditions. However one interprets the specifics of the claim, its general intent is clear: the worshiper claims to be totally forsaken with only God as a hope for support.

In verses 11-12, the tone of the prayer shifts to very specific requests. Earlier the psalmist spoke of dwelling in the house of God, of beholding the beauty of God, and of inquiring in the temple (verse 4). All of these reflect a desire for mystical and extraordinary experiences. The threefold petitions in verses 11-12 are much more down to earth. (1) The worshiper prays to be taught, to be instructed in the way of the Lord. To place oneself in the posture of a pupil, to renew the status of a learner is an act of humility. To pray to be taught is the expression of a willingness to make a new beginning, to start afresh. (2) There is a second request: that one be led on a level path. The request may be nothing more than the hope that henceforth life will be more predictable, more normal, less filled with the canyons and crags of uncertainty and turmoil. Or it may be a request for life to assume a new shape and a new form. To pray to be led on a level path suggests a commitment to follow the straight and narrow. A willingness to be led implies a willingness to walk. These first two requests are made "because of my enemies"—so that the enemies would have no real grounds to accuse or so they could not attack from ambush. (3) The third request expresses a negative desire—not to be given up to the greed or will of his opponents. The person may have been charged with a crime or slandered about (note the reference to false witnesses in verse 12) and thus requests that God support his cause (perhaps by giving a verdict in his favor; see Deut. 17:8-13).

The concluding verses of the psalm are to be understood as a final confession made by the worshiper (verse 13) and an oracle of encouragement addressed to the worshiper by the priestly functionary (verse 14) who presided at the ritual when this psalm was utilized. The worshiper's confession is life-affirming. In spite of the distress of the hour, he is convinced that he will see the goodness of God, that is, experience divine blessing as long as he lives. "In the land of the living" is a circumlocution to avoid making a reference directly or indirectly to one's death when it is not imminent. The priestly word is upbeat. Wait, be strong, take courage. The Greek translator here has the text say, "Be manly."

James 4:13-17; 5:7-11

The two parts of today's epistolary lection are related only indirectly, if at all. The first may be said to deal with presumption, the second with patience. In the former, the one who presumes to have a claim on the future is roundly condemned. In the latter, the one who is impatient before the future is also condemned.

The first section actually continues the polemic against the rich begun in chapter 2, but this is obscured by the omission of the following verses (5:1-6). In this omitted section, the level of polemic becomes especially severe, but more adequately catches the flavor of the prophetic style already introduced in 4:13-17. Clearly, our text speaks of those with mercenary interests, whose business it is to "trade and get gain" (verse 13). This is but another way of setting up the remarks that follow in 5:1-6.

The outlook and tone is truly reminiscent of the denunciation of the rich by the Old Testament prophets, such as Amos. The oral style is indicated by the opening words, "Come now, you who say . . . you rich" (4:13; 5:1). The tone is sermonic and may reflect a diatribal style in use in early Christian preaching.

Those who make plans about today or tomorrow, or even next year, are called into account for their arrogance: "You boast in your arrogance" (verse 16). Though it is not said here that such an attitude is folly, such warnings were common in the wisdom tradition. For example, "Do not boast about tomorrow, for you do not know what a day may bring forth" (Prov. 27:1; cf. also Sir. 11:18-19). Similar advice is given in *The Sentences of Pseudo-Phocylides*, a Jewish writing roughly contemporary with the book of James: "Nobody knows what will be after tomorrow or after an hour. The death of mortals cannot be foreseen, and the future is uncertain" (116-17). The folly of making premature claims on the future was also noted by pagan authors, such as the Roman philosopher Seneca (d. A.D. 65), who wrote, "But how foolish it is to set out one's life when one is not even owner of the morrow!" (*Epistles* 101.4).

We should note that it is those bent on acquiring possessions who plan so confidently with time that is not really theirs. There seems to be a direct correlation between the acquisition of possessions and the confidence with which one lays hold on the future. We are reminded of the story of the rich fool whose huge acquisitions led him to false hope about the future (Luke 12:16-21). Closely related are the sentiments expressed in the Jewish apocalyptic work I Enoch, "We have become rich with riches and have possessions; and have acquired everything we have desired. And now let us do what we purposed" (97:8-9).

To such ones, the question is asked, "What is your life, really?" (verse 14). In response, the text stresses the transitoriness of life, comparing it with a "mist," or perhaps "smoke," a common metaphor used to illustrate the evanescence of life (cf. Hos. 13:3; Ps. 37:20; 39:4-6, 12; 68:2; 102:3; Wisd. of Sol. 5:14). Earlier, the fleeting life of the rich has been compared with fading flowers and withering grass (1:9-11).

But the future is not ours, insists our text; it is the Lord's. Thus, all plans should be prefaced with the phrase, "If the Lord wills" (verse 15), as was often the case in the early church (Acts 18:21; Rom. 1:10; 15:32; I Cor. 4:19; 16:7; Heb. 6:3). Recognizing that human plans were often subject to the divine will was not a unique Christian outlook. We find the phrase, "if the Lord wills," or rough equivalents, in Greek writers from Plato on, and it is especially frequent in many Greek inscriptions. That this was a general recognition within the ancient world should have been all the more reason for Christians to temper their arrogance in making claims on the future as if it were theirs to use and dispose of.

The first section concludes with a proverb on sins of omission. How it relates to the earlier verses is not clear. Perhaps it too is directed against the rich for their failure to use their resources to alleviate the need of others. There has been a general recognition that one's failure to do what is right is as grievous a wrong as overt transgression (cf. Deut. 23:21-22; 24:5). Job himself, the subject of today's Old Testament reading, acknowledged as much (Job 31:16-23).

In the second part of today's lection, the key theme is patience: "Be patient, therefore, brethren, until the coming of the Lord" (verse 7). Already in the New Testament, we find those who are overly anxious for the Lord to come, even to the point of quitting work (I Thess. 2:19; 3:13; 4:15; 5:23; also cf. II Thess. 2:1, 8; I Cor. 15:23). The other extreme in the early church was that some concluded that the Lord would never come and consequently abandoned all hope in the Second Coming (II Pet. 3:8-10). In either case, it is required that Christians wait in hope and do so patiently.

In good diatribal style, our text offers examples. First, from the natural order, the farmer serves as the paradigm of patience, for he must do his work in hope (I Cor. 9:10), waiting patiently for the early and late rains (cf. Deut. 11:14; Jer. 5:24; Hos. 6:3). Second, the prophets are cited as examples of those who rarely lived to see their own hopes realized. In fact, their steadfastness in the face of persecution made them memorable examples for posterity (Matt. 5:12; Heb. 11:33-38). No one was any more exemplary in this respect than Job, whose name has become synonymous with patience (Job 1:21-22; 42:1-6). In the end, the Lord was seen to be "compassionate and merciful" (Exod. 34:6; Ps. 103:8; 111:4).

On this note, our text ends and recalls a theme with which the book of James began: the one who proves to be steadfast in endurance is blessed (1:12).

Mark 9:38-50

The Gospel reading for today poses for the interpreter-preacher two immediate problems: what is the relationship of Mark 9:38-50 to the preceding material and what gives to Mark 9:38-50 any internal unity? These cannot be regarded as questions only for the academic study of the text if the preacher is to treat these verses in sermons.

If it is any comfort, Matthew and Luke, while often following Mark as a primary source, encounter difficulties here. Matthew, for example, omits altogether the story of the strange exorcist (verses 38-39), places Mark 9:40 in another context and in a stronger form (12:30), joins Mark 9:37 and 41 in one passage (10:40-42), and scatters in the Sermon on the Mount many of the sayings in Mark 9:42-50 (5:13; 29-30). Luke, on the other hand, preserves the story of the strange exorcist (9:49-50) without Mark's verse 41, and, like Matthew, scatters to other points the sayings on conduct (14:34-35; 17:1-2). We must conclude that the present arrangement of Mark 9:38-50 is the writer's own, gathering to this place stories and sayings for which we have no original context.

We can only conjecture, but there are clues in the text that point us toward Mark's intention in these verses. First of all, instruction on what it means to be a disciple was introduced earlier in verses 33-37. Verses 38-50 do not really depart from that for they treat the questions of who really is a disciple (verses 38-40), hospitality among disciples (verse 41), taking care not to offend new disciples (verse 42), the moral earnestness of the life of a disciple (verses 43-49), and the call to unity among disciples (verse 50). Second, behavior "in the name" of Christ is introduced in verse 37. This is to say, living and acting in Christ's name is clearly a signal that all this material is addressed to the post-Easter church. During his ministry, Jesus did not teach his followers to wear or use his name. In fact, Jesus himself did not accept the name of Christ (verse 41) prior to his passion (14:61-62). The repetition of the phrase referring to Christ's name (verses 37, 38, 39, 41) therefore joins this apparently divergent material as early Christian teaching on discipleship. Third, the use of a child for instruction in humble service (verses 36-37) might have prompted the inclusion here of the unit of teaching which begins, "Whoever causes one of these little ones who believe in me to sin" (verse 42). This association of "child" and "little ones" could have been made even though the addition of the modifier "who believe" indicates that the "little ones" of verse 42 refers to disciples, very likely new to the community, and not to children as such. In keeping with this idea of instructing new believers is the suggestion that the sayings in verses 43-50 may have been taken from a catechism. Catchwords and phrases such as parts of the body, "it is better," salt, and fire hold these unrelated statements together. These could have served the catechumens as memory devices.

What, then, is being said in Mark 9:38-50? At least four areas of instruction are imbedded here. (1) "Not being one of us" is not an adequate criterion for determining that a person is not a Christian. Granted, standards for discerning who is and who is not a disciple were a serious problem for the early church, especially in the case of itinerant exorcists (verse 38), healers, and prophets. Ethical conduct, said Matthew (7:16, 21-23); doctrinal confession, said John (I John 4:2); confession of Jesus as Lord and service to others, said Paul (I Cor. 12:1-7). But not being in our circle, at least in Mark's church, was no ground for exclusion. (2) Hospitality was to be practiced freely, and with minimal requirements. Even a cup of cold water given and received (verse 41) was not unnoticed or unrewarded. (3) New converts are to be accorded special care and consideration (verse 42). Causing one of them to stumble was as grave a sin for Mark as for Paul (I Cor. 8:7-13). (4) The life of a disciple must be morally earnest inasmuch as our present behavior has eternal consequences (verses 43-50). Nowhere in the Gospels is the language of Jesus more vivid and emphatic than in these calls to self-discipline and to arms against temptation.

Proper 22

Sunday Between October 2 and 8 Inclusive

Genesis 2:18-24; Psalm 128; Hebrews 1:1-4; 2:9-11; Mark 10:2-16

Genesis 2:18-24

Except for the text from Hebrews all the readings for the day concern a single matter, marriage and family. The Old Testament lection is the account of the creation of woman, explaining the forces that lead men and women to form new families. Psalm 128 celebrates marriage and children as blessings upon the one who is pious and righteous. The first part of the Gospel reading (Mark 10:2-12) gives Jesus' sayings concerning divorce, citing both Genesis 1:27 and one of the concluding verses of our Old Testament text (Gen. 2:27) in support of the conclusion that marriage is ordained by God.

Genesis 2:18-24 is a crucial part of the Yahwistic account of creation and the fall (Gen. 2:4*b*–3:24). In contrast to the Priestly Writer's account of creation (Gen. 1:1–2:4*a*), in which the activity of God is central, this one focuses upon the human situation. The purpose of the narrative in 2:4*b*-24 is to account for human existence as it was intended to be. Chapter 3 then accounts for human existence as it is experienced, full of ambiguities, pains, and troubles.

The Yahwistic story of creation reports how Yahweh made the first human being from the "dust of the ground, breathed into his nostrils the breath of life" (Gen. 2:7), and then established all the conditions necessary for fully human existence. Those factors were (1) life itself as a gift of God, (2) a supportive environment (2:8-9), (3) work as both physical labor (2:15) and intellectual endeavor (2:19-20), (4) freedom ("freely eat," 2:16) and limits ("but of the tree . . . you shall not eat," 2:17) which together leave the creature with moral decisions to make, and (5) community, if only in the presence of a single other (2:18-25). The situation described is not paradise as popularly understood, but, as the concluding verse indicates, things were right, as they should be; the first pair had no shame (2:25). The features described here are always present, however much they are obscured by pain and suffering. The final verse also prepares us for the next episode, when things change.

The story of the creation of woman is a lively and compelling one. At the end the writer provides us with an interpretation of the events in the form of a narrative aside (verse 24). The account is not without humor. After observing that "it is not good that the man should be alone" Yahweh creates the animals, acknowledging that not one of them is sufficient to solve the problem. Then after creating woman Yahweh, like the father of the bride, leads her to the man, who exclaims his pleasure in poetic lines (verse 23).

Several points in the text call for particular comment. The term translated "helper" (verses 18, 20) by no means indicates the subordination of the woman to the man. The same Hebrew word frequently applies to God (Exod. 18:4; Ps. 121:1-2). In this context it is better translated "partner." The "deep sleep" (verse 21) is not some divine anesthesia, but is for the purpose of concealing the creative act from the man. The creation of woman is a mystery which he must not observe.

The man's poetic reaction (verse 23) includes a play on words and is a popular explanation of the fact that the terms for "woman" and "man" are similar. More important, it expresses that fundamental identification of the sexes with one another, also expressed in the next verse. Both verses are responses to a deep question, How does one explain the attraction between male and female, one so strong that they leave the homes of their parents to be together? Answer: They were originally one flesh. "One flesh" here does not refer to a romantic or spiritual union of the two, but is quite concrete. Two persons do indeed become one, specifically in sexual union and its results, children.

The main point of the narrative is clear and unambiguous. The union of male and female—marriage as such is not mentioned—is both good and necessary. Full humanity, by

197

implication, is found only in community. Moreover, human sexuality is affirmed without qualification. It is neither the cause nor the result of the fall, but part of God's good creation.

Psalm 128

This psalm opens with a beatitude (verse 1) which is then followed by an address in the second person to the righteous. The beatitude may be said to state a general principle and the address expounds or illustrates the principle with certain specifics.

Proclaimed blessed is the one who fears the Lord and walks in his ways. These two expressions, "fearing the Lord" and "walking in his ways" are synonymous ways of saying the same thing. They both refer to obedience to the revealed will of the Deity.

The second-person address in verses 2-3 which expounds on the consequences of being blessed form an excellent accompanying reading to the Genesis text. Luther described Psalm 128 as a "marriage song," and its contents would have been appropriate for a marriage setting in antiquity. Four conditions are promised the righteous man who obeys God.

1. He will reap the benefits of his work, "eat the fruit of the labor of your hands" (verse 2a). In the ancient world, it was not a foregone conclusion that one would benefit from and enjoy the products of his labors. Many factors could keep the labor of the Israelite peasant from accruing to his benefit. (a) One such set of circumstances was climatic. Drought, disease, locusts, and what have you could devastate the crops from which the average Israelite made his living. (b) International factors could deprive one of the consequences of his labor. Many years, the Israelites planted their crops and Egyptian armies marching north harvested them. The next year's crops were planted only to be harvested by Mesopotamians marching south. Living as they did on the narrow land bridge joining the continents of Africa and Asia meant that the Israelites lived a very precarious existence, often at the mercy of stronger neighbors. (c) Social matters

could provide a third set of circumstances in which one profited little from his labor. Slaves, those in debt, and day laborers saw others enjoying the fruits of their work. In Palestine, where one had to lubricate the working of his hands with the sweat of his brow before the earth was coaxed to produce (see Gen. 3:19), the promise of enjoying the fruits of one's labors was indeed a source of hope.

2. Work that is personally profitable is conjoined with happiness and well-being (verse 2*b*). The ideal life not only involved reaping the benefits of one's labors but also enjoying a state of well-being.

3. A third promise assures the faithful that his wife would be a fruitful vine in the innermost parts of his house (verse 3*a*). The grapevine could refer to the wife's fruitfulness and productivity but it could also refer to her care, succor, and protection. One of the ideals of Israelite life was to sit securely under one's own vine, beneath one's own fig tree (see Mic. 4:4).

4. A person's offspring, in the ideal life, would be like olive shoots around his table (verse 3*b*). That is, they would be numerous and healthy, assuring the continuation of the family name as well as being social security for one's old age. The table around which the children congregate was the center of the Jewish home. At its head, the father presided over the sacred meals like a high priest in the temple.

In what appears as a priestly benediction, two further wishes are made as part of the blessing (verses 5-6). The first asks that the person see the prosperity of Jerusalem. This would mean that Jerusalem, one of the most fought over cities in the world, would know a time of peace and tranquility. Since Jerusalem was the heart and soul of the nation, the spiritual center of the people, its prosperity would be emblematic of the people's prosperity. If Jerusalem fared well, so would its "citizens." Thus the blessing of Jerusalem was a blessing upon those who called it "home."

Finally, there is the wish for a long life. "May you see your children's children." May you live to be a grandparent and know the blessings and promises of cuddling in your arms those of the third generation.

Hebrews 1:1-4; 2:9-11

Today's epistolary lection is the first of seven semi-continuous readings from the Letter to the Hebrews. The first part of this lection was treated in the set of additional lessons for Christmas Day in the volume *Advent, Christmas, Epiphany, Year B,* which the reader may wish to consult. Since our epistolary readings for the next several weeks are taken from Hebrews, some preliminary remarks about the epistle are in order.

Even though the epistle was for a long time associated with Apostle Paul, it is in fact anonymous. The scholarly consensus is that it is not a Pauline writing. To call it an epistle is something of a misnomer, since it bears little formal resemblance to other New Testament epistles. It lacks a formal greeting which mentions the author and addressees. Only at the end of the letter (13:22-25) does it really resemble other New Testament epistles. It is more in the nature of an essay, or treatise, although it is clearly sermonic. By its own definition, it is a "word of exhortation" (13:22). The concern throughout the letter is to bolster the readers' faith by demonstrating the incomparable superiority of Christ. In terms of its style and literary composition, it is a finely crafted work, demonstrating an excellent command of Greek and rhetorical sensitivity.

In many ways, the preface (verses 1-4), which serves as the first part of today's lection, sets the tone of the work with its clear christological focus. The finality and fullness of the revelation of Christ is contrasted with the partial revelation of the past. The author does not deny that God has spoken effectively in times past "to our fathers by the prophets" (cf. Hos. 12:10; Luke 1:55). But he does insist that a new stage of God's revelation has begun "in these last days" (cf. Jer. 23:20; Heb. 9:26; I Pet. 1:20). There is the clear conviction that a new age has dawned and that if one wants to hear God's new revelation, one must do so through Christ.

Packed into these few verses are numerous claims about Christ, and they are quite staggering. Some scholars have seen in these opening verses an early Christian hymn, and this may account for the confessional nature of these christological claims.

1. He is "a Son . . . appointed the heir of all things" (verse 2). A few verses later, Christ is identified with the "Son" of Psalm 2:7 (verse 5), and in this capacity obviously becomes the Father's heir (Matt. 21:38).

2. Christ is God's assistant in creation (verse 2). Here, the author is influenced by the Jewish wisdom tradition in which Wisdom had become personified, elevated to preexistent status, and given a role as God's agent in creation (Wisd. of Sol. 9:2). Christ is similarly depicted elsewhere in the New Testament (John 1:3; I Cor. 8:6; Col. 1:16-17; Rev. 3:14).

3. He is a reflection of the glory, or radiance, of God, and also the imprint of God's nature (verse 3). Here, again, the language is drawn from the wisdom tradition in which Wisdom is said to be "a reflection of eternal light . . . an image of [God's] goodness" (Wisd. of Sol. 7:25-26). The image suggested by the text is that of Christ as a ray of dazzling light from which the radiance of God emanates (cf. II Cor. 3:18; Rom. 8:29; Col. 1:15).

4. Christ upholds "the universe by his word of power" (verse 3). Christ has both creative and sustaining power, or in the words of Colossians 1:17, "in him all things hold together." The creative power attributed to God's Word is now extended to Christ through whose "word of power" the universe holds together (cf. Wisd. of Sol. 9:1).

5. Christ "made purification for sins" (verse 3). In these few words, the atoning work of Christ is summarized (cf. Heb. 9:14, 26; cf. Job 7:21).

6. His resurrection is seen as an exaltation to the right hand of God (verse 3). The image is more specific. Christ is said to be seated at the "right hand of the Majesty on high" (cf. Ps. 110:1; 113:5; Heb. 8:1; 10:12; 12:2; Eph. 1:20; Mark 16:19).

7. His exalted position beside God renders Christ superior to the angels (verse 4). The theme of Christ's superiority to the angels is developed further in the remainder of chapter 1. The "name" is doubtless that of "Son" (cf. verse 5; cf. Eph. 1:21; Phil. 2:9; I Pet. 3:22).

The second lection relates to the preface thematically with its reference to Jesus, made a "little lower than the angels." This, of course, is a reference to Psalm 8:5 (cf. Heb. 2:7). But, here the emphasis shifts to his incarnate status as one who received glory through his suffering and death. However, some new images are introduced: Jesus whom God made the pioneer of our salvation (cf. Heb. 12:2; Acts 3:15) through his suffering (cf. Heb. 5:8-9). Also, he is the one who sanctifies us (cf. Heb. 9:13; 13:12; also John 17:19; cf. Exod. 31:13). The image here is Jesus as the perfect sacrifice through which our purification is achieved (cf. Heb. 10:10, 14, 29; 13:12; cf. I Thess. 4:3).

As one looks at this second lection closely, one discovers that verse 11 ends in the middle of a sentence! For this reason, the lection should end with verse 11*a*.

With the wealth of christological images packed into these verses, today's epistolary lection obviously offers a cornucopia of christological possibilities. Any one of these images might be fruitfully explored homiletically. Or, one might wish to address the theological question of the finality of God's revelation in Christ and the way modern Christians might appropriate this in our pluralistic world.

Mark 10:2-16

With striking and, to many preachers, welcome unity, all the lections for today focus on primary human relationships, and they do so by affirming God's purpose in creation. In fact, in the Gospel reading Jesus quotes a portion of the Old Testament lesson (Gen. 2:24).

Mark 10:2-16 belongs to the larger block of material 8:27–10:45 which we have characterized in earlier comments. This text falls between the second and third predictions of the passion. Jesus and the Twelve are "on the way," literally and theologically, to Jerusalem. The location has changed (10:1) but the pattern in the narrative is familiar: Jesus is teaching, crowds have gathered. Pharisees raise a question touching the interpretation of Scripture, Jesus responds, and then in private ("in the house") he further instructs the Twelve. The rubrics of public and private teaching (4:1-12; 7:14-23; 9:14-29;

13:1-8) enable Mark to present the tradition from Jesus and then interpret it for his church. Mark 10:2-12 falls, then, in two parts, verses 2-9 and 10-12. To the discussion of marriage Mark joins a story about children, variations of which are found elsewhere (Mark 9:36; Matt. 19:13-15; 18:3; Luke 18:15-17).

That the question about divorce was raised not for information but to test Jesus should not lessen for the reader the importance of the inquiry or of the response. The issue is divorce and the Pharisees quote the law (Deut. 24:1-4) which permitted a man who found something unseemly in his wife to give her a bill of divorce and send her away. Jesus shifts the issue from what the law allows, which Jesus judged to be a concession to human weakness (verse 5), to what God intends. The subject, then, is not divorce, but marriage, in support of which Jesus also quotes Scripture, from the two creation stories (Gen. 1:27; 2:24). God's act and God's intent are not negated or superseded by legal permissions.

Jesus' shift of attention to marriage and God's creation of "one flesh" leaves the disciples with the lingering question of divorce. Here Mark places a statement from the sayings of Jesus to the effect that divorce and remarriage constitute adultery (verses 11-12). That the saying assumes that either spouse may divorce the other indicates that Jesus' teaching has already been adjusted to fit the possibilities in the Greco-Roman society of Mark's church. The Judaism of Jesus' time made no provision for a wife to divorce her husband. But Mark's church is not alone in seeking to address a problem in its membership in a way which honored Jesus' teaching that marriage not divorce expressed God's will. Matthew (5:32; 19:9) allowed for divorce on grounds of adultery. Paul, while adhering to the tradition from Jesus, offered the Corinthians a different interpretation for marriage in which only one partner was a Christian (I Cor. 7:10-11). The church from that time until now has been most wise when continuing in the way of the New Testament writers, struggling with God's will in each situation rather than quoting that particular Scripture which seems to smile most favorably upon one's preference.

It may seem surprising that the same disciples who were taught about the kingdom by Jesus as he held a child before them (9:35-37) would here rebuke those bringing children to Jesus (verse 13). But these are the men who argued over greatness and who had keen appetites for power. Thinking of the kingdom in terms of place and power they had no time for children. After all, children could not march, organize, plan, lead, or provide financial support. But that, says Jesus, is just the point. A child can receive the kingdom without offering, without claim, without calculation. Such is a clear transaction of grace. The preacher will want to avoid, therefore, the fruitless and questionable exhortations about how we should all be like children. Equally inappropriate are those pink and blue lists of children's qualities which we are to emulate. If children *qualified* for the kingdom, then what happens to grace? And if we imitate children in order *to qualify,* what happens to us? Children are brought to receive Jesus' blessing, and so are we.

Proper 23
Sunday Between October 9 and 15 Inclusive

Genesis 3:8-19; Psalm 90:1-12; Hebrews 4:1-3, 9-13;
Mark 10:17-30

Genesis 3:8-19

The Old Testament reading comes from the story of the results of the first sin of the first human beings. Psalm 90, a corporate prayer, is a highly appropriate response, particularly because of its somber tone and the lament over the brevity of life. Just as Genesis says the first pair could not hide their sin, so Hebrews 4:13 affirms that no creature is hidden from God. Genesis 3:19 confronts Adam with the awareness of his death; Mark 10:17-30 presents the possibility of eternal life.

Between the reading for last week and the one for today stands only the account of the act of rebellion itself, remarkably filled with insight into human psychology. Especially in view of a long and frequently misleading history of the interpretation of this story several matters in those verse require comment. The serpent here is not the devil. In fact, the narrator carefully circumscribes his place and role. The translation "serpent" is too elegant; "snake" is more appropriate. He is part of creation, a "wild creature," made by the Lord God (3:1). He created neither sin nor suffering, but his role is to pose the questions in a subtle way, making possible and even encouraging the act of disobedience. He symbolizes and represents the experience of evil as external, coming from outside the person. Nor is the woman a temptress, as her husband will later suggest (verse 12). She simply offered the forbidden fruit to the man and he accepted (verse 6).

The Yahwist's story is not so much one of the origin of sin as the origin of its painful effects in human life. In combination with the account of creation, it means to give an explanation of the way human beings have experienced their existence—and especially its brokenness—from the time of the writer down to the present day. It deals with the most profound theological questions in a typically biblical mode, by telling a story. Brokenness, pain, ambiguity, and suffering are given a moral explanation: they are the result of sin.

By no means are all of the effects of the sin presented as curses or punishments imposed by Yahweh. Some of them are simply set into motion by the act itself. The first of these is noted in the verse which precedes our lection. The snake promised that eating the fruit—the text does not say what kind—would bring knowledge, and it does. When the eyes of the man and woman were opened they knew they were naked (3:7); that is, they experienced shame (Gen. 2:25). The next effects were guilt and estrangement from Yahweh, to the point that they hid from him (verses 8-10), but he immediately knows what they have done (verse 11). The next result, estrangement from each other and from their environment, is presented with an incredibly sensitive combination of the comic and the sad (verses 12-13). Each in turn blames the other, and the man even blames Yahweh: "The woman whom thou gavest to be with me . . . ." The sin which they had committed in common did not bind them together, but separated them from each other and from God.

Then follow the curses upon each in turn. Here the theological interpretation of facets of present existence becomes quite explicit. Behind the curse upon the snake (verses 14-15) is probably an old explanation of why snakes crawl on the ground, and why people—not just women, all the "seed" of the first woman are included—dislike snakes so much.

The man and woman are not cursed directly, but pain, dissonance, and contradictions come into their lives. The address to the woman (verse 16) concerns her role as mother and wife in Israelite patriarchal society. Her excessive pain in childbirth and the anguish of her subordination to the husband, says the Yahwist, were not part of the plan of creation, but the effects of human sin. She will desire her

206

husband, but instead of giving her fulfillment and rest he will dominate and humiliate her.

The man's curse (verses 17-19) is neither work nor death. Before the violation of Yahweh's prohibition he had to till the garden (Gen. 2:15), and he named the animals (Gen. 2:19-20). To be a full human being one must have work to do. The dissonance is that now his work is full of failures, time wasted, fruitless efforts. To punish the man Yahweh curses the ground. Moreover, the final word does not introduce death as a new factor. This creature had always been dust. But the difference is a monumental one: the man's death is placed before his eyes. Now the awareness of it will cripple life. It is true, however, that as the man and wife are driven from the garden they are prohibited from ever attaining immortality (Gen. 3:23). In ancient Israel that was a divine prerogative.

The aim of the story as a whole is to explain the broken state of human existence. Life is filled with ambiguity. On the one hand, there is in all of us a deep awareness of the way things should be or could be. That is characterized here as life before the first sin. On the other hand, while those facets can always be recognized, life is not like that. The Yahwist raises the question of the origin of some forms of suffering and explains them in moral terms, as the results of sin.

The value of the story for us—and its place in Christian preaching and teaching—does not lie in the completeness of its answers. The meaning of human suffering is, finally, a mystery which is beyond us. Its contribution lies rather in the profound way that it mirrors our lives. It interprets us to ourselves. As with all tragic literature, we enter into and identify with the lives of all the characters and comprehend some of the forces which have led to tragic results. We thus achieve a deeper understanding of our own lives and of those around us.

Psalm 90:1-12

This psalm is a communal lament in which the community offers its complaint to the Deity about the transience and the brevity, the toil and the trouble of life. As such it forms an excellent accompaniment to the narrative of Adam and Eve's sin and the subsequent divine curse. The psalm like Genesis 3:8-19 sees an intimate connection between human disobedience and human misery and mortality, between divine wrath and the human predicament.

Two basic contrasts are drawn in the psalm between the Deity and humanity. The one contrast, and the most overt, is that between the eternal, everlasting nature of God and the transitory, dying character of humankind. The second contrast is that between the holy God, who reacts with anger and wrath against disobedience, and humanity with its overt iniquity and secret sin, its unholiness and rebellion.

There is a certain undercurrent of animosity toward God in this psalm. While it doesn't stand out starkly revealed, nonetheless it is there. The psalm writer must have felt, even if he did not say it, that there seems to be some injustice to the way things are. On the one hand, God exists forever and is in no way conditioned by the calendar or subservient to time. On the other hand, human life is so fleeting, so time-bound, so insubstantial. In spite of this disparity between the human and the divine, the psalmist however is not led to despair. Instead the writer sees the one eternal God as the dwelling place for the endless generations of human beings (verse 1) and asks for divine assistance in coming to terms with the length and shape of human existence (verse 12).

The opening invocation, hymnic in style, anchors human and communal life with its everflowing generations in the embrace of the eternal God (verse 1). The eternity of God is expressed by affirming his existence prior to the earth's giving birth to the mountains and even prior to the divine formation of the earth and the world (verse 2). When compared to God, the earth and the mountains which watch the generations come and go are but youngsters. These symbols which stand for continuity and endurance are but the creations of the everlasting.

The first stanza (verses 3-6) laments the brevity and frailty of human life which ends in death. God is described as the timeless one, for whom a millennium, a thousand years, seems like a yesterday to humans or passes as quickly and quietly as a (four-hour) watch in the night to a sleeping person. Yet the everlasting, hardly conscious-of-time God, has decreed that humans should return to the dust from whence they came (Gen. 3:19). The One who bestowed life is the One who withdraws it. Human life must be lived knowing that death is awaiting. (The minister preaching on this or similar texts should make it clear that they were written at a time in Israel's history before the people believed in resurrection from the dead or in the doctrine of immortality.)

Even life itself—the dash between two dates—is subject to dissipation. Like a dream, or grass in the morning, life has a fading quality (verses 6-7). Life at its peak, its best, here symbolized by the morning grass covered with the invigoration of the dew, soon encounters the noonday heat and by evening has faded and withered. The psalmist here gives expression to that recognition that once we pass the child-producing, child-rearing phase of life, nature or God has a way of sweeping us away. Strength, vitality, and spirit atrophy and wither.

In the second stanza (verses 7-10), human existence with its attendant sorrows and sighs and ultimate demise are related to the anger of God and human sinfulness. Life's troubles and death are related to human sinfulness just as in Genesis 3. Life is lived and brought to its termination under the shadow of divine wrath. Here one can see the psalmist struggling with the realization that death and life's disorders and dissipations are somehow intrusive into the created order. Existence was never meant to be so. Only disruptions in the created order and the wrath of God could explain the dark, shadowy side of life.

Even at its best in longevity, the normal limits (not the average) of a life-span, according to the psalm writer, were seventy, perhaps eighty, years. Yet these years are full of toil and trouble and end with a sigh—soon gone; soon forgotten.

Verse 11 is difficult to interpret. It seems to ask if anyone takes seriously the nature of divine wrath and the necessity of fearing (obeying) the Divine. The answer to this rhetorical question would seem to be "no one."

In spite of the psalmist's rather dark and pessimistic (realistic?) reading of life, the writer does not end in absolute discouragement or counsel despair or contemplate suicide or encourage hedonistic abandonment. Verse 12 is, of all things, an appeal for instruction. To be taught! As if life itself were not a lesson hard enough! The psalmist prays for wisdom so we will be able to number our days, to calculate our calendars, to live aright so that we may not die awry.

Hebrews 4:1-3, 9-13

Both parts of today's epistolary lection contain a word of exhortation typical of Hebrews: "Let us . . . " (verses 1 and 11). In one instance, the author encourages his readers to be fearful before the possibility that the promised rest will elude them as it did the disobedient Israelites. In the other instance, he urges his readers to be diligent in striving to enter "that rest."

The theme of "rest" is introduced earlier in chapter 3, where the author discusses the rebellion and disobedience of the Israelites. In this context, he quotes from Psalm 95, whose concluding section consists of a denunciation of Israel's disobedience in the wilderness. In the psalm, Yahweh himself speaks and concludes by saying, "Therefore I swore in my anger that they should not enter my rest" (verse 11). Quite often in the Old Testament the promised land of Israel is described as place of "rest." In Exodus 33:14, God tells Moses, "My presence will go with you, and I will give you rest." Even more to the point, in the Book of Deuteronomy the land of Israel is spoken of as "the rest and . . . inheritance which the Lord your God gives you" (Deut. 12:9-11; also 3:20; 25:19; Josh. 1:15; 21:44; 22:4). What is usually implied in these passages is that the land of promise would be a place where the Israelites would enjoy "rest from their enemies," that is, peace and stability.

In chapter 4 of the book of Hebrews, this theme of "rest" drawn from the experience of Israel in the wilderness is supplemented with the "rest" God experienced at the end of the period of creation. Genesis 2:2 is quoted in this connection, "And God rested on the seventh day from all his works" (verse 4). The author combines this theme with that of the wilderness experience to develop an eschatological understanding of rest. Thus, "there remains a sabbath rest for the people of God; for whoever enters God's rest also ceases from his labors as God did from his" (verses 9-10). This eschatological vision of rest is depicted even more vividly in Revelation 14:13, "Blessed are the dead who die in the Lord henceforth . . . that they may rest from their labors, for their deeds follow them!"

For the author of the book of Hebrews, then, "rest" remains a promise in which the faithful can hope. Using Israel as a negative example, he appeals to his readers to be responsive to the "good news" that "came to us just as to them." Then, in a very illuminating phrase, he says that "the message which they heard did not benefit them, because it did not meet with faith in the hearers" (verse 2). This suggests that the Word of God can be nullified unless it is received by hearts of faith that respond in obedience (cf. I Thess. 2:13).

This mention of the message (of God) that must be met with responsive hearts ties in directly with the second part of today's lection in which the central theme is the living and active Word of God. We miss the significance of these words if we equate the Word of God with a book. Rather, what is in view here is the spoken Word in all its dynamic force, illustrated, for example, in the creation (Gen. 1:3-31; cf. Wisd. of Sol. 9:1). The powerful force of the spoken word is rightly compared with a sharp sword, as for example, in Isaiah 49:2, when the prophet says that the Lord "made my mouth like a sharp sword." The same metaphor is used in Wisdom of Solomon in a description of God's visitation of the Egyptians in the Exodus: "For while gentle silence enveloped all things, and night in its swift course was now half gone, thy all-powerful word leaped from heaven, from the royal throne, into the midst of the land that was doomed, a stern warrior carrying the sharp sword of thy authentic command, and stood and filled all things with death, and touched heaven while standing on the earth" (18:14-16).

It is against this background that our author speaks of the Word of God as "living and active," having the capacity to penetrate the very soul and spirit of human beings. The final image is particularly graphic as it depicts every creature as naked before "the eyes of him with whom we have to do" (cf. I Enoch 9:5; Ps. 139; Rev. 1:14).

Mark 10:17-30

Last Sunday in the Gospel lesson Jesus was asked a question by persons looking to the law of Moses and Jesus set them before God. The subject was marriage and divorce. Today a man asks Jesus a question about eternal life. The man knows and has kept the law of Moses and, unsatisfied, comes to Jesus the Good Teacher for an answer. He, too, is set before God. Neither Moses' law nor Jesus' wisdom gives life; life is a gift of God. Between the gift of eternal life and this seeker lies a problem: wealth. As in last Sunday's text, Jesus and the Twelve are on the way to Jerusalem and the cross. Mark has already prepared us to expect in these journey narratives radical demands from Jesus and confusion from the Twelve.

Mark 10:17-30 consists of three parts joined by Mark to create not only a description of an event in Jesus' ministry but out of it a clear word to the church. The first part, verses 17-22, is a complete unit, telling the story of Jesus and a man seeking eternal life. The man is unnamed; that he was Saul of Tarsus is the creation of a novelist. In fact, our identification of him as "the rich young ruler" is possible only by borrowing "young" from Matthew's account (19:20) and "ruler" from Luke's (18:18). The man's sincerity appears in his kneeling (verse 17) and his frustration in his contradictory question, "What must I *do* to *inherit*?" (verse 17). Jesus responds in a clearly discernible process. He first sets the man before God as the giver of eternal life (verse 18). Jesus wants the man to understand that what he seeks only God can give (Christians who become so Jesus-centered as to forget God should take note). Second, Jesus sets the man within his own faith tradition (verse 19). The Commandments cited are rather randomly drawn from the second half of the Decalogue and even include a new one, "Do not defraud." All of them have to do with human relationships (Matthew adds the love of neighbor command from Lev. 19; Matt. 19:19). Finally, Jesus leads the man to complete what is lacking: go, sell, give, come, follow (verse 21). Here Jesus is not adding anything to be done by a man who has been doing his religion since his youth. On the contrary, Jesus is calling him to cast aside all other dependencies and in radical trust stand bare before the

God who gives. In other words, this is an invitation to discipleship. There is here no praise of poverty or an attack on the wealthy. The world's goods can be passed around without love or trust in God, and many plans for such have been devised. But here stands a person whose life has been defined by wealth, and sadly, he will not accept a new definition of himself: a man rich before God (verse 21). In a very rare use of the word "love" in Mark (here and 12:29-31), the writer says, "Jesus loved him" (verse 21). The man asked a big question and he got a big answer; small answers to ultimate questions are insulting. He was allowed to say no to Jesus. Where there is no room to say no, a yes is meaningless.

The second part of Mark 10:17-30 consists of verses 23-27 which contain, in addition to the portrait of the disciples as amazed at Jesus' words (verse 24), a group of sayings related to wealth. Mark has appropriately placed these sayings after the story of the rich man who sought eternal life. By the typical pattern of having Jesus elaborate to the Twelve on the teachings given others (verse 23), Mark is able to say to the church that what Jesus said back then he is still saying to us. The message is clear: riches constitute a formidable obstacle to persons who seek discipleship. But the difficulty is not an impossibility. The Good News does not lie in changing "camel" to "rope" (a very similar word in Greek) or in interpreting "the needle's eye" as a small gate through which kneeling, unburdened camels could barely pass. Such interpretive efforts to make the kingdom humanly possible are out of order. "With men it is impossible, but not with God; for all things are possible with God" (verse 27; Gen. 18:17; Job 42:2). That is the Good News, and just as Jesus looked intently at the rich man (verse 21), so does he look at his church when he speaks (verse 27).

The third part of our text, verses 28-30, is a word of assurance to Peter, to the Twelve, and to the church. Those who leave everything for Jesus and the gospel (verse 29; also 8:35) will be vindicated. Even amid persecution (verse 30) they shall have life now and in the age to come, life eternal. The rich man asked about eternal life and Jesus answered not only him but us as well.

213

Proper 24

Sunday Between October 16 and 22 Inclusive

Isaiah 53:7-12; Psalm 35:17-28; Hebrews 4:14-16; Mark 10:35-45

Isaiah 53:7-12

The readings for the day share significant common themes and motifs. The concluding part of the fourth Servant Song describes the suffering of the servant at the hand of enemies; Psalm 35, an individual lament, is a prayer for deliverance from enemies. The servant "bore the sin of many" (Isa. 53:12), and Jesus came "to give his life as a ransom for many" (Mark 10:45). Moreover, Jesus tells the disciples that the one who would be great must be a "servant" (Mark 10:43). According to Hebrews, Jesus is a high priest who, because of his experience, can "sympathize with our weaknesses" (Heb. 4:15).

This reading is part of the fourth Servant Song in Second Isaiah (Isa. 52:13–53:12). The entire song is the traditional and most appropriate Old Testament reading for Good Friday. No other passage in the Hebrew Scriptures more clearly describes the Messiah as a suffering servant of God, one who was obedient to death, and one whose suffering and death were vicarious. The song, more than any other in the Old Testament, enabled the earliest Christians to understand and to communicate to one another and to the world at large the meaning of the death of Jesus (see Acts 8:34; Rom. 5:25; I Cor. 15:4).

The structure of the entire poem is relatively easy to recognize if one is attentive to the shifts in the speakers. It has three parts, and in none of them does the servant himself speak: (1) at the beginning (52:13-15) God speaks to proclaim the exaltation of the servant before the astonished response of nations and kings; (2) in the central section (53:1-11a) some unidentified group speaks to report on the life and death of the servant and their response to it; and (3) finally (53:11*b*-12), God speaks again to confirm the meaning and effect of the servant's suffering; he will be exalted because "he bore the sins of many."

Though the poem is quite distinctive in terms of style and literary genre, it probably was written by the same prophet who wrote Isaiah 40–55 and it has some affinities with other Old Testament literature. The account of the servant's suffering is similar to the cultic tradition of individual laments such as Psalms 22 and 35. However, in such songs it is usually the individual in trouble who gives an account of that suffering and, in songs of thanksgiving, of deliverance. Here the suffering of a third person is described. There are words of confession by the unnamed speakers (verses 4-6), suggesting a service of penitence. Finally, the direct quotation of the words of God at the beginning and the end is like that in prophetic speeches.

It seems unlikely that the question of the identity of the servant in the poem's original historical context can be resolved decisively. Analysis of the form, however, suggests an answer to part of the eunuch's question in Acts 8:34: "About whom, pray, does the prophet say this, about himself or about some one else?" He speaks about another. It is also clear from Isaiah 52:13-15 that he is speaking of the same one introduced in the first servant song (Isa. 42:1-4). But whereas the context of the first song takes the servant to be Israel as a whole, this one clearly speaks of an individual. Commentators who interpret the servant of all the songs as Israel take the personal language of Isaiah 52:13–53:12 metaphorically to mean: Israel's suffering and humiliation through the exile were on behalf of the world, so she shall be vindicated. Far more important, however, than the historical identity of the servant is the meaning of his life and death.

All of the major themes of the poem as a whole are expressed in the part which forms our reading. (1) The basic message is stated at the outset and reiterated in the conclusion (53:12*a*): God will vindicate and exalt his suffering servant. That point, not only in the original context but in all others, is a reversal of expectations, including those of the disciples in Mark 10:43-45. God's power and authority are manifested in weakness; God acts through one whose suffering made him repulsive to all who saw him. (2) We are asked to identify with the life of the innocent sufferer, recounted here from youth (53:2) through a trial and death (53:7-8). (3) The servant's life of suffering and humiliation is both vicarious and efficacious. It is on behalf of others, and it effectively removes their sin (53:6, 8, 12). (4) Not only will the servant be vindicated before the whole world, but also his suffering is on behalf of the transgressions of all ("the many," 53:12).

The association of this text with the New Testament readings for the day certainly will emphasize its understanding of the Messiah. But the Markan and Hebrews lections also call attention to the reaction of believers to their encounter with the servant. In Isaiah 53:1-11*b* it is those who have seen the suffering servant who acknowledge and accept the fact that his suffering was for them. Mark goes further, with Jesus rebuking ambitions for glory, telling the disciples that they too must suffer like he will, and that the last shall be first. Those who follow the servant of God will also become servants.

Psalm 35:17-28

Psalm 35 is a rather long and complicated composition. The various components of a lament are interwoven throughout the psalm. Descriptions of the distress or trouble (verses 7, 11-16, 19-21), pleas and petitions for help (verses 1-6, 8, 22-27), and vows (verses 9-10, 18, 28) are interlaced throughout the psalm. The section selected for this lectionary, verses 17-28, could be seen as a complete psalm insofar as its content is concerned. It contains all the basic features of a lament.

The psalm appears to have been written for use in cultic services by persons who were or felt themselves to be wrongly accused of some sin or crime and who had undergone suffering and torment as the consequence of such accusations. It thus forms an excellent accompanying reading for the servant passage in Isaiah 53:7-12.

The last half of the psalm, and today's lection, opens with a cry to God. The cry constitutes an indirect complaint and accusation against the Deity for dereliction of duty (verse 17). The question—"How long wilt thou look on?"—allowed the worshiper to give expression to the sense of being abandoned by the Divine. The complaint against God (renewed in verses 22-23) who appears to be looking on the worshiper's plight with indifference, however, passes quickly into a plea for redemption. References to "their ravages" and "the lions" provide strong metaphorical descriptions for the person's opponents. Thus to the sentiment of divine abandonment is added the feeling of human oppression. Forsaken by God and plagued by humans constitute the predicament of the petitioner. Although such sentiments may suggest that the people using this psalm were psychologically overwhelmed and were bordering on paranoia, the psalm must be seen at the same time as giving vent to those deep feelings of human and divine estrangement that are so commonly our companions in life. When this text is used in worship or in preaching, some way should be sought to permit people to bring such sentiments to the surface, to recognize them, and to realize their authenticity and legitimacy.

The vow in verse 18, as in verses 9-10, allowed the worshiper to anticipate already the joys and benefits of being redeemed and to make a firm commitment for future action. Such a vow which obligated one to do something in the future had the psychological advantage of shifting the focus of attention away from being absolutely immersed in the present and its traumas toward thoughts of a time beyond the soul's momentary impasse. The vow or self-obligating promise constitute an anchor harpooned into the future, giving hope a firmness and commitment that some mere vague statement about the future would never do. Here the vow is to offer thanksgiving and celebration in a public ritual of worship, a vow that was taken seriously (see Eccles. 5:4-5).

In the description of distress (verses 19-21), the psalm returns to the individual's troubles and the feeling that enemies are out to get him. The foes and opponents appear to be persons who have falsely accused the psalmist of some wrong or crime (see verse 11) and claim to be witnesses of the deed (verse 21). In speaking of the distress, the psalmist does two things: first of all, the person affirms his innocence: note the references to "wrongfully" and "without cause," and second, the opponents are described as the opposite of the petitioner. They rejoice over others, wink the eye (suggesting backhanded tactics or the claim to some special, shared, secret information), hate, raise trouble, torment the peace-loving quiet citizens, and cook up fabricated stories.

In understanding this portion of the psalm and also in attempting to see how it might be employed in preaching, we should recognize the context within which one could so strongly assert one's own innocence and at the same time condemn others. A person using this psalm would have been participating in a temple ritual the purpose of which was to resolve the question of guilt. If the participant were guilty, the participant was required to assert his innocence to the point where a crisis of conscience would occur. Such strong claims of innocence would have added more guilt to the guilty perhaps triggering genuine confession and penitence.

Verses 22-27 constitute the worshiper's appeal, the requests for action on God's behalf. Verses 19-21 assert the case and offer some reasons why the worshiper's cause should be upheld and the opponents' denied. The appeal then lays out the desired consequences: (1) The worshiper requests that God no longer be indifferent to the person's conditions, that a verdict and decision be forthcoming (verses 22-23). (2) The worshiper wants his cause to be vindicated so that his enemies will not have the pleasure of having "done him in" (verses 24-25). (3) The worshiper wants to see a reversal not only in his fate and status but also in that of his opponents. Thus the person prays that his enemies will get what they have handed out or what they hoped would come about. They should be put to shame and suffer confusion (verse 26). This may seem to us to be a bit revengeful but Old Testament law stipulated that false witnesses and those bringing false charges were subject to the penalties which might have been given to their victims (see Deut. 19:15-21). (4) The vindication of the worshiper is seen as the occasion for others to learn and to rejoice (verse 27; the NEB translates, "But let all who would see me righted shout for joy"). Divine vindication is the means of seeing that right has a place in the divine order of things and that God delights in the welfare of his servant or in the fortunes of those who would live according to divine principles. In other words, vindication would affirm that God is not indifferent.

The psalm concludes with a vow: the worshiper promises to offer testimony and praise, to affirm and testify to God's righteousness if the worshiper receives the requested aid.

Hebrews 4:14-16

Since this passage serves as part of the traditional epistolary reading for Good Friday, it has already been treated in the *Lent, Holy Week, Easter, Year B* volume. In that liturgical setting, quite obviously we tend to focus on Jesus' full identification with humanity as it is expressed in this passage. Other notes are sounded in the passage, however, and it is appropriate here to listen to them.

The passage actually unfolds in a two-part structure. It opens with a bold and dramatic statement about Christ, the exalted high priest (verse 14), but then speaks of his priestly capacity to identify with human suffering (verses 15-16). In both instances, it is the image of Christ, the "great high priest," exalted as the Son of God, that is in view. But what is worth noting is that he sits on the heavenly "throne of grace," listening to our prayers, not as one who has known only heavenly exaltation but earthly temptation as well. Even though in his exalted state, he has no needs, in his earthly life he too had occasion to ask for "help in time of need." And this ability to listen as one who is able to identify with the petitioner's experience is the critical difference.

First, his exaltation. Jesus as the "great high priest" is a recurrent christological image developed in the book of Hebrews (2:17; 3:1; 5:5, 10; 6:20; 7:26; 8:1; 9:11; 10:21). In the following chapter, which is treated in next week's epistolary lection, this high priest image is linked directly with the figure of Melchizedek. But here the emphasis is on the "great high priest who has passed through the heavens," indeed who has been "exalted above the heavens" (7:26). In fact, there is no distinction here, as there is in Luke-Acts, between his resurrection and his ascension, as if there were a two-stage exaltation. It is viewed rather as a single, pioneering journey through the heavens where he is finally "seated at the right hand of the throne of the Majesty in heaven" (8:1; cf. Eph. 4:10). Moreover, it is "Jesus, the Son of God," who is interpreted as the object of Yahweh's words in Psalm 2:7, "Thou are my Son, today I have begotten thee" (1:5; 5:5; also cf. 6:6; 7:3; 10:29). The perspective throughout is post-Easter. Christ's exaltation is treated as axiomatic, "since then we have . . ." (verse 14). And it is this Easter conviction that becomes the basis of the exhortation: "Let us hold fast our confession" (verse 14; cf. 3:6; 10:23). The exhortation to fidelity is grounded in the Easter faith. At the heart of the confession lies the triumph of Easter.

But our text then moves from exaltation to temptation, with emphasis on Jesus as the "one who in every respect has been tempted as we are" (verse 15). Most immediately, the wording here recalls the Gospel accounts of Jesus' temptation (Matt. 4:1-11 and parallels), although the experience of Gethsemane is not far away (cf. Matt. 26:41; also Luke 22:28). In trying to understand what is implied by "in every respect," we do well to use the Gospel accounts of Jesus' temptation as the interpretive device, for there the three temptations are clearly seen as tests of his vocation. That Jesus was "made like his brethren in every respect" is affirmed by a variety of New Testament witnesses (2:17; Rom. 8:3; Phil. 2:7; Col. 1:22). Yet, just as uniformly, the New Testament conviction is also that in spite of his full participation in humanity, he did so "without sinning" (7:26; John 8:46; II Cor. 5:21; I Pet. 2:22; 3:18; I John 3:5). Again, the clue to what this means is provided by the Gospel accounts of the temptation: he was fully faithful to his divine vocation. The Passion narrative even further reinforces this as it depicts his obedience to the will of the Father (Mark 14:36 and parallels).

His full humanity, and in particular the way in which he identified with human suffering by suffering himself, enables him to be sympathetic with our weaknesses. "For because he himself has suffered and been tempted, he is able to help those who are tempted" (2:18). Consequently, just as the first part of our passage concluded with an exhortation, so does the second part. But this time, it is not an appeal to "hold fast to *the* confession." It is rather an appeal to "draw near with confidence to the throne of grace," or, in other words, an exhortation to confident confession. Elsewhere, the author stresses that such drawing near is possible with the fullest assurance of faith (10:22; cf. 10:19, 35; also I John 2:28; 3:21; 4:17; 5:14; Rom. 5:1-2).

What emerges, then, from today's epistolary lection is a twofold exhortation: to confess the creed and to confess our sins. We are urged that both can be done in full confidence, the first because Christ, our high priest, has been exalted, the second because he has also been tempted—fully exalted, fully tempted.

Mark 10:35-45

All the lections for today speak of the suffering of God's servant and of the meaning of that suffering for the people. Against such a backdrop the request by James and John for positions in the kingdom is a most discordant note. But the inappropriateness of their request is no less evident when placed in the context Mark has provided.

Between last Sunday's Gospel and the reading before us is Mark's account of the third and last prediction of the Passion (10:32-34). With that prediction and the story of James and John this entire section of Mark (8:27–10:45) comes to a close. Following Jesus' first prediction (8:31), Simon Peter strongly objects and rebukes Jesus. Following the second (9:31), the Twelve engage in a discussion as to who is the greatest. And now, after the third and most detailed of the predictions, James and John ask for the favored positions in glory. With their request the blindness, not only of the Twelve but of the inner circle (Peter, James, John) in particular, is complete. Also complete is the vast difference between Jesus and his followers on the nature of the messianic mission. In the crisis, they will abandon him (14:50). Some scholars believe Mark has taken a position over against the Twelve and the church they represent. More likely Mark is addressing a church which, though having the advantage of hindsight, has not embraced the cross as the definition not only of the Messiah but of discipleship as well.

The story of James and John is told in verses 35-40. Matthew, who follows Mark closely otherwise (20:20-28), has the request come from the mother rather than James and John. That this is editing by Matthew, perhaps protecting the two apostles, is evident in that Jesus answers not her but James and John, exactly as in Mark (Matt. 20:22; Mark 10:38). Luke, for whom the apostles are the guarantee of the church's continuity with Jesus, omits the story altogether and relocates the dispute which follows (verses 41-45) in the upper room at the Last Supper (22:24-27). In response to the request of James and John, Jesus promises suffering but cannot guarantee positions in glory. To describe that suffering Jesus uses two Old Testament metaphors: the cup of wrath (Isa. 51:17, 22; Lam. 4:21) and baptism in the overwhelming flood (Ps. 42:7; 69:1-2; Isa. 43:2). Here Jesus may be drawing on current views of the messianic woes which would initiate the eschatological age.

In verses 41-44, the indignation of the ten toward James and John provides the occasion for Jesus to instruct the group on the matter of service in the kingdom. In these sayings Jesus separates true greatness from the exercise of authority over others and reverses the usual categories of service and greatness. That all four Gospels repeatedly record this instruction (Matt. 20:24-27; 23:11; Mark 9:35; Luke 9:48; 22:24-27; John 12:24-26; 13:12-16; 15:20) is not only an argument that these sayings represent an authentic tradition from Jesus, but it also testifies to the widespread and persistent condition of a church that remained enamored of power and position. And Jesus' words continue to be difficult to hear and to obey.

Verse 45 not only closes this lection but also this entire section of Mark. It is appropriate to the immediate context in that it presents Jesus as the Son of man whose entire mission is to serve not to be served. However, this verse transcends the context in that Jesus' giving of himself has salvific value, unlike the serving and dying of his disciples. The death of Jesus, says Mark, is a ransom; that is, his death sets free captives and hostages. The statement launches, but does not contain within itself, elaborate theories of atonement. Almost as significant as the content of verse 45 is its location in the Gospel. Predictions of the Passion are past; instructions about discipleship are past. With Jerusalem and Golgotha now within view, past teaching and impending fate are joined in one statement about Jesus' entire purpose: to serve, to die, to set free.

Proper 25

Sunday Between October 23 and 29 Inclusive

Jeremiah 31:7-9; Psalm 126; Hebrews 5:1-6; Mark 10:46-52

Jeremiah 31:7-9

The Old Testament lection announces salvation to Israel, specifically as return from exile. Psalm 126, with its prayers for restoration and cries of celebration, directly continues and responds to both the content and mood of the Jeremiah passage. Both the Gospel reading and the Old Testament text speak of the blind; in the former it is blind Bartimaeus and in the latter the blind whom God brings back to the land of Israel. The affinities, however, are deeper. Both readings proclaim that God's power of salvation is at work in very concrete—even physical—ways.

Even the new *Common Lectionary* with its expanded list of Old Testament readings includes surprisingly few readings from the Book of Jeremiah in contrast, for example, with the Book of Isaiah. And the reading for this day is very similar in style and content to the material in Second Isaiah (chapters 40–55). There is not sufficient evidence to determine authorship, but it probably came, like Isaiah 40–55, from the time of the Babylonian exile (597-538 B.C.). The prophet Jeremiah was active from about 627 B.C. until at least 586 B.C., the decades immediately preceding the first and second Babylonian invasions.

Jeremiah 31:7-9 is a part of what has been called "the book of consolation" (Jer. 30–31), a collection consisting mainly of announcements of salvation. Within that collection it stands as a distinct and independent unit of tradition. Certainly there are similarities of theme with what precedes and follows, but the opening formula in verse 7 signals a new unit as does the summons to hear in verse 10.

As the messenger formula which begins it shows, the unit is a prophetic speech, one in which the prophet conveys not his own words but those of the Lord. The speech itself is a prophecy of salvation with three distinct parts. (1) In verse 7—except for the introductory formula—Yahweh gives instructions to an unidentified addressee. That the imperatives are in the plural indicates that he addresses the people as a whole. The Lord calls for them to shout for joy, and then tells them what to say: "The Lord has saved his people, the remnant of Israel." (Compare Isaiah 40.) (2) Yahweh then announces what he will do for the people, those now scattered from the land (verses 8-9*b*). He will bring them back, including the blind, lame, and women, pregnant and even those in labor who have difficulty traveling. The road back will be smooth, and water will be easy to find. (3) Finally, Yahweh gives his reason for what he plans to do, and the reason why he can be trusted to do it—"for I am a father to Israel, and Ephraim is my first-born" (verse 9*b*).

The prophetic books, especially the earlier ones, are filled with prophetic announcements, usually of punishment. Such speeches generally have Yahweh speak to indict Israel for her sins, and the indictment functions to give the reasons for the punishment that is on the horizon. Prophecies of salvation often give no reason at all for the Lord's graceful action. If they do, it is in terms similar to the ones used here. The "reason" lies in God's free decision, out of love for the people. The metaphor of Yahweh as parent and Israel as a child is not uncommon (see Isa. 1:2-3; Hos. 11:1-9).

The speech is unqualified good news. Several features remind us, however, of the dark backdrop of the proclamation, that these are words of hope to the hopeless. The "remnant of Israel" (verse 7) are those left after the disaster, the ones who have been through the fire. The words are for those presently scattered to the "north country," even "the farthest parts of the earth" (verse 8). The latter expression may be poetic hyperbole or it may reflect the awareness that the people are dispersed from Babylonia to Egypt. Moreover, the glorious description of the road home (verse 9) reminds us that it was anything but smooth and easy.

The vision of the future is based on that worldly spirituality of the Old Testament. The Lord is a saving God whose gifts include a place to live, and whose people—"a great company" (verse 8)—include the blind, the lame, the pregnant women, and the women in labor.

Psalm 126

This psalm has been selected as a companion reading to Jeremiah 31:7-9 because of the assumed connection of the psalm with the return from exile which is predicted in the prophetic text. The association of the psalm with the exile appears to be a secondary development, however. The psalm was probably originally written for use in the fall festival which fell just before the autumn rains and the fall planting. The theme of the psalm—the reversal of fortune—fits nicely, however, with the Jeremiah text.

The first half of the psalm (verses 1-3) looks back to the past, probably to the preceding year's festival time, while the last half (verses 4-6) looks forward with intercession to the future.

The opening verse is translated in various ways. An alternative to the RSV is the translation, "When the Lord determined the destiny [or "set the fate"] for Zion." Such a determination was probably considered part of the annual fall festival which marked the end of the old year and the beginning of the new. It was believed that during the festival, God decreed what would happen in the coming year and thus set the destiny for the future. Remnants of a similar perspective can be seen in our beliefs about beginning anew with resolutions and a clean slate on New Year's Day. The past restoration or determination of fortunes is recalled in the psalm as a glorious time. The expectations of the future on that previous occasion made the people seem as if they were dreaming, that is, the expectations were uninhibited by the normal limitations of reality. Laughter and joy were the characteristics of the experience. God had done or decreed great things, things to be recognized even by the nations, the Gentiles (see Ps. 98:1-3 which also belongs to the fall festival context).

The prayer of petition and appeal in verses 4-6 requests a good future in the coming time that would reverse the status of the present. (Just as our New Year's resolutions and expectations exceed the realities of the year, so it was in ancient Israel.) The dry wadi beds, the dusty gullies of the Negeb desert, are used to symbolize the present and the way in which these could be transformed into watercourses with growing vegetation by the coming rainy season symbolize the hoped-for future. Such imagery may have been a proverbial picture indicative of a sudden and drastic change.

Mythological and primitive concepts underlie the references to sowing with weeping, reaping with joy. The association of tears with sowing is based on several factors: tears symbolize rainfall, sowing involves death since the seed must "die" to appear as new grain growth, planting is a gamble and a risk, and the scattering of seeds resembles the shedding of tears. Such customs as weeping when sowing are found in many cultures around the world. Significant also is the idea of performing one type of action in the present so as to achieve the opposite at a later point in time. Deprivation in the present, the temporary suspension of gratification can be seen as the means to fuller realization in the future. Weep now and shout for joy later.

Hebrews 5:1-6

In the preceding verses, the author has treated Jesus, the "great high priest." Now, he elaborates more fully on the Levitical priesthood.

First, he notes that the Levitical priest is appointed "to act on behalf of men in relation to God" (verse 1). He is, in other words, a mediator between humans and God, commissioned to act in behalf of his constituents. Though the term is not used here, "advocate" *(paraklētos)* comes close to expressing the thought. The roles of both Jesus and the Holy Spirit come to be interpreted in this way (John 14:16; 15:26; I John 2:1). The work of the high priest in this respect is adequately described by Jethro, the father-in-law of Moses, when he said to Moses, "You shall represent the people before God, and bring their cases to God" (Exod. 18:19; also cf. Exod. 4:16). Or, as the author earlier writes, the high priest acts "in the service of God, to make expiation for the sins of the people" (2:17). This obviously involved the offering of "gifts and sacrifices for sins" (cf. 8:3). Interestingly, similar language is used by Paul in describing his own apostolic ministry, when he speaks of working "in the priestly service of the gospel of God," and calls his work among the Gentiles "work for God" (Rom. 15:16-17).

Second, our text speaks of the humanity and vulnerability of the Levitical high priest. "He himself is beset with weakness" (verse 2; 7:28). In spite of the fact that the standards for becoming a high priest were quite rigorous, he was nevertheless human, and therefore subject to sin. Accordingly, in the various descriptions of his work, it is usually stressed that he must offer sacrifices not only for the people but for his own sins as well (7:27; 9:7; Lev. 9:7; 16:6, 15-16). But, our text is quite specific in noting that his task is to deal with "the ignorant and wayward," or more literally, "those who do not know and who wander off." The Mosaic law took a hard line on sins committed deliberately, or in the words of the Old Testament, "sins done with a high hand" (cf. Num. 15:30; Deut. 17:12; Ps. 19:12-13). By contrast, those who committed "unwitting sins" were dealt with mercifully (cf. Num. 15:27-29; Lev. 4:2).

The language of today's text is closely related to that used in Jesus' parable of the "sheep gone astray" (Matt. 18:10-14; Luke 15:3-7). One also thinks of numerous New Testament references concerning those who act "in ignorance" (Acts 3:17; 13:27; 17:30; Luke 23:34; I Tim. 1:13). Since each of us, at one time or another, has behaved in a way that is "ignorant and wayward," this phrase may be a useful avenue to explore homiletically.

From the human weakness of the high priest, the author finally turns to the nature of his appointment. Even the Levitical high priest was divinely appointed (Exod. 28:1), and in this respect Christ was no different, for he was not self-appointed as a high priest, but received his appointment from God (cf. John 3:27). The author interprets Psalm 2:7,

"Thou art my Son, today I have begotten thee," as words spoken by Yahweh directly to Christ, his Son. Originally, this psalm celebrated the coronation of the king, but was appropriated by Christians early on to express their conviction that Christ, the Son of God, had been exalted to a position of divine kingship (cf. 1:5; Acts 13:33). In addition, the words of Psalm 110:4, "Thou art a priest for ever, after the order of Melchizedek," were similarly appropriated to underscore the permanent nature of Christ's appointment to the high priesthood of God. Christ's similarity with the priesthood of Melchizedek receives full elaboration in chapter 7 (cf. also I Macc. 14:41).

Mark 10:46-52

Mark 10:46-52 joins Jeremiah 31:7-9 and Psalm 126 in the mood of joy as the blind, lame, and sorrowing shout and sing their way up to Zion. By placing the story of the healing of blind Bartimaeus immediately prior to Jesus' entry into Jerusalem, Mark has made this healing a prelude to that festive occasion and in a sense has put Bartimaeus in that parade. However, to find the meaning of this story one must, as with other Markan texts, look in two directions: within the account itself and in the location of the narrative in the Gospel as a whole.

Internally, Mark 10:46-52 is a healing story, bearing some traits common to other such stories in the Gospel, but with other familiar characteristics missing. It is an "on the way" story with the usual cast of characters: Jesus, the Twelve, a huge crowd, and a person in need. In this case the one in need is named, perhaps an indication that Bartimaeus was known to the Markan church. Bartimaeus is the very image of one without anything to offer, anything to claim; he is a blind beggar. In his call for help, Bartimaeus addressed Jesus as "Son of David" (verse 47). By including a messianic title which he dislikes, is Mark simply passing along an unedited tradition or is he implying that such a title for Jesus is something a blind man would say? In Jerusalem, the crowds will shout, "Blessed is the kingdom of our father David"

(11:10). It is difficult to know what either Bartimaeus or Mark intended here. The attempt to silence Bartimaeus recalls the response of the disciples to the approach of the woman with the blood flow (5:30-32) and to those who brought children to Jesus (10:13-16). But persistence wins (7:25-29), the blind man makes his plea to Jesus, and Jesus pronounces him healed by faith. Although released to go his own way, the healed Bartimaeus chooses to follow Jesus "on the way" (verse 52). Noticeably absent are the attempts to find privacy for the healing and the charge to silence. Apparently the last healing story in Mark belongs not with the itinerant ministry marked by Jesus' repeated demands for silence, but with the Jerusalem ministry in which Jesus even acknowledged to the Jewish court that he was the Christ (14:61-62). Events in Jerusalem will reveal the meaning of Galilee's secret.

Perhaps Mark's location of this healing story just prior to the entry into Jerusalem helps the reader understand why it differs so noticeably from the account of healing a blind man in 8:22-26. We noted in an earlier lesson that the block of material, 8:27–10:45, is governed internally by three predictions of the Passion and is bracketed on either side by stories of Jesus healing the blind (8:22-26; 10:46-52). The earlier healing is performed with great difficulty, in private, followed by Jesus' charge that the one healed not return to tell what happened. In the stories which follow, the disciples are given inside information about Jesus' fate but repeatedly show themselves to be blind. With that instruction of the Twelve now concluded, Mark tells of the healing of another blind man, but this time the healing is without difficulty, without privacy, and without a charge to secrecy. In fact, the blind man who now sees becomes a disciple.

Whatever a preacher may make of Mark's dramatic arrangement of his narrative, one thing is clear: there is no room here for any sense of superiority over the characters in the text. The crowd tried to silence a blind beggar whose cries for help were an annoyance to their triumphant parade with Jesus. But who among us has not? And the Twelve, insiders all the way and privy to Jesus' painful disclosures about his approaching Passion, heard all and heard nothing, saw all and still were blind. Both pulpit and pew still ask, "Lord, is it I?" In John 9 there is a story of Jesus healing a blind man. It is not at all parallel to Mark in content or in style, but it concludes with a comment that is fitting here: the blind see, the seeing are blind.

Proper 26

Sunday Between October 30 and November 5 Inclusive

*Deuteronomy 6:1-9; Psalm 119:33-48; Hebrews 7:23-28;
Mark 12:28-34*

Deuteronomy 6:1-9

The semi-continuous reading of the book of Hebrews for this season leads the epistolary text in its own direction—toward christological reflection—but the other lections converge on a single issue, the heart of the law. Mark 12:28-34 contains the earliest tradition of the Great Commandment, quoting Deuteronomy 6:4-5 in combination with Leviticus 19:18. The selection from Psalm 119, with its prayer for the capacity to know the law and respond in obedience, is a highly appropriate response.

Virtually the entire Book of Deuteronomy is presented as the farewell speech of Moses to the assembled people of God. (The exceptions are narrative introductions or transitions such as 1:1-4; 4:41-43; 10:6-9, and the account of Moses' final deeds and his death in chapter 31.) While there are differences in style and form in various parts of the book that indicate a long history of growth and composition, almost everything is second person address and hortatory or homiletical in style. The law and the saving history are interpreted, explained, and laid on the heart of the addressees.

Deuteronomy 6:1-9 consists of two distinct parts, verses 1-3 and 4-9. Read together, the first paragraph will serve as the introduction to the second, but in the composition of the book 6:1-3 actually concludes one section concerned with the law while 6:4 begins a new one.

Verses 1-3 are in that repetitious, hortatory language common to the book. The preacher seeks every possible way to urge the law upon the hearers and to persuade them to obey. He holds out the promises of possession of the good land, long life, and well-being to faithful Israel. Elsewhere threats will also be used, but here the view that rewards follow faithfulness is presented warmly: Be obedient so that Yahweh can do what he desires to do, fulfill his promises.

The crux of the reading, and of the book as a whole, is verses 4-9. The passage is known in Judaism by its first word, "Hear," in Hebrew *shêma'*. In Judaism the term describes a distinct section for liturgical and devotional use, variously including only verse 4, verses 4-5, or verses 4-9. Its beginning imperative, "Hear," is more than a call to attention; it is a summons to listen actively and respond. We may take that summons as a directive to consider seriously the meaning of the words in their original context, without rejecting the rich history of liturgical use and theological reflection in synagogue and church.

What follows the initial imperative in verse 4 is a statement in the indicative. The Hebrew of the statement can be legitimately translated in various ways, as comparison of translations or even a look at the RSV footnotes will reveal. When Hebrew philology, grammar, and syntax leave several possibilities the context must be decisive, and in this case the context is the book as a whole and the convenantal traditions here reflected. On those grounds the third RSV alternative is the most appropriate: "The Lord is our God, the Lord alone." Neither monotheism nor the unity of God is the meaning, but undivided allegiance to Yahweh. The covenant and the Decalogue stand behind this verse, and undivided devotion is the point of the first commandment (Deut. 5:7; Exod. 20:3). Moreover, the problem which Deuteronomy repeatedly, almost constantly, addresses is not the more-or-less abstract one of monotheism, but the danger of worshiping false gods, the possibility of corrupting the faith with Canaanite beliefs and practices. The fact that Israel's God is a single one, Yahweh, is the foundation not only for the Decalogue but also for all of life.

Verse 5 is in the imperative form of a command. In substance it is the positive form of the first commandment, "You shall have no other gods before me" (Deut. 5:7; Exod. 20:3), but the injunction to "love the Lord your God" makes it distinctive. In the context of the covenant and the law, "love" is not simply a feeling but a total response of devotion and obedience, with the emphasis on its permanence. "Heart," "soul," and "might" stress that love is to entail all of one's faculties and abilities. The foundation of this command is Yahweh's love for his people: "The Lord set his heart in love upon your fathers and chose their descendants after them, you above all peoples, as at this day" (Deut. 10:15; see also 4:37; 6:7; 7:7, and elsewhere).

In view of the Great Commandment's addition, with Jewish tradition, of the command to love one's neighbor, we should point out that such concern is by no means lacking in Deuteronomy. The love of God, through obedience to the law, expresses itself in love and concern for the other, including slaves, the poor, foreigners, the widow, and the orphan (see Deut. 10:18; 15:7-18; 16:11; 24:17-18).

The remainder of the reading (verses 6-9) urges obedience and provides guidance for the way it is to be done. Take the words to heart, teach them to your children, speak of them at all times in your everyday conversation. Love of God must become a habit of heart and mind. The injunction to talk of the law "when you lie down, and when you rise" (verse 7) led to the twice-daily recital of the shema in Judaism, and the binding of the words as a sign led to the practice of phylacteries, copies of the shema worn in small leather containers. The fundamental concern of these verses is that the tradition remains vital and is passed on through the generations, lest it be forgotten (Deut. 6:12).

The two points here which cry out for proclamation and interpretation in the context of worship are singleness of devotion to God and the love of God. Concerning the first, it is easy to name false gods, but we must struggle with the complexity of the matter in our own time. At one level it was simple for the preachers of Deuteronomy as for the prophets and even the priests: worship only the Lord, not the Canaanite deities. But it was also complicated for them, To what extent can we follow the customs of the culture and still be faithful? The authors of Deuteronomy took a radical course, setting out to destroy all vestiges of foreign religion and centralize worship in Jerusalem. They did not do that, however, without constant attention to the concern that faith in the God who had brought them out of slavery in Egypt must be acted out day to day in society.

The command to love God is even more difficult. How can one command such a thing? Love cannot be coerced. Two mutually supportive directions are suggested by Deuteronomy 6:1-9. (1) How does anyone learn to love? Only by being loved can one respond in kind. That is why Deuteronomy will constantly remind the congregations of Israel—and ours as well—that obedience in love is the response to being chosen and loved by God. (2) One's actions, emotions, and even passions are affected by training, habit, practice, and education. We are shaped by what we hear, read, discuss, and do. That is why Deuteronomy insists that the command and its foundation be taught, discussed, and kept constantly before one's eyes.

Psalm 119:33-48

This psalm selection is the *he* and *waw* stanzas of this long alphabetic composition on the law. (On Ps. 119, see Proper 18 pages 161-64). In the eight lines of each stanza, eight synonyms are used to speak of the will of God. In the former occur statutes, law, commandments, testimonies, ways, promise, ordinances, precepts. In the latter appear promise, word, ordinances, law, precepts, testimonies, commandments, statutes.

The fifth stanza of the psalm, the *he* strophe, contains a number of causative verbs in Hebrew since the causative forms were produced by prefixing a *he* to the basic verbal root. Note "teach me" ("cause me to learn"), "give me," "lead me," and so on.

As throughout this psalm, the emphasis is on love for and obedience to the law. The stress in verses 33-40 is on the divine function in imparting the law to the would-be observer. The assumption that lies behind the requests of this section is the realization that more is required in a person's relationship to the law than merely the law and a desire to learn. Theologically, one can say that what is required is that third ingredient, namely, the presence of the Divine which creates the possibility of union between the law and the learner. (A variation on this theme is the later rabbinical saying, "Where two study the law together there God is in their midst.") Psychologically, one could say that what is required is that enlightenment or illumination in which truth becomes real and existential. Sometimes this is reflected in the assertion that knowledge must become understanding. In this regard, the text speaks of the law as a "way" (verse 33) and as a "path" (verse 35). The law thus invites one to a way of life, to an orientation of the whole being. It is, if one understands this in the best sense, an obsession.

Verses 33-40 also refer to those things that intrude into life and siphon off devotion to the law: "gain" or, to use the New Testament term, "mammon" and "vanities" (those things which are unsubstantial and/or morally unsound). These either distract the attention or else blur the vision, either of which dissipate the ability to focus the will.

Note that the law is perceived as the means to life. "Teach me," "give me understanding," and "give me life" are all synonymous expressions. In the law is life.

The NEB translates verse 33 as: "Teach me, O Lord, the way set out in thy statutes, and in keeping them I shall find my reward." Although there is some question about how to translate this verse, the NEB reflects one perspective on the law. Obedience is its own reward. "Be good for goodness' sake" may not be just a special plea for a way of life but a deep insight into the nature of how one integrates life.

In verses 41-48, three emphases are noteworthy: (1) knowledge of the law and its incarnation in one's life is the means to handle the taunts and accusations hurled one's way; before taunters and before kings, the knowledgeable and the obedient have an answer and no need to fear; (2) to walk in the law is to walk in liberty or as the Hebrew says literally, "in a broad place"; in obedience there is freedom; and (3) the law is the object of love and devotion. For the psalmist, the law is the object also of delight, a worthy recipient of one's passion.

Hebrews 7:23-28

These verses conclude the discussion of the priesthood of Melchizedek, a theme introduced earlier (5:6, 10) and developed more fully in the first part of chapter 7. As far as our author is concerned, the only real analogy for Jesus' priesthood supplied by the Old Testament is that provided by Melchizedek, the mysterious king of Salem and "priest of the Most High God" (Gen. 14:17-20). That he had "neither beginning of days nor end of life" (verse 3) supplied the point of contact with Christ, the Son of God, who had become a "priest for ever" (verse 3).

The fact that Jesus was not of Levitical descent (verse 14) was of no consequence. Neither was Melchizedek a Levitical priest, yet according to Scripture, Abraham clearly acknowledged the superiority of Melchizedek's priestly status by paying tithes to him (verse 4). This clearly shows that genealogical descent has nothing to do with establishing the relative value of one's priesthood. Thus, Jesus has become a priest "not according to a legal requirement concerning bodily descent but by the power of an indestructible life" (verse 16). Convinced that Christ, through his resurrection, now lives forever, the author sees no one else to whom the words of Psalm 110:4 can be applied, "Thou art a priest for ever, after the order of Melchizedek" (verse 17). But, the author also saw the two preceding lines of the psalm as especially significant: "The Lord has sworn and will not change his mind" (verse 21). For him, this constituted a divine oath. It not only meant that Christ was a high priest forever, but that his status had been confirmed by an oath from God.

Jesus, then, was "the surety of a better covenant" (verse 22). The superiority of the "new covenant" is a major theme of the book of Hebrews (8:6-10; 9:15-20; 12:24; cf. Luke 22:20; II Cor. 3:7-18). But, in precisely what respects is it better? Today's epistolary lection supplies the answer.

First, Christ's priesthood is permanent (verses 23-25). The Levitical priesthood could only survive through a succession of high priests. Since they were mortal, replacements had to be found when they died. There could be continuity of office, but no continuity of person. With this setup, the Levitical priesthood was subject to all the vagaries of human institutions that are passed on from one person to another. As we all know, with each new president, boss, CEO, or dean, we have to begin negotiations all over again. Policies change with the person.

By contrast, the priesthood of the new covenant has only one occupant, Jesus, who "continues for ever" (verse 24; 5:6). To deal with one high priest, as opposed to a succession of them, offers distinct advantages, not the least of which is permanent availability: "He is able *for all time* to save those who draw near to God through him" (verse 25). He is always on call: "He always lives to make intercession for them" (verse 25; cf. 9:24; Rom. 8:34). Not only does he hold office permanently, but he remains unvarying: "Jesus Christ is the same yesterday, today, and for ever" (13:8).

Second, the moral character of Christ far exceeds that of any given Levitical high priest. Earlier in the letter, in noting the humanity of Christ, the author stressed his identification with human weakness. Here, however, there is a vast chasm between Christ the high priest and the Levitical priests. Among other things, Christ is "holy, blameless, unstained, separated from sinners, exalted above the heavens" (verse 26). By contrast, Levitical priests are men appointed "in their weakness" (verse 28). The contrast is clear and the difference broad: Christ is everything they are not.

Their own imperfection is shown by the fact that they must offer sacrifices for their own sins, according to the Mosaic law (5:3; 9:7; Lev. 16:6, 11, 15). The sacrifices they offer are "continual" (Exod. 29:38-46; Num. 28:3-31), and this in itself attests their relative ineffectiveness. Were they of permanent value, they would only need to be offered "once for all," as was the case with Christ's sacrifice. In his case, once was enough, and this stress on the absolute finality of the sacrificial death of Christ further extends the remarks made in the preface to the letter (1:1-4; 9:12, 26-28; 10:10; also Rom. 6:10; I Pet. 3:18).

Third, Christ's status as high priest was sealed with a divine oath. As noted above, the crucial Old Testament phrase has already been introduced from Psalm 110:4 (verse

21). And the obvious point has been drawn: Levitical priests were installed without an oath. By contrast, Christ's appointment as high priest was secured by God's own vow, and one that superseded the law (verse 28).

Quite clearly, the outlook throughout this passage is confessional. The author's exegesis of the Old Testament, his interpretation and appropriation of the Melchizedek story, and his assessment of the many shortcomings of the Levitical priesthood all hold only because of his unwavering faith in the "indestructible life" of Christ (verse 16). But, given this as a hermeneutical principle, the priesthood of Christ is seen to be a "better covenant." Numerous themes suggest themselves for homiletical appropriation, not the least of which is the permanence of Christ's high priesthood. This becomes all the more attractive in view of the way in which we moderns know and experience change.

Mark 12:28-34

All the lections for today join in permitting, or rather urging, continuity between Christianity and Judaism by focusing upon the heart of both: love of God and love of neighbor. As Paul expressed it, the commandments "are summed up in this sentence, 'You shall love your neighbor as yourself' " (Rom. 13:9). In fact, the Old Testament readings remind us that not every Israelite experienced the law as oppressive, breeding despair and hypocritical displays of religion. And our Gospel reminds us that even in contexts of disputes with Jewish leaders, Jesus claimed and affirmed the fundamental tenets of his tradition. Too often Christians forget this, creating generalized and largely false dichotomies between law and gospel, work and faith, act and motive.

Mark 12:28-34 is a complete story, only lightly tied to its present context (verse 28*a*) and rounded off at the end (verse 34*b*). It could effectively be placed in any context without loss of meaning. In fact, Luke, who recasts the story, places it earlier in his narrative (10:25-28). Mark, and Matthew after him (22:34-40), has located this exchange between Jesus and a scribe in the block of material that presents Jesus in Jerusalem, teaching and debating, and in general pronouncing

God's judgment upon a Judaism gone awry (11:1–13:37). The time sequences in the events we traditionally place in Holy Week are impossible to recover. Mark has framed this material upon a series of visits to the temple by Jesus (11:11, 15, 27; 12:35, 41; 13:1). It is probably because the scribe responds to Jesus by saying that love of God and neighbor are "much more than whole burnt offerings and sacrifices" (verse 33) that Mark sets the story in the temple. At any rate, in the institution which was the heart of Judaism, Jesus and a scribe go straight to the heart of their common tradition.

The scribe who approaches Jesus with a question is presented in a positive light. Of the nineteen references to scribes in Mark, this one is alone in that regard. Matthew (20:35) and Luke (10:25) portray the questioner as a lawyer seeking to test Jesus, but the preacher must not let that influence how our text is heard. Mark's story is most refreshing. After a series of entrapment questions from Pharisees, Herodians, and Sadducees (12:13-27) the sincerity and perception of this scribe are welcomed. His question was appropriate to Judaism's continued reflection upon its tradition and faith in the effort to keep perspective and not to stray from the center. And Jesus' answer was not original with him. Rabbis before him had joined the Shema ("Hear, O Israel, . . . ," Deut. 6:4-5) and the command to love one's neighbor (Lev. 19:18*b*) in a capsule statement of Israel's faith and ethic. It would be totally inaccurate, therefore, to portray Jesus as the first to understand the point of Judaism. In fact, by his citations from Deuteronomy and Leviticus and by his agreement with the scribe that these take precedence over rituals, Jesus places himself in the prophetic tradition which included Isaiah, Jeremiah, and Amos. Law can lose its heart; ritual can lose its reason; a relationship can lose its love. But both Mark and we know all too well that Judaism has no monopoly on such distortions of faith.

The scribe agrees with Jesus and Jesus agrees with the scribe. It is a rare and pleasant moment. But agreeing is not enough. The scribe is "not far from the kingdom of God" (verse 34). Like the rich man in an earlier story (10:17-22), the scribe is lacking something. For Mark, it is following Jesus on the way and all the way to the cross. The kingdom of God is not agreeing on the right answers, important as the search for truth is. It is rather living, doing, and relating which the love of God and love of neighbor inspire, inform, and discipline.

Proper 27

Sunday Between November 6 and 12 Inclusive

I Kings 17:8-16; Psalm 146; Hebrews 9:24-28; Mark 12:38-44

I Kings 17:8-16

In the readings for the day we meet two unnamed widows with a great deal in common, the one who gave what she had to the prophet Elijah and the one whom Jesus observed contributing her two pennies. Psalm 146 continues the theme of the righteous poor as well as its other side, God's execution of justice for the oppressed and concern with the feeding of the hungry.

The Old Testament reading is one episode in the stories of the prophet Elijah, found in I Kings 17:1–19:21; II Kings 1. The setting of the stories is the Northern Kingdom during the reign of Ahab (874-852 B.C.) of the dynasty of Omri. The Elijah stories are an old collection doubtless handed down in prophetic circles before they were incorporated by the Deuteronomistic historians into their account of Israel's past. Such stories were particularly important to the Deuteronomistic circle because of their conviction that history was set on its course by the word of God through prophets.

Elijah had appeared on the scene abruptly and without introduction, announcing to Ahab that there would be "neither dew nor rain these years, except by my word" (I Kings 17:1). The word of the Lord then led him first to a brook east of the Jordan to be fed by ravens (I Kings 17:2-7) and then to Zarephath to be fed by a widow.

In the background of the story in I Kings 17:8-16, then, is the conflict between prophet and king, but that is set aside for the moment. More immediately there is the drought. The story is complete and self-contained, though it is followed by the account of Elijah's miraculous raising of the widow's dead son.

It is the drought which provides the narrative tension, the uncertainty which creates suspense. That suspense is heightened by Yahweh's command that it is to be a widow who will feed him, and even more by the revelation that she is so poor that her life and that of her son are threatened (verse 12). It is not the greatness of the man of God that will save them all, but the power of the word of Yahweh through him. "Fear not," he says, and not as simple reassurance but as an oracle of salvation. Then in typically prophetic form he announces the word of God concerning the future: "The jar of meal shall not be spent, and the cruse of oil shall not fall, until the day that the Lord sends rain upon the earth" (verse 14). And that is the way it turned out.

The episode is a miracle story with legendary and folkloristic features. It is told, however, not to glorify Elijah, but to show how the power of God, in the form of the prophetic word, was made manifest through him. While the Bible contains more dramatic miracle stories than this one, we are still meant to be astonished. To provide a rationalistic explanation—the generosity of the widow moved her neighbors to bring meal and oil—may serve only to reduce the astonishment that the divine word could solve such a problem.

When this story is considered in connection with Mark 12:38-44, the role of the widow becomes crucial. That the widow was poor is not surprising. In ancient Israelite society economic well-being generally required a male head of the household. Even all the Old Testament texts, including our psalm for the day, which express God's concern for the widow and the fatherless indicate that there was need for such concern. She is not only poor; she is a foreigner. All the more dramatic then is her willingness to be generous with what little she had, trusting that his word was indeed the word of God.

Psalm 146

This psalm is the first in a small collection (Pss. 146–150) all of which begin and end with a call to praise, hallelujah

("Praise the Lord"). The psalm praises God, describing the divine character and divine activity, while simultaneously contrasting the divine with the human. The composition could be aptly described as a theological synopsis summarizing aspects of Israel's belief about God.

Verses 3-4 warn against placing one's faith in humans even if the humans are extraordinary and exceptional ("princes"). Humans are ultimately helpless: they all die and with death their planning ceases and their thinking terminates. Such death-oriented creatures are not proper objects of trust.

On the other hand, God is a worthy object of trust and one who brings blessedness and happiness in his train. A series of four characteristics of God are presented as supporting the contention that "happy is the one whose help and hope is in God." (1) First of all, appeal is made to God as creator. As the one who made heaven, earth, and sea—that is, the totality of the universe—God is himself not bound by the structures and limitations of creaturehood. As creator, he is owner and ruler. (2) Second, appeal is made to the fidelity and constancy of the Creator "who keeps faith forever." Unlike humans whose plans and programs die with them, God and his help endure forever. Unlike humans, God is not threatened by the possibility of nonbeing. (3) God is the one who is not only concerned for but also executes (guarantees) justice for the oppressed. In this affirmation and throughout verses 7-9, one finds a consistent emphasis of the Old Testament: God takes a special interest in and acts on behalf of the downtrodden, the powerless, and the despairing. (4) The satisfaction of physical needs is also the concern of God who "gives food to the hungry." As the maker of heaven and earth, God does not will that humans be oppressed nor that they should suffer from hunger.

Following these four divine characteristics, the psalmist speaks of seven activities of God in which the Divine acts to alleviate human distress and to defend those without rights. Most of those noted as the object of God's care are persons without full authority and potential to assume responsibility for and to exercise rights for their own welfare: the prisoners (at the mercy of the legal system or perhaps in slavery), the blind (at the mercy of the seeing), those who are bowed down or with bent backs (in debt or oppressed by others thus carrying burdens not their own), the righteous (the innocent in the legal system who however were at the mercy of the upholders of justice), the sojourners (foreign settlers or visitors, not members of the native culture and thus aliens), and the widow and fatherless (who were without the support of a male patriarch in a male-dominated culture). God is declared to be committed to the care of all these while at the same time seeing to it that the wicked come to their just reward—ruin.

The psalmist here obviously presents the basic nature and character of God but does not claim that conditions and circumstances conform to this idealized divine will. In the list of attributes, God is primarily contrasted with human leaders (verses 3-4 over against 5-9). Verse 10 adds an eschatological note to the text and perhaps points to the future as the time when the intervention of God on behalf of society's rejects and subjects will occur.

In preaching from this psalm, attention should be focused on its attempt to define the divine disposition as in favor of the downtrodden and the destitute, the powerless living at the peripheries of society, in the basements of humanity's houses.

Hebrews 9:24-28

In the last epistolary reading from the book of Hebrews, the high priesthood of Christ was compared with the Levitical priesthood and found to be superior. Today's passage continues this comparison, but advances it even further.

Christ is said to have entered "not into a sanctuary made with hands, a copy of the true one, but into heaven itself" (verse 24). In the preceding verse, the author speaks of the vessels of the tabernacle as "copies of the heavenly things." Earlier in the chapter, the author mentions the "greater and more perfect tent" (not made with hands, that is, not of this creation) that Christ entered. All these references presuppose the discussion earlier in the letter where the author contrasts the earthly tabernacle in the wilderness with the heavenly tabernacle (8:1-6).

Underlying this comparison appears to be a Platonic outlook which conceived of two worlds, or levels of reality. The world we experience is the world of things perceived with the senses, the phenomenal world, and it has as its counterpart the world of ideas perceived with the mind, the noumenal world. Each "thing" in the real world has its counterpart in the ideal world, in fact may be regarded as a "shadow" or "type" of its corresponding "idea." Of the two worlds, the world of ideas is the more "real," more basic, since every "thing" in the real world is thought to have been derived from its corresponding "idea" in the noumenal world. Thus, the world of ideas is the "unseen world," but not for that reason imaginary. It is both more basic and more permanent in every respect.

Drawing on this outlook, our author conceives of the earthly tabernacle as a "copy and shadow" (8:5) of the heavenly tabernacle. Of the two, the latter is "the true tent" (8:2). Thus, in today's text, he insists that the sanctuary Christ entered was not "a sanctuary made with hands," or some "thing" manufactured, modeled, or handcrafted from an original. It was no mere "copy," but was itself "the true one." The heavenly tabernacle where Christ carries out his priestly work is far more original and closer to the actual presence of God, for he entered "into heaven itself, now to appear in the presence of God on our behalf" (verse 24). In one sense, God's presence had dwelt in the Most Holy Place of the earthly sanctuary by proxy; it was there, but only as an extension of God's heavenly presence. But now, in the heavenly tabernacle, Christ officiates in the very presence of God not in an earthly tabernacle far removed in distance from the realm of "true" reality.

At this point, our text resumes points of contrast treated in previous epistolary lections. Basically, there are two: (1) the Levitical priesthood involved repeated, or "continual" offerings, whereas Christ's priesthood involved a single offering made "once for all"; and (2) the Levitical high priest offered "blood not his own," that is, the blood of bulls and goats (9:12, 19; 10:4), whereas Christ, "by the sacrifice of himself" (verse 26), offered his own blood. In each of these respects, the form of Christ's priesthood is found to be superior. The "continual" offerings of the Levitical priests merely attested their ineffectiveness (10:1-3). Had Christ's offering been of the same kind, it would have been necessary for him to have made an annual offering "since the foundation of the world" (verse 26). This is obviously absurd.

The author's Christology is aptly summarized in verse 26: "He has appeared." This is a clear reference to his incarnation. The same word is used, and elaborated, in I Timothy 3:16, an early Christian confession: "He was manifested in the flesh."

"Once for all." This phrase is typically used by the author to express the absolute finality of the work of Christ (7:27; 9:12; 10:10; cf. I Pet. 3:18). Christ is the "last word" God has spoken (1:2).

"At the end of the age." The phrase expresses the Christian conviction that Christ's coming to the earth signaled the final stage of salvation history (Matt. 13:39-40, 49; 24:3; 28:20; I Cor. 10:11; I Pet. 1:20; 4:7; I John 2:18; also Gal. 4:4; I Enoch 16:1; IV Esdras 7:113).

"To put away sin by the sacrifice of himself." The death of Christ is seen as the ultimate sacrifice through which purification for the sins of humanity was achieved (1:3; cf. I John 3:5; also Testament of Levi 8:9). He was "offered once to bear the sins of many" (verse 28; 9:6; 10:12, 14; also Rom. 6:10; I Pet. 2:24; 3:18).

At the conclusion of our passage, there is a shift in the argument. Up to this point, the author has been contrasting the work of Christ with that of the Levitical priesthood. Here, however, he sees a similarity between that which all humans experience and that which Christ experiences (verses 27-28). The argument seems to be that just as everyone of us experiences death "once," and from death pass to another stage, in our case, "judgment," so Christ experienced death "once," and from death passed to another stage of his work. The final stage of his work was not judgment, however, but salvation. At his second coming, his task will no longer be to "deal with sin," since that was accomplished once and for all

PROPERS AFTER PENTECOST

in his sacrificial death. Rather, it will be to "save those who are eagerly waiting for him" (verse 28).

Obviously, our text provides additional material for preaching on the work of Christ as presented in the book of Hebrews. One may wish to explore the intercessory work of Christ in the "heavenly sanctuary" as it occurs "in the presence of God," and relate this to other New Testament passages, such as Romans 8:34. Or, the eschatological theme introduced at the conclusion of today's lection might be fruitful to explore, especially since it resonates with themes and texts used in the All Saints service.

Mark 12:38-44

Today's Gospel lesson continues the selected teachings and events within Mark's larger unit, 11:1–13:37, a body of material set within Jerusalem and primarily in the temple. This setting provides not only a context for dispute with Jewish leaders over the proper understanding of life before God, but also a backdrop for instructing the disciples in what constitutes good and bad models of leadership. In the text before us, those instructions are drawn from observing the scribes at work and a widow at worship.

Mark 12:38-44 consists of two distinct parts: verses 38-40 which warn against the influence of scribes, and verses 41-44 which praise the example of a widow. The first part is clearly intended by Mark as only one sample of what Jesus taught: "And in his teaching he said" (verse 38a). Verse 40 is rather awkwardly joined to what precedes and may have existed earlier in another context. Part two, verses 41-44, is an independent story with its own introduction and conclusion. It is absent from Matthew and is preserved in briefer form in Luke (21:1-4). How can one account for these two units being placed together here in Mark? Several possibilities suggest themselves. Since the widow story is set in the temple (verse 41) it is congenial to a context of many temple events. It may also be the case that the reference to widows in verse 40 attracted the poor widow story. This may seem a reason without substance, but in oral cultures ease of memory may take precedence over logic. (Was a similar principle at work in the lectionary for today, with three of the four readings having to do with poor widows?) A more practical reason may lie in Mark's desire to place before the church two contrasting models of behavior: scribes who are proud and greedy and a widow who is humble and generous.

The behavior of the scribe in last Sunday's Gospel (Mark 12:28-34) makes it clear that the indictment in today's text did not apply to all scribes but to those whose behavior is described in verses 38-40. In a community centered in its regard for the Torah, its interpretation and application, the scribe was an important and duly honored person. But places of honor tend to attract persons who are not honorable, and regrettably, this applies also to the field of religion. And as positions in the worlds of politics and commerce provide temptations to greed and self-aggrandizement, so does the world of the spirit. In fact, history has demonstrated that power and greed can be unusually demonic here, given the naïveté and simple trust of many of the faithful who do not realize what transactions are taking place beneath robes, prayers, and sacred texts. The "greater condemnation" (verse 40) which comes to such leaders is calculated on a simple formula: greater knowledge means greater responsibility; from the one to whom more is given, more is expected. As the Epistle of James states it: "Let not many of you become teachers, my brethren, for you know that we who teach shall be judged with greater strictness" (3:1).

The brief story in verses 41-44 is so dramatic and evocative of emotion that the reader has to be attentive to avoid missing its point. The principal character is a figure of pathos in that culture: a poor widow. And her small act, unnoticed except by Jesus, is performed among the rich pouring out abundant gifts, a fact that would have further diminished her offering, except for Jesus. It is he who properly evaluates her two lepta, the smallest coins in circulation, because it is he who knows this is all she has. The canon by which Jesus weighs her gift is not sentiment, but the comparison of one's gift to what one has remaining for oneself. He does not inveigh against large gifts or romanticize small ones; he simply notes that some, after giving large amounts, still have abundance while the widow, after her gift, has nothing. Nothing, that is, except complete trust in God. No wonder that Jesus, who earlier had taken a child in his arms and taught the Twelve, again calls his disciples to him and says in effect, "You have been very interested in greatness. Look at her; she has done something great."

Proper 28

Sunday Between November 13 and 19 Inclusive

Daniel 7:9-14; Psalm 145:8-13; Hebrews 10:11-18; Mark 13:24-32

Daniel 7:9-14

It is highly appropriate that this selection from Daniel occurs with the Markan reading from the so-called Synoptic Apocalypse. Not only is Daniel 7:13 the background of the vision of "the Son of man coming in clouds with great power and glory" (Mark 13:26), but both lections present us with a thoroughly apocalyptic understanding of the last days. The responsorial psalm echoes the vision of God and God's reign in Daniel: it is an everlasting kingdom, a dominion enduring throughout all generations. Even the reading from Hebrews continues the point of the enthroned God with the Messiah at hand to act on his behalf.

Chapter 7 occupies a central place in the Book of Daniel, which was written during the Maccabean revolt, when faithful Jews were being persecuted by the Seleucid ruler Antiochus Epiphanes (167-164 B.C.). Much of the symbolism of the book relates directly to that situation.

Daniel 7 is the first of four vision reports in the book. Though similar in superficial ways to earlier prophetic visions, the apocalyptic visions are quite distinctive. Like most prophetic visions, they report a vision and then give its interpretation, and often the visionary sees himself in the revelation. But apocalyptic visions are much longer, and their symbolism is striking, bizarre, and detailed. The more significant contrast is that while prophetic visions generally concerned the immediate future, apocalyptic visions set the immediate situation of the visionary into the framework of world history as a whole and its imminent radical transformation. The writer of Daniel thus believed that the events of

251

the wars and persecutions were the last throes of the forces of evil, and that God would soon act to establish his kingdom.

Our reading must be read in the context of Daniel 7 as a whole. The first and last verses provide a narrative framework. The remainder consists of the report of what was seen (verses 2-14) and its interpretation (verses 15-27), which at points reverts to the description of the scene before Daniel. Everything is recounted in the first person, from the perspective of the visionary. Today's reading thus is the second part of the description of the revelation. It was preceded by the appearance of four great and horrible beasts out of the sea, finally focusing on the little horn of the last beast to appear.

The vision of the appearance of "one that was ancient of days" (verse 9) contrasts dramatically with the foregoing scene. But the dark backdrop of terror is not forgotten. As myriads of worshipers come before the glorious throne, the sound of the little horn can still be heard (verse 11).

The scene in Daniel 7:9-14 includes three distinct movements. First, (verses 9-10) there is the vision of the appearance of the Ancient of Days and his court. This is doubtless a description of God himself and is remarkable in its visual detail. In the Old Testament God is never described so specifically. Other features of the description, however, are indebted to traditions found elsewhere in the Old Testament. Prophets and others often envisioned God's heavenly court (I Kings 22:19; Job 1:6; Ezek. 1; Isa. 6; Ps. 82). The fiery throne with wheels appears in Ezekiel 1-3. The "court" may be simply the reflection of a royal throne room, but here it is juridical, for "judgment" (verse 10). Second, (verses 11-12) judgment is executed on "the beast," apparently the last one with the horns. This amounts to a death sentence upon the Greek empire, including its Seleucid descendants. Third, (verses 13-14), "one like a son of man" appears before the Ancient of Days and is granted dominion and glory, a kingdom that shall not end.

The "one like a son of man" is not named, and his identity has been a lively question in the history of the interpretation and application of the text. A very similar expression, "son of man," occurs numerous times in the Book of Ezekiel, as the

form of address when Yahweh speaks to the prophet. There
it means simply "human being." The phrase is used this way
in Daniel 8:17 in an address to Daniel, but in 8:15, "one
having the appearance of a man" means an angelic figure.
Since his kingdom will not pass away (verse 14), and the
same thing is said of the kingdom given to the "saints of the
Most High," some have taken "the one like a son of man" as a
collective reference to the "saints," the righteous faithful
worshipers. But the expression here must have in view an
angelic, messianic figure. To be "like a son of man" must
mean not human but having some human characteristics or
appearance. It is easy to see why such vocabulary became
important in expressing the meaning of the incarnation of
God in Jesus, both fully human and fully divine.

The purpose of this text in the framework of chapter 7 is to
communicate and publish a divine revelation concerning the
course and end of history, which will be the reign of God in
justice. God will put an end to the worldly enemy and set up a
kingdom in which the faithful will participate. Even suffering
under bestial powers has meaning, and it will only last for a
while.

The proclamation of apocalyptic texts is not easy, but such
texts lie at the heart of the Christian faith. God's kingdom has
already come, but it is not yet consummated. We live, said
the earliest Christians with the Book of Daniel, already in the
light of the New Age which is dawning upon us. The vision of
that age must inform all we say and do. One way to proclaim
such texts is to look for signs of that reign of God around us.
Here the hungry are fed. There people live together in peace.
Here a family is reconciled. None of these is the kingdom. But
the kingdom of God is like that.

Psalm 145:8-13

An alphabetic psalm, 145 consists of a series of short
affirmations which extol the reign and kingship of God. The
text oscillates between words addressed to the Deity (verses
1-2, 4-7, 10-13*a*) and words spoken about the Deity but
addressed to a human audience (verses 3, 8-9, 13*b*-21). The
lection for this Sunday consists of both types of material—

speech about God (verses 8-9, 13*b*) and speech to God (verses 10-13*a*).

Verses 8-9, which speak about God, offer a formulaic definition or description of God as he is in himself or what classical theology calls the attributes of God. The same description, in almost exact terminology, appears in Exodus 34:6; Joel 2:13; Jonah 4:2; and Psalm 86:15; 103:8. Six characteristics of the Deity are emphasized, all of which stress the benevolent aspects of the divine: gracious (or perhaps "dutiful" as in the appropriate relationship between master and servant), merciful (or "compassionate"), slow to anger (or "patient, long-suffering"), abounding in steadfast love (or "extremely loyal"), good to all (or "universally concerned"), and compassionate to all that he has made (or "tenderly caring for all his creatures"). Such a text as this is the nearest one finds in the Old Testament to a descriptive definition of the Divine. Although the emphasis is placed on the benevolence of God, verse 20 indicates that moral considerations—the issue of justice and injustice—which receives so much emphasis elsewhere in the Hebrew Scriptures is not ignored in the theology of this psalm.

The central topic in the praise of God in verses 10-13 is the kingdom of God. The kingdom of God is here understood, as in most places in the Bible, as the dominion or rule of God. In verse 13*a*, "kingdom" and "dominion" are parallel to each other and thus can be seen as synonyms. Thus the focus of this text is concerned with the present manifestation of God's kingdom—his rule as king at the moment—rather than an eschatological emphasis which comes to dominate in the New Testament. Nonetheless, the futuristic elements do appear in verses 10-11 where the verbs can be translated, as in the RSV, in a future tense.

Both the deeds and the devotees of God, that is, the world of creation at large and the world of his special people, offer their testimony regarding the rule of God (verses 10-11). Both offer witness to humanity at large ("the sons of men"; the NEB translates "their fellows"). Thus the creation and the covenant community point to the reign of God, a reign which is eternal and forever enduring (verse 13*a*). Verse 13*b* reiterates the emphasis on the eternal and continuing reign of

God. He keeps faith with all his promises ("is faithful in all his words") and is unchanging in all that he does ("gracious in all his deeds"). Thus one can trust God and rely on his word.

The preaching on this text should stress the eternal, consistent, abiding character of God's reign. As creator, God is king and the world and all that is in it are his subjects. The remainder of the psalm (verses 14-20) like verses 8-9 focuses on the benevolent character of the God who reigns as king (see Ps. 146 and Proper 27).

Hebrews 10:11-18

Further contrast between the Levitical priests and Christ is seen in the respective posture they adopted for officiating. The Levitical priests stood before God to minister to him (Num. 16:9; Deut. 10:8; 18:7), whereas Christ made a sacrifice "for all time" and then "sat down at the right hand of God" (verses 12; 1:3, 13; 8:1; Ps. 110:1; Matt. 22:44; Acts 2:34-35; Rev. 3:21). The Levitical priests' standing position is itself a symbol of impermanence. The image of Christ "seated at the right hand of the throne of the Majesty in heaven" (8:1) symbolizes, by contrast, that his work has been completed. So effective was the single sacrifice that he offered, no work remains to be done in this respect. All that is left is for him to await the final subjugation of his enemies (verse 13). His task now is one of intercession with God on behalf of those who "draw near to God through him" (7:25; 9:24).

Themes echoed earlier in the epistle continue here. The Levitical sacrifices were offered repeatedly, and their very repetition is a sign of their ineffectiveness. The only conclusion our author can draw from this is that such sacrifices "can never take away sins" (verse 11). They never get through to the "conscience of the worshiper" (9:10). Since annual sacrifices do not succeed in cleansing the conscience of the worshiper, they only serve as a "reminder of sin year after year" (10:2-3). This leads to the inevitable conclusion: "It is impossible that the blood of bulls and goats should take away sins" (10:4; cf. 7:18-19; 9:9, 13-14).

By contrast, Christ made a "single sacrifice for sins" and it was done "for all time" (verses 12; 7:27; 9:28; Rom. 6:10; I Pet.

2:24; 3:18). In doing so, he achieved full sanctification for those who worshiped him (1:3, 10:10, 29; 13:12; I Thess. 4:3). Whereas "the law made nothing perfect" (7:19), Christ's sacrifice made it possible for us to be "perfected for all time" (verse 14). He was able to do in a single sacrifice what the Levitical priests were unable to do through hundreds of years of annual sacrifices: offer genuine forgiveness of sins.

To clinch this point, the author cites the well-known promise of Jeremiah that was introduced earlier in the epistle (8:8-12). Here, he quotes only parts of the longer passage that bear directly on his argument, noting by way of introduction that the witness of the Holy Spirit bears him out (cf. 3:7). First, the new covenant of which Jeremiah spoke promised an "inward law" written on the hearts and minds (verse 16; Jer. 31:33). Second, it offered the hope that sins and misdeeds would be remembered no more (verse 17; Jer. 31:34). True forgiveness would mean no more annual reminders. Thus, "where there is forgiveness of these [sins], there is no longer any offering for sin" (verse 18).

Since this lection concludes the readings taken from the book of Hebrews, it may be useful to make some summary comments. As we have seen, the image of Christ as our high priest receives extensive and elaborate treatment. In numerous ways, the author contrasts the Levitical priesthood with that of Christ and consistently finds the latter superior. In one sense, this translates into a denigration of the Levitical priesthood, but in another sense this form of comparison only attests the richness of the set of metaphors provided by the tabernacle and priesthood.

As a way of setting our author's exegetical work into context, it should be noted that other authors of the period, such as Philo and Josephus, conceived of a cosmic tabernacle corresponding to the one on earth. From this they developed an elaborate symbolic interpretation of the tabernacle and Levitical priesthood. The author of Hebrews is working in this same hermeneutical tradition, but with the chief difference made by the Easter faith. It was the conviction that Christ had risen and was seated at the right hand of God that helped our author reinterpret the priestly cultus. Accordingly, Christ was for him a "priest for ever." Because he did his intercessory work in the very presence of God, in the "heavenly tabernacle," it was efficacious in a way that the Levitical sacrifices could never be. By the very fact that theirs was "earth-bound," it had temporary value. Above all, the way in which it dealt with the most pressing and persistent human need—sin and its forgiveness—was finally ineffective. What was needed was a sacrifice to end all sacrifices, one that could bring about full and final purification and forgiveness of sins. The testimony of the book of Hebrews is that Christ "by a single offering . . . has perfected for all time those who are sanctified" (10:14).

Mark 13:24-32

Mark 13:24-32 drops the reader down in terrain remarkably different from the biographical-type narrative of the remainder of the Gospel. Were the material not identified as Markan one would guess it to be from Daniel or Revelation. From one point of view, Mark 13 sits awkwardly where it is, and the reader of the Gospel could without loss of continuity move from chapter 12 to chapter 14. But from another point of view, this apocalyptic discourse of Jesus could hold a key position in the entire narrative. Many find the Gospel coming to an unsatisfactory conclusion, emphasizing the cross, having no resurrection appearance, calling the disciples to reassemble with Jesus in Galilee, and describing frightened women fleeing silent from the tomb. If there is an incompleteness, perhaps the answer is in chapter 13: the final climactic events are yet to occur. Let us move in for a closer reading.

Jesus entered Jerusalem (11:1), went to the temple, looked around, and the next day (?) went again to the temple, this time to cleanse it in an act that signaled the end of its function. Now in 13:1, for the final time Jesus leaves the temple and predicts its complete destruction. Seated on the Mount of Olives opposite the temple, Jesus is asked by the first four disciples whom he had called (verse 3) when this destruction would occur and what signs would announce it. In the discourse which follows, the end of the temple, the end of all things, and the glorious coming of the Son of man to gather his own (the Parousia) are interwoven themes. But perhaps clarity will be served by looking at the passage as a response to the two questions of the disciples: When? What signs?

The first part of the discourse makes the point that the end is not yet (verses 5b-23). Calamities of war, famine, and persecution will mark the beginning of the messianic woes that precede the end, but they are not signs of the end. False prophets and false messiahs who so interpret the times and claim the end has come are not to be believed (verses 6, 21-22). When the end does come it will be announced with cosmic signs that no one can miss, with the appearance of the Son of man, and with the gathering of the elect from all nations (verses 24-27). While the end is not yet, it is very near (verses 28-31). However, since only God knows when, calculating should cease and everyone should be alert and watch (verses 32-36). Verse 37 then addresses the call to the whole church to watch.

Amid a number of uncertainties as to the meanings imbedded here, several lines of thought are quite clear. Mark is writing to a church that is struggling not only to survive but to interpret the confusing events which are almost overwhelming to their faith and their understanding of discipleship. Severe persecution has begun (verses 9-13) and Jerusalem is under the merciless onslaught of Titus and the Roman army (verses 14-20). What does it mean? False prophets preach that this is the end and some claim to be the returned Christ (verses 6, 21-22). Mark's task is to counter these false teachers (cf. II Thess. 2:1-5), to encourage the church to endure (verse 13), and to keep alive the hope of the Parousia while saying the end is not yet. Being discouraged into thinking Christ will never return was to Mark a danger to the church as threatening as believing that Christ had already come. The message, then, is to be neither falsely optimistic or falsely discouraged. Christ will come and with signs that no one can miss. Appropriate Christian behavior is enduring, without trying to guess when; it is continuing the mission to the nations (verse 10), not giving up. Any teaching about the Parousia and the end time which either by panic or neglect pulls us away from Christ's mission to the world is from a false prophet.

Proper 29 (Christ the King)

Sunday Between November 20 and 26 Inclusive

Jeremiah 23:1-6; Psalm 93; Revelation 1:4b-8; John 18:33-37

Jeremiah 23:1-6

The festival of Christ the King, as the last Sunday of the liturgical year, is an eschatological celebration. This intention is expressed in all the readings for the day. A human and historical image—kingship—is the symbol for the eternal reign of Christ. Jeremiah 23:5-6 is the promise of a righteous king in the line of David that the earliest followers of Jesus saw fulfilled in him. Psalm 93 does not celebrate the enthronement of the Davidic king but of Yahweh himself. Revelation 1:4b-8 praises God as king forever and Christ as "ruler of kings on earth" (verse 5). In the Johannine pericope Pilate asks Jesus if he is king of the Jews and he responds indirectly, "My kingship is not of this world" (John 18:36).

Jeremiah 23:1-6 consists of two distinct paragraphs, as all modern translations indicate. Verses 1-4 are an announcement of judgment against the "shepherds who destroy and scatter the sheep" and an announcement of salvation to the "flock": the Lord will remove their reasons for fear by giving "shepherds who will care for them." The second paragraph (verses 5-6) is an announcement of salvation: Yahweh will raise up a just and righteous king in the line of David. As they stand in the final form of the Book of Jeremiah, the second unit is both a contrast with and an extension of the first. But there are disjunctions between the units which suggest that they originated independently, and perhaps even come from different authors. The first paragraph speaks of "shepherds" (plural) while the second has a single king; the first is prose and the second poetic.

259

Commentators on this passage have disagreed about its authorship and historical provenance. Certainly verse 3, if not all of the first unit, assumes a situation after the time of Jeremiah, namely, the exile. On the other hand, the bad shepherds could very well be the last kings of Judah during the time of Jeremiah. Authorship of verses 5-6 is likewise an open question, though most recent commentators tend to attribute it to Jeremiah. The problem with that conclusion is that this would be the only point where Jeremiah, unlike Isaiah, expresses his hope in terms of the Davidic dynasty. However one resolves that question, the entire unit comes either from the era just before or during the Babylonian exile.

The "shepherds," both good and bad, certainly represent political and religious leaders. Concluding a section of the Book of Jeremiah concerning the last kings of Judah, the reference certainly is to the series of rulers, but it could just as well apply to the officials as a whole. The "shepherds who will care for them" (verse 4) could be either the succession of righteous kings or political and religious leaders.

The juxtaposition of the unit about shepherds with the promise of a king in the line of David calls attention to the importance of the pastoral imagery in the biblical messianic expectations. Certainly that imagery is indebted to some extent to the tradition that David himself was a shepherd. (See I Sam. 16:19 and the commentary for Proper 5 in this volume.) It is a rich combination of power and gentle care: the pastoral king, the royal shepherd.

Verses 5-6 provide a concise summary of the major features of the messianic hope in the Old Testament. The one who is to come will be a king in the line of David (II Sam. 7; see commentary at Propers 9 and 10 in this volume), and raised up by the Lord to prosper in all that he does. Justice and righteousness will characterize his reign (Isa. 9:6-7), bringing salvation to the people of God, in this case those of Israel and Judah. That he will reign as king means he will be king with real power and autonomy, not be a vassal of a foreign power or be controlled by officials of the royal court. The throne name given to him, "Yahweh is our righteousness," suggests that through him the Lord vindicates the people as righteous.

Though the king is an ideal one the promise is rooted in flesh and blood and history. This is the promise that the earliest followers of Jesus saw fulfilled in him, the divine will incarnate. Theologically, the Old Testament text enables us to keep our eyes fixed on two points also fundamental to the New Testament witness, the humanity of the Anointed One, and the faith that through him God is at work.

Psalm 93

This text, with its focus on the kingship of God and the divine rule over the chaotic powers of anarchy, is fitting for the celebration of Christ the King. The psalm was probably used originally as part of the fall festival (the Feast of Tabernacles). During the festival, there was a declaration and celebration of God's reenthronement as king. Thus the opening line of the psalm can be translated, "The Lord [Yahweh] has become king," that is, he has resumed and reasserted his role as king of the world, and like an earthly king, is dressed in regal robes.

The content of the psalm moves from the kingship of God to the theme of creation. The kingship of God is manifest in his establishment of the world. In establishing the world, his throne and divine rule are simultaneously secured (verses 1-2). This idea of the divine establishment and permanence of the world seems to modern persons a rather insignificant concept. For the ancients it certainly was not, for to them the world was far more uncertain, unknown, and threatening than it is now. In the rhythm of the seasons, people experienced the regularity of nature; but in disease, drought, distress, and death, the ancients experienced life and the world in enigmatic terms. To confess and believe that God had founded the world meant that God's will was seen as the basis of the natural order and that life and the world were under his control and thus possessed an order and rationality. People could live with a certain sense of "at-homeness" in the world and with confidence in the world's operations.

Psalm 93:3-4 proclaims God's rule over chaos and anarchy. He is mightier than the floods, mightier than the thunders of many waters, and mightier than the waves of the sea. The imagery of waters, waves, floods, and the sea has its roots in general Near Eastern thought. In Mesopotamia, where the lands were subject to periodic floods, it was believed that cosmic order and structures ruled over and were created out of turbulent waters. These waters and the depths they represented embodied the constant threat of chaos just as they had at the beginning of creation. In Canaanite religion, the god Baal had to fight and defeat the chaotic waters personified in the god Sea. (Note that it is the sea which God splits to allow the Hebrews to leave Egypt; Exod. 14.) After his defeat of Sea, Baal was acclaimed king of the gods and a house or palace was constructed for him. Much of this Near Eastern imagery has been applied to Yahweh in Psalm 93. It is he who establishes the earth and against whom chaotic powers may struggle but over whom they cannot triumph.

The last verse of the psalm is short and terse and has often stumped interpreters. The decrees referred to are probably best understood as the laws established by God to regulate creation. These decrees find reflection in the opening chapter of Genesis, where God is depicted as regulating the orders of creation (see also Gen. 8:22). The idea that God has set bounds and limits to creation occurs in Jeremiah 5:22-24 where the prophet compares the regularity and obedience of the "natural world" with the disobedience of Israel. Elsewhere the prophet compares the permanence of the fixed orders of creation to the eternal character of God's love. (See Jer. 31:35-36.)

Just as God created laws to regulate human life and institutions, so also he ordained decrees and laws by which the created order operates. The reference to the house of God in verse 5 probably does not refer to the earthly temple but instead refers to God's heavenly abode or to the world of creation itself. Just as on earth, cosmic order and holiness befit the house of God. What establishes divine order in the cosmos (verses 1-2) and subdues the powers of chaos (verses 3-4) are God and his decrees (verse 5).

Revelation 1:4b-8

The Feast of Christ the King was instituted by Pius XI in 1925 to celebrate the kingship of Christ as a way of combating the destructive forces of this age. Originally, it was celebrated on the last Sunday of October and was seen as prelude to the celebration of All Saints Day. This was a fitting symbolism since the triumphant Christ was seen to have motivated the saints and lived on in the church's memory of their noble deeds. The feast is now celebrated, however, on the last Sunday of the liturgical year as the climax toward which the celebration of the year moves and toward which individual Christians orient their own lives. Its eschatological dimension should be duly noted, as did Vatican II in acknowledging the significance of this feast at the end of the liturgical year celebrating the Lord of glory as "the goal of human history, the focal point of the desires of history and civilization, the center of mankind, the joy of all hearts, and the fulfillment of all aspirations . . . . Animated and drawn together in his Spirit we press onward toward the consummation of history which fully corresponds to the plan of his love: 'to unite all things in him, things in heaven and things on earth' (Eph. 1:10)" (*Pastoral Constitution on the Church in the Modern World*, no. 45 [Flannery, p. 947], as cited in A. Adam, *The Liturgical Year* (New York: Pueblo), 179).

It would be difficult to find a text more suitable for the occasion than today's epistolary lection with its powerful images of vindication and triumph, its stress on Christ as "the ruler of kings on earth" (verse 6), and its eschatological motif (verse 7). First, however, it should be noted that in form, it is an epistolary greeting from "John to the seven churches that are in Asia" (1:4a). Typical of the way many New Testament letters begin, the book of Revelation as a letter begins with a prayer addressed to the readers. Perhaps it is even more appropriate that the final epistolary lection of the liturgical year is in the form of a prayer that magnificently addresses those in whom the hopes of every Christian lie: God "who is and who was and who is to come" (4:8; 11:17; 16:5; Exod. 3:14; Isa. 41:4), the Holy Spirit here conceived as "the seven spirits who are before his throne" (3:1; 4:5; 5:6;

cf. esp. Isa. 11:2-3), and Christ who is given multiple acclamations that we will note later. Though not fully Trinitarian as the term later came to be understood by the church, the opening greeting at least pays homage to the fullness of Christian Deity.

The centerpiece of the prayer, however, is Christ who is acclaimed with a veritable cluster of rich and powerful images, any one of which the preacher could profitably explore on this final Sunday of the liturgical year:

Faithful witness (verse 5). Taken one way, the Greek wording may actually imply two acclamations: "the witness," or literally "the martyr" *(martus)* and "the faithful one." Jesus as a martyr figure who was slain is obviously a dominant image of the book of Revelation (cf. 5:9; 13:8), and one that doubtless heartened the readers who themselves were being persecuted, and in some cases martyred (6:9-10; 20:4-6). This might be developed along with the emphasis in the Passion narrative of the Gospel of Luke where Christ's death is portrayed especially as that of a martyred figure, an innocent prophet unjustly convicted and killed. But, not only was he a "martyr," but one who demonstrated absolute fidelity to his calling. He is thus the "faithful and true witness" (3:14; also 19:11; cf. Ps. 89:1-2; Jer. 42:5). It may be that the phrase "faith of Jesus Christ" (Rom. 3:22) is a reference to such fidelity on his part, that is, the faithfulness which Christ demonstrated in his sacrificial death. In any case, the example of Christ emphasizes the exhortation to these readers, "Be faithful unto death, and I will give you the crown of life" (2:10).

Firstborn of the dead (verse 5). By his resurrection, Christ became the "first fruits of those who have fallen asleep" (I Cor. 15:20), or to use another metaphor, the "firstborn of the dead" (cf. Col. 1:18). As the "first child" of the resurrected life, he enjoys the status and esteem that rightly falls to the firstborn, and therefore, oldest child (Ps. 89:27; also 2:7).

Ruler of kings on earth (verse 5). Just as David had been described as the "leader and commander for the peoples" (Isa. 55:4), so Christ as David's heir enjoys the rank of the "kings' king" (cf. Luke 1:32-33), or in the words of our author, "King of kings and Lord of lords" (17:14; 19:16; also I Tim. 6:15).

After these words of acclamation about Christ, the prayer turns to the work of Christ and what he has done on our behalf. First, it is noted that he "loves us and has freed us from our sins by his blood" (verse 5). The language here recalls earlier epistolary lections, such as, Ephesians 5:1: "Christ loved us and gave himself up for us." His sacrificial death and redemption achieved through the shedding of his blood call to mind the epistolary lections from Hebrews that have just been concluded (cf. Heb. 9:14), but can also be related to a host of other biblical readings (I John 1:7; also Isa. 40:2; Ps. 130:7-8).

Not only did he effect true and lasting forgiveness for us, he also elevated us to priestly status, making us "priests to his God and Father," thereby fulfilling the prophetic hope (Isa. 61:6; also I Pet. 2:5, 9). But priestly service also implies sharing in his kingly reign. Israel was called to the service of Yahweh as "a kingdom of priests and a holy nation" (Exod. 19:6), and this double honor Christ has made possible for us (5:10). Those who remain faithful are promised to be made "priests of God and of Christ" and to "reign with him a thousand years" (20:6).

Because of what he has made possible on our behalf, his is "glory and dominion for ever and ever" (verse 6). Such universal adoration is typically given to both God and Christ throughout the book of Revelation (4:11; 5:13; 7:10, 12; 11:15, 17; 12:10; 15:3-4; 19:1-2, 5, 6-7). Other New Testament doxologies similarly acknowledge their preeminent position (Rom. 11:36; 16:27; Gal. 1:5; Eph. 3:21; Phil. 4:20; I Tim. 1:17; II Tim. 4:18; Heb. 13:21; I Pet. 4:11; II Pet. 3:18; Jude 25).

With verse 7, there is emphatic stress on the eschatological work of Christ as the one who "is coming with the clouds" (cf. Dan. 7:13; also Matt. 24:30 and parallels). His coming will be universally visible (cf. Zech. 12:10), especially to those who were party to his crucifixion (cf. John 19:37). Judgment will be handed out to "all tribes of the earth" and they "will wail on account of him."

After the conclusion of the prayer, the Lord God proclaims, "I am the Alpha and the Omega . . . who is and who was and who is to come, the Almighty" (verse 8). Standing at the beginning and end of time and all things (cf. Isa. 44:6), God encompasses all time: past, present, and future (21:6; 22:13; also 4:8; 11:17; 16:5). As the victor of time, God is unquestionably "the Almighty" (4:8; 11:17; 15:3; 16:7, 14; 19:6, 15; 21:22; also II Cor. 6:18; cf. II Sam. 7:8; Amos 3:13; 4:13).

With this multifaceted text, rich with christological symbolism and packed with powerful confessional statements, the preacher will find it difficult to decide what not to explore. Almost any single element of the passage could serve as the springboard for the sermon on this occasion.

John 18:33-37

The Season of Pentecost concludes with the service of Christ the King. The Gospel proclamation for this service draws on Jesus' response to Pilate's question, "Are you the King of the Jews?" (John 18:33). In order properly to hear that response we need first to attend to the occasion that prompted the question.

Many efforts to reconstruct the trial of Jesus use the Synoptics primarily, inserting from John any phases of the procedure not reported by the other Evangelists. Unique to the Fourth Gospel is the interrogation by Annas (18:13, 19-24), high priest and father-in-law of Caiaphas who was functioning as "high priest that year" (18:13). Since the high priesthood was for life, the reference to Caiaphas as high priest "that year" is probably the writer's caustic comment on the power of Roman politics to determine even the religious institution. But using John to supplement the Synoptics is hardly a proper way to read this Gospel. The fact is, John has an entirely different perspective on the trial, as he does on the entire ministry of Jesus.

In the Gospel of John, Jesus is from God, is going again to God and is, throughout his ministry, aware of this origin and destiny. He carries out God's will according to "his hour" and is not determined in word or deed by outside forces. In 12:23 Jesus says, "The hour has come for the Son of man to be glorified," and the reader senses that all the subsequent events will unfold to that end. Judas, the soldiers, the priests, Pilate: all are responsible for their actions, but for this Evangelist what really needs to be seen is the purpose of God at work through all the contingencies of historical events. From this perspective, Jesus is presented clear-eyed, firm, and totally in control while all about him other characters are running around filling their roles in the drama.

With this in mind, let us notice more closely the trial scenes. The interrogation by religious leaders occupies verses 13-27. The appearance before Annas is sketchily presented, Annas being high priest but not really high priest. Caiaphas is mentioned four times, but there is not one word about his encounter with Jesus. After all, Caiaphas is high priest but not really high priest. Of the four brief paragraphs, two are devoted to Simon Peter (verses 15-18, 25-27). Why? Because that is where the real trial is taking place, outside by the charcoal fire. Inside Jesus is being questioned but it is meaningless; Jesus moves with firm purpose to his own glorification. But outside, Simon Peter (and the disciples, and the church) is being questioned, and that trial is not going well at all. The Evangelist proves himself as much the preacher as the historian.

The trial before Pilate is, unlike the Synoptics, very lengthily told (18:29–19:16). Our lection records the second of seven episodes (18:29-32, 33-38a, 38b-40; 19:1-3, 4-7, 8-11, 12-16) in that trial during which Pilate is portrayed as a tragi-comical figure who shuttles back and forth between the Jews outside and Jesus inside. He claims the power of the state, not knowing that his power has been given to him from above (19:11). He shouts his authority, but performs in confusion and fear, submitting to petty politics and prejudice. He says he is in charge, but it is obvious that Jesus is in charge. Jesus counters Pilate's question with a question (verse 34), offers logical proof that his kingdom is not of this world ("not of this world" does not mean otherworldly but that his kingdom is not determined by or grounded in the values and strategies of the world), and tells Pilate the reason he cannot understand this (verse 37). In the two-level drama of this Gospel, the writer and reader understand what the characters in the story do not.

Pilate can ask, "So you are a king?" (verse 37) but he cannot understand the answer. But the church did, and does. The church stood and stands before powers and authorities, being interrogated. And in that hour the church recalls this scene. "So you are a king?" Yes, but not because of the world's authorities or in spite of them. Because human hands did not place the crown on his head, human hands cannot remove it.

Visitation, May 31

I Samuel 2:1-10; Psalm 113; Romans 12:9-16b; Luke 1:39-57

I Samuel 2:1-10

Without a doubt this is the most appropriate Old Testament reading for the celebration of Visitation. Primarily because Hannah was seen as a type of Mary, her song provided some of the motifs and expressions for the Magnificat. The responsorial psalm, with its specific references to God's gift of children to the barren woman, is well chosen.

Hannah's song was not originally a part of the story of the birth and dedication of Samuel but has been added subsequently, functioning for the readers of the book in much the same way that responsorial psalms serve us in worship. Apart from the narrative introduction, nothing in the song refers specifically to the situation of Hannah or Samuel, though there is the reference to barrenness and birth (verse 5). Moreover, the mention of the "king" in verse 10 is anachronistic for the story of Samuel's beginnings, and the song as a whole corresponds to later psalms that were used in the temple. Consequently, exegesis of this passage should be attentive to the meaning of the song on at least three levels: (1) the song in its present literary context, (2) its meaning in itself independent of the narrative, and (3) its appropriation and interpretation in the early church as reflected in Luke 1:39-57.

1. In the Book of First Samuel the song is part of Hannah's act of worship when she brings her son Samuel to the sanctuary at Shiloh to "loan him" to the Lord (I Sam. 1:28). It is preceded by the story of Hannah's barrenness, her prayer for a child and vow that he would be dedicated to Yahweh

(I Sam. 1). In every respect she is a woman of faith, presented as a model to all who hear her story. She is also a woman of destiny, for the account of Hannah and her son Samuel is an important key in the history of the people as a whole. It comes at a decisive turning point, between the chaos of the period of the judges—"In those days there was no king in Israel; every man did what was right in his own eyes" (Judg. 21:25)—and the rise of the monarchy, first with Saul and then David, both of whom Samuel anointed. Samuel's birth heralds a new age, and his mother is more than a passive participant.

2. Hannah's song itself is a thanksgiving psalm with many elements of a hymn of praise. It begins with the declaration of intent to praise God (verse 1) and then affirms that Yahweh is the incomparable God who knows all (verses 2-3). Next (verses 4-9) God is praised as the one who protects and cares for the weak, who is indeed Lord of life and death, and who executes justice. The song concludes (verse 10) on a distinctly messianic and cosmic note: Yahweh will defeat those who oppose him, judge the entire earth, and elevate his anointed.

3. In the early church context it was not only the parallels between Hannah and Mary that were picked up but also the fundamental point of the song. It is God who acts to save the weak, the lowly, the poor, and the needy. The God of justice, who sets the world on its pillars (verse 8), chooses to be known through humanity at its most vulnerable stages, a baby just weaned from his mother's milk, or even one yet unborn.

Psalm 113

Psalms 113–118, the so-called Egyptian Hallel psalms, were used as part of the celebration of Passover. They were sung, first by the Levites in the temple when the Passover lambs were being slaughtered, and later in the evening by the families as they ate the Passover meal. Psalm 113 does not seem to have been written initially for use during Passover, but was adopted for this occasion because of its central themes: God's concern for the oppressed and the unfortunate and the divine reversal of the fate of the poor and needy.

The psalm illustrates the Exodus theme—from oppression to freedom, from humiliation to joy, from servitude to service. In Judaism, this theme is found in the Passover ritual when the father instructs the family, represented by the younger son, by telling the story of the Exodus "beginning with the disgrace and ending with the glory."

Psalm 113 is a hymn that praises God, speaking of the Deity in the third person. Three factors about the Deity are stressed in this text: his universality, his transcendence, and his redemptive concern for the underprivileged. This last theme is also found in the song of Hannah and the Magnificat and serves to bind together the three texts of today's lections.

1. The universality of God finds expression in verses 2-3. Two aspects of this universalism are noted. Verse 2 focuses on the chronological universality: God's name is blessed from now until forever. Verse 3 stresses the geographical universality: from the sun's rising to its setting.

2. The transcendence of God who is high above the nations and above the heavens and who looks down upon creation (the heavens and the earth) is the content of verses 4-6.

3. Against this backdrop of universality and transcendence, the central thrust of this psalm, in verses 7-9, proclaims God's special concern for those destitute and despairing in life. Those whom society has in its midst and so frequently ignores and misuses are the special concern of the God who might appear to be too remote and too removed to even notice much less aid them. Two examples of the class are noted: the poor and the barren mother. The poor on the dust piles and the ash heaps of life, and the barren woman unable to be a mother are visited by the Deity. God is proclaimed as the one who reverses the fate, who alters the fortune of these underlings of society. The poor and needy (like Moses in the Exodus story) are made to sit with princes (in Pharaoh's palace). The barren whose womb yearns to embrace and nurture new life (like Sarah or Hannah) is made the joyous mother of children.

That God is concerned for the disposable, throwaway members of society is revolutionary theology; that the church should imitate the Divine in this regard is revolutionary ethics. A revolutionary God and a revolutionary church are both gifts from the beyond, not the products of a theology homegrown and self-engendered in the human heart.

Romans 12:9-16*b*

Today's epistolary lection consists of a catalog of Christian exhortations, notable for their proverbial form. Among them is the charge not to be haughty and to associate with the lowly, which picks up on a major theme from today's Gospel reading, the Magnificat (cf. esp. Luke 1:52). In a similar vein, Psalm 113 praises Yahweh as one who favors the humble.

Even though this is but one motif of the epistolary reading, it is part of a larger set of concerns that give thematic unity to Paul's instructions here. He opens by insisting that love should be genuine, literally "without hypocrisy" (verse 9), and many of his remarks that follow are but variations on this theme. In his own apostolic ministry he was motivated by genuine love (II Cor. 6:6), and elsewhere the New Testament insists that love should issue from a pure heart (I Tim. 1:5; cf. I Pet. 1:22).

"Hate what is evil, hold fast to what is good" (verse 9). These words are reminiscent of Amos 5:15, "Hate evil, and love good, and establish justice in the gate." And as the psalmist reminds us, "The Lord loves those who hate evil" (Ps. 97:10).

"Love one another with brotherly affection" (verse 10). Here, the general injunction to love is given specific content, as Paul urges Christians to model themselves after the family where siblings experience mutual love and concern (cf. I Thess. 4:9; Heb. 13:1; I Pet. 1:22; 2:17; I Pet. 1:7).

"Outdo one another in showing honor" (verse 10). Later, Paul urges that honor be given to those to whom honor is due (13:7).

"Never flag in zeal, be aglow with the Spirit" (verse 11). It is quite possible to grow fainthearted even in doing good works, or perhaps especially in doing good works (cf. Gal. 6:9). Accordingly, one should look to the Spirit as the source of strength (cf. Acts 18:25).

"Serve the Lord" (verse 11). The object of Christian service is the Lord Christ (Col. 3:24; cf. Acts 20:19).

"Rejoice in your hope, be patient in tribulation" (verse 12). This continues his instruction introduced in Romans 5:2-3. The object of Christian hope was the resurrection hope, and this enabled them to develop patience in facing tribulation. Earlier, he stresses that one can face suffering creatively by seeing in it an occasion to strengthen one's character (Rom. 5:4).

"Be constant in prayer" (verse 12). Vigilance in prayer is held out as a common expectation for Christians (Acts 2:42; Eph. 6:18; Phil. 4:6; Col. 4:2; I Thess. 5:17; I Tim. 2:11). Here is another theme that relates directly to today's Gospel reading. It is, after all, a prayer in which Mary magnifies the Lord. In fact, one should note the number of prayers that occur in Luke 1–2.

"Contribute to the needs of the saints, practice hospitality" (verse 13). At the outset of his ministry to the Gentiles, Paul had agreed to "remember the poor" (Gal. 2:10) and thus devotes considerable time, energy, and space to the relief fund for the Jerusalem saints (cf. I Cor. 16:1-2; II Cor. 8–9). Extending hospitality was but another form of this, and in fact was so important that it became a criterion for judging the worthiness of potential church leaders (I Tim. 3:2; 5:10; Tit. 1:8; Heb. 13:2; I Pet. 4:9).

"Bless those who persecute you" (verse 14). The language echoes the teachings of Jesus (Matt. 5:44; cf. Luke 23:34; I Cor. 4:12; Acts 7:60; I Pet. 3:9; Luke 6:35; Eph. 5:1).

"Rejoice with those who rejoice, weep with those who weep" (verse 15). Here is another point of connection with the Gospel reading, for we recall that when Elizabeth's neighbors and kinsfolk heard that she had given birth, "they rejoiced with her" (Luke 1:58). This also echoes the sentiments of Sirach 7:34: "Do not fail those who weep."

"Live in harmony with one another" (verse 16). Christian community implies living together in harmony and love (cf. Rom. 15:5; II Cor. 13:11; Phil. 2:2; 4:2; cf. I Cor. 1:10; I Pet. 3:8).

"Do not be haughty, but associate with the lowly; never be conceited" (verse 16). In keeping with Old Testament warnings against pride and conceit (Prov. 3:7; Isa. 5:21), Paul excludes arrogance from permissible Christian behavior (cf. Rom. 11:20, 25; I Tim. 6:17).

Luke 1:39-57

The reader of the first two chapters of Luke has to attend to two dominating characteristics of the section: Luke's literary achievement and his theological achievement.

Luke's literary achievement in these chapters is twofold. First, he is able to interweave the narratives of the births of John the Baptist and Jesus is such a way that God is praised in both, the greatness of neither figure is diminished, and yet clearly John's greatness lies in his witness to the lordship of Jesus. To this point we will return. Second, Luke is able to carry the stories on the wings of song, prayer, and blessing. Very likely the reader is here being treated to liturgical materials from early Christian worship which consist primarily of direct and allusive uses of Old Testament materials. Obviously in Luke's church the Hebrew Scriptures provided content not only for preaching (the sermons in Acts 2–5) but also worship. That Nativity stories were conveyed in song and praise has continued to instruct the church as to how best to proclaim this portion of the faith.

Luke's theological achievement is also twofold. First, the relation of John and Jesus is clear at the outset, from their births. Both are gifts of God, have divine missions, are within six months of the same age (1:26), and are, in fact, kinsmen (1:36). But notice: John not only is to go before Christ in the spirit of Elijah to prepare the people (1:17), but while still in the womb, honors Jesus who is also yet in the womb (verses 41, 44). Notice also that Elizabeth calls Mary "the mother of my Lord" (verse 43), and when Mary arrives at her home, Elizabeth is inspired by the Holy Spirit to pronounce upon Mary and her child the blessing of God (verses 41-45). The scene is beautiful and moving, but it also has polemic force against those who followed John and claimed him to be the Messiah.

Second, Luke's theological achievement is the announcement of the eschatological reversal which will fulfill God's ancient promise to the children of Abraham (verses 46-55).

Two women, both chosen to be servants of God, meet in the hill country of Judah. One is old and barren and the birth of her son will continue the stories of God's favor as told in the births of Isaac, Samson, and Samuel. But the Magnificat, based on Hannah's song in I Samuel 2:1-10 is not sung by Elizabeth as might be expected, but by the one who is young, still in her virginity. Elizabeth's son symbolizes continuity with the old, but Mary's son is God's new and unique act. Through Mary's child shall come the promised reversal of fortunes: the weak, the poor, the humble, and the hungry shall be exalted, filled, freed, and blessed.

The firmness of faith that this shall occur is expressed in the uses of the past tense in Mary's song. To speak and act as though God had already fulfilled a promise is to join memory and hope in the creation of a way of life appropriate to the people of God.

Holy Cross, September 14

Numbers 21:4b-9; Psalm 98:1-5 or Psalm 78:1-2, 34-38;
I Corinthians 1:18-24; John 3:13-17

Numbers 21:4*b*-9

The imagery is strange and striking, with all the appearances of "folly" (I Cor. 1:1): Jesus lifted up on the cross "as Moses lifted up the serpent in the wilderness" (John 3:14). However, when we examine more closely the story of the serpent in the wilderness, the meaning of the metaphor and the theological logic of the New Testament typology become apparent. The selection from Psalm 78 is the more direct response to the Old Testament reading itself. Psalm 98:1-5 celebrates God's victory and vindication of the faithful.

The larger context of Numbers 21:4*b*-9 is the account of Israel's wandering in the wilderness, the period between the Exodus from Egypt and the entrance into the land (Exod. 13:17–Deut. 34). The account of the covenant at Mount Sinai (Exod. 19:1–Num. 10:10) is a distinct episode in the story. When ancient Israel handed down the tradition of the wandering in the wilderness, two themes were emphasized, God's gracious care for the people and their rebellion by murmuring against the Lord. They expressed the tradition both in the narratives of the Pentateuch and in cultic songs such as Psalm 78, which emphasizes the people's rebellion and God's forgiveness. Some prophets remember the period as one of faithfulness (Jer. 2:2-3) and others stress Israel's disobedience (Ezek. 20:10-26).

If we have followed the people of Israel through the wilderness, the pattern of events about to unfold in Numbers 21:4*b*-9 will already be a familiar one. The people complain about the lack of food or water or both, addressing their words "against" God and Moses (verse 4). The Lord responds either with food and water (Exod. 14:10-31; 16; 17:1-7) or with anger and punishment (Num. 21:4-34; 14; 21:4-9). In the latter instances Moses intercedes and the people are spared the full effects of the divine wrath. In either case the problem is resolved for the moment and the people move on toward the promised land.

The reason for the complaint is not entirely clear. On the one hand the people say, "There is no food and no water." On the other they "loathe this worthless food" (verse 5). The latter may be an objection to the manna—after all it looked like bdellium and tasted like coriander seed (Num. 11:6-7)— or a complaint about the boredom of wilderness fare. In any case, the important fact is that they spoke against God and Moses, "Why have you brought us up out of Egypt to die in the wilderness?" That amounts to rejection of their election and of God's saving work on their behalf.

God's response is to send death–dealing "fiery serpents" among them. (NEB, taking the name as a reference to the reptile's bite, translates "poisonous snakes.") Deuteronomy 8:15-16 lists "fiery serpents and scorpions" along with the need for water and manna as the Lord's means of testing the people in the wilderness.

Next (verse 7) the people appear before Moses to confess their sin and implore him to pray to the Lord on their behalf that he take away the dangerous snakes, and he intercedes for them.

Note that the Lord does not grant the prayer. Instead of taking away the serpents the Lord instructs Moses to make a "fiery serpent, and set it on a pole; and every one who is bitten, when he sees it, shall live" (verse 8). Moses follows the instructions by making a "bronze serpent" and setting it on a pole, and it has the promised effects (verse 9).

The bronze snake must reflect the ancient idea that an image of a dangerous animal could serve as protection against it. Moreover, the snake as a symbol for healing is well-known. But does not the construction and use of this image violate the second commandment (Exod. 20:4)? Furthermore, the term translated "serpent" here occurs in Isaiah's vision in the temple as the name for the six-winged creatures (Isa. 6). Second Kings 18:4 reports that King

Hezekiah, as part of the purification of worship, destroyed "the bronze serpent that Moses had made," obviously because it had become the object of idolatry. That interpretation is quite different from Numbers 21:4*b*-9, in which the bronze figure is not an idol but the means by which God heals the people.

Perhaps the most important theological dimension of this passage is the understanding of the relationship between sin, punishment, and the divine response. When the people confess their sin, the death-dealing snakes are not removed. The effects of rebellion still are present with them. God responds, however, with the gift of life in the midst of death. The stricken Israelites have only to look at the figure on the pole to be healed. Presumably they still have the scars and pain, but they do not die. That paradigm, not just the elevation of the snake on the pole, must lie behind the Johannine typology (John 3:14).

Psalm 98:1-5

This text is one of the enthronement psalms (93–99) which were used in the fall festival as part of the ritual reenthronement of Yahweh. The festival celebrated, as the psalm proclaims, the triumph and reign of Yahweh as king. In the first five verses of the psalm emphasis falls on the victorious triumph of God (verses 1-3), which is paralleled in the triumph of Christ on the cross, and on the call to praise (verses 4-5), which is paralleled in the cross as the exaltation of Christ.

The term "victory" is repeated three times in the opening three verses. The victory of God is declared to be (1) the consequence of his power symbolized by his right hand and holy arm, (2) his vindication among the nations or the establishment of his status and reputation among the peoples of the world, and (3) the manifestation of his love and fidelity to Israel. God himself, the nations of the world, and all his chosen people are thus seen as involved in the divine victory.

The response to the victory of God is human praise. Verses 4-5 call upon the world to respond in song and sound with voice and instrument.

Psalm 78:1-2, 34-38

This psalm is a long composition offering a recital of the historical epochs of Israel's past. The following epochs are covered: (1) the patriarchal period (verses 5-11), (2) the Exodus and wilderness wanderings (verses 12-53), (3) the settlement in the land of Canaan (verses 54-66), and (4) the election of David and Zion. These epochs and the events associated with them are used as points of departure for preaching and proclamation. In this psalm, most of the past is interpreted as times of disobedience and is utilized to engender a sense of guilt and shame on those addressed in the psalm.

The two sections selected for this lection are part of the introduction (verses 1-2) and a portion of the psalmist's interpretation and preaching on the wilderness theme (verses 34-38). The opening verses present the historical synopsis and interpretation that follow as a teaching or a parable, that is, not as a pure recital of history but as an interpretative reading of the past intended to speak to the present.

Verses 34-38 are a portion of the homily on Israel's behavior in the wilderness. Although cared for, preserved, and fed in the desert, the Hebrews are described as having constantly sinned. The people are depicted as demurring and demanding, unappreciative and uncooperative. Over and over again, God has to act to reprimand them. Verses 34-38 proclaim two things about the people. (1) They were not repentant until they were punished; they did not turn toward God until God had turned against them. Their repentance was the product of divine coercion. (2) Their devotion was superficial and temporary. Their mouths and their tongues were committed to religious expression, not their hearts. Flattery and lies not fidelity and loyalty were their hallmarks.

In spite of the people's behavior and their transient faith, they depicted God as their refuge and redeemer (verse 35). Long-suffering and forbearing, God forgave and did not destroy; he withheld his anger and did not give vent to his wrath (verse 38).

I Corinthians 1:18-24

Since I Corinthians 1:18-31 serves as the epistolary lection for Tuesday of Holy Week, the reader may wish to consult the remarks made about it in the previous volume *Lent, Holy Week, Easter*. Even so, for a special day of celebration devoted to the cross, this passage from Paul is singularly appropriate since it is a *locus classicus* for his theology of the cross. As he remarks later in writing to the Corinthian church, "Jesus Christ and him crucified" formed the center of his proclamation (I Cor. 2:2). Nor did this serve merely as the object of his preaching. As is well-known, the "crucified Christ" became the mold into which he cast his own personal existence, so much so that he could claim that he had been "crucified with Christ" (Gal. 2:20). It is not as if Christ's death on the cross served as some external model over against which he patterned his life, although this was true to a certain extent. Rather, the language here is that of true participation. He has actually reenacted the crucifixion in his own life, not as an event that occurred "back there" in his conversion, but an act that continued to shape his identity and apostolic vocation (II Cor. 4:7-12).

Central to today's epistolary reading is Paul's claim that the message of the cross is folly (verse 18). In Paul's own experience, he found this message disquieting and unnerving to Jews and Greeks alike. The former saw it as a "stumbling block," the latter as "folly" (verse 23). For most first-century Jews, a crucified Messiah was not only a contradiction in terms, but a violation of Scripture. When they read Deuteronomy 21:22-23, they concluded that to be hung on a tree was a sure sign of criminality. They could draw no other conclusion than that "Jesus crucified" bore the stigma of scriptural condemnation. Quite simply, he died under the curse of the Torah. Greeks, by contrast, found the message incredible, not because of troubling passages from the Hebrew Scriptures but because they had difficulty reconciling the message of a crucified hero with their expectations of savior-figures. To be sure, many of them saw the death of Socrates as a noble death for a noble cause. And they also knew myths of dying and rising gods from the

280

mystery religions. Even so, the death of a Jewish messianic pretender did not strike them as particularly commendable as an event in and through which they might experience salvation and eternal life.

This, at least, was Paul's own experience. Yet he saw the consistent rejection of his preaching of the "crucified Christ" as a clear instance of human presumption. For him, it was an unassailable axiom of faith that in Christ God had acted to justify humanity. This, after all, was his own saving experience. Above all else, Paul had experienced God in Christ (II Cor. 5:19). For anyone to interpret the Christ-event otherwise was to call God into question. Consequently, in our passage Paul assails God's detractors as those who would dare to put God in the dock. How can humans subject God to a test (verse 20)?

What emerges is Paul's understanding of the cross as paradox. Ostensibly, it looks foolish. But, to whom? To human beings who pretend to be wise. Yet, true wisdom is God's domain, and it is revealed in this instance in what appears to be an act of consummate folly. But so be it, for it is precisely in such unexpected ways that God has acted in the past. The Corinthians' own conversion was perhaps the most immediate example of this, for they had very little to commend themselves before God, yet God performed the miracle of creation in them (verses 26-31).

Paul recognizes full well that for one to see the cross as a display of God's wisdom is a confessional act. It is the power of God "to us who are being saved" (verse 18). It presupposes that we are "called" (verse 24). Then, as now, the best perspective on the cross is found by those who have experienced saving power through the crucified God.

John 3:13-17

The preacher may wish to review the comments on the Gospel lection for Trinity Sunday (John 3:1-17), not only to see our text in its larger literary and theological setting but also to be reminded of the difficulties in dividing the Fourth Gospel into discrete units for preaching. To what extent such problems are shared in a sermon is a matter of purpose, need, and individual capacity; after all, the proclamation of the cross does not wait on the settling of a centuries-old debate among scholars. However, the proclamation of the cross suffers at the hands of the preacher who does not struggle with the difficulties the text may offer.

It is reasonable and supportable to say that today's lection consists of three sub-units: verse 13; verses 14-15; verses 16-17. Verse 13 concludes the conversation with Nicodemus in which two radically different perspectives are described as "of heaven" and "of earth." Jesus calls for a birth from above and Nicodemus thinks of the physical impossibility of being born again. Jesus grounds his qualification to speak of heavenly things (verse 12) with the claim that he alone is of heaven, having descended and ascended (verse 13). To speak of having ascended in the past tense is momentarily disconcerting since the statement is in a pre-resurrection context. However, John's Gospel presents Christian preaching after the fact and the text here and elsewhere has already assumed the tenses appropriate to that preaching.

Verses 14-15 make a self-contained statement about the ways in which Christ's redemptive act is analogous to the event of the bronze serpent recorded in Numbers 21:4b-9. In that story, people suffering under God's punishment for sin are granted relief and given life if they will look in faith upon the elevated serpent. The analogy is clear enough. However, it must be remembered that in John's Gospel, the lifting up of Christ refers not only to the manner of his death (12:32-33) but also to his ascension to God. In both Numbers 21 and John 3, God is presented as gracious, taking the initiative for human redemption.

Verses 16-17 begin the theological summary that extends through verse 21. This is but one of many such summaries following conversations and signs in this Gospel. In this and all the summaries the subject is God. Nicodemus and all of us need to understand that the purpose of Christ's coming is not to help us become successful in religion but to know God. And the God revealed in the Son is a God who loves, who loves the whole world, who desires none to perish but that all have life eternal. God does not simply wish this; God sends the only Son to offer life as a gift. In continuing to make this

282

appeal to the world, God not only has to counter the forces and structures of evil, but also sometimes has to contradict preachers who are trapped in the Jonah syndrome, announcing condemnation even after God has "repented," embraced the penitent, and granted new life.

All Saints, November 1, or on First Sunday in November

Revelation 21:1-6a; Psalm 24:1-6; Colossians 1:9-14; John 11:32-44

Revelation 21:1-6*a*

On All Saints Day, we remember those who have preceded us in the life of faith. We recall their noble lives as examples of courage and fidelity and celebrate the heavenly hope to which they aspired. In doing so, we find ourselves linked with them as sharers of a common hope and destiny.

This first reading sketches the eschatological vision of a "new heaven and new earth." It is a vision that has captured the imagination of saints in every century. They have been drawn to it and motivated by it, as we are. If the first reading speaks of the heavenly Jerusalem, Psalm 24 speaks primarily of the earthly Jerusalem as it confesses God as the Creator of the earth and calls for a life of uprightness and holiness as a prerequisite for entering the temple. This theme of moral rectitude is continued in the epistolary reading from Colossians 1:9-14 which calls us to a "life worthy of the Lord," lived with "endurance and patience with joy." The epistolary reading also makes explicit our sharing in "the inheritance of the saints." In recounting the story of the raising of Lazarus, the Gospel reading brings to the fore themes of resurrection and eternal life.

The vision of "a new heaven and a new earth" in 21:1-6*a* should not be viewed in isolation. It is only one in a series of visions in which the seer has been shown the victorious Christ (19:11-21), the binding of Satan and the millennial reign of the martyrs (20:1-6), the loosing of Satan and the Great Assize (20:7-15). Today's passage is actually the first segment of the lengthy vision of the new Jerusalem (21:1–22:5). This broader literary context is worth noting since today's passage makes no explicit mention of the saints who inhabit the new Jerusalem. They are in view, however, as the larger context makes clear. The seer has been shown those saints martyred for the faith who have been raised to share in the millennial reign (20:4-6). He also describes the inhabitants of the new Jerusalem as "those who are written in the Lamb's book of life" (21:27).

The vision opens with a cosmic transformation in which the "first heaven and the first earth" have "passed away" (verse 21; cf. II Pet. 3:7). In apocalyptic thought, the created order is subject to the more powerful sway of the divine will and may be said to "vanish" or "flee" (6:14; 16:20; 20:11). But even in the pictorial language of the Psalms the created order is similarly viewed (Ps. 114:3, 7). The disappearance of the sea indicates that it is a complete transformation. The primeval waters that serve as the home of dragons and beasts no longer separate heaven and earth (13:1; 17:1). This vision of the new heaven and earth is informed by the prophetic vision of Isaiah (65:17-18; 66:22).

Descending from heaven is "the holy city, the new Jerusalem" (verse 2; cf. 3:12; also Gal. 4:26; Heb. 11:16; 12:22). It became proverbial to speak of Jerusalem as "the holy city" (Isa. 48:2; Dan. 9:24; Neh. 11:1, 18; Matt. 4:5; 27:53; Rev. 11:2; 21:10; 22:19). So closely was the city identified with Israel itself, that the city could virtually signify the people of God whose character was expected to be consonant with the holy character of the city itself (Isa. 52:1). This emphasis on moral purity as a prerequisite for admission to the temple is seen in today's psalm. To compare the "holy city" with "a bride adorned for her husband" only serves to reinforce this image of wholeness and purity. It also introduces the image of the messianic feast, which is frequently used as an eschatological image (19:9, 17; 21:9; Matt. 9:15; 18:23; 22:2; Isa. 61:10).

The reference to "the voice from the throne" recalls an earlier vision where God sits enthroned on a "great white throne" (20:11; cf. 16:7; 19:5). The message of the voice is that God's presence is now fully realized. God's dwelling, or literally his "tent," is now pitched "with men," thereby fulfilling Old Testament hopes (Lev. 26:11-12; Ezek. 37:27; I Kings 8:27; also Zech. 2:13; cf. John 1:14; Rev. 13:6). To experience the full presence of God is to become identified as "God's people" (Isa. 8:10; Jer. 31:1; Ps. 95:7).

Especially striking about this "new world" is what is not there: tears, death, mourning, crying, pain (verse 4). Each of these should be understood as having specific reference to the martyrs who have been mentioned earlier (cf. 7:17). Yet, this eschatological vision also expresses the realization of prophetic hopes (Isa. 25:8; Jer. 31:16).

In the final words of today's lection, the seer is reassured that this is a genuinely new reality: "Behold, I make all things new" (verse 5). The new creation begun in the Christ-event (II Cor. 5:17) has now come to full fruition. He is also assured that these revelatory words are "trustworthy and true" (verse 5). This has been the confident hope of every believer who has lived and died for the faith. Finally, there is the declaration, "It is done!" The work of God has now been completed fully and finally. And the one who has brought history to its end is "the Alpha and the Omega, the beginning and the end" (verse 6). To speak of God in this way is more than a claim that God brackets time and history on both ends. It is rather a way of saying that God is both the source and purpose of history.

As we have seen, today's text has in mind in particular the saints who have been martyred for the faith. On All Saints Day we remember the acts of Christian martyrs, as well as the deeds and works of "canonized" saints. But we also celebrate the lives of all the faithful, living and dead, for whom the new Jerusalem is their ultimate destiny. The words of the preface in the festal Mass are especially appropriate: "Today we keep the festival of your holy city, the heavenly Jerusalem, our mother. Around your throne the saints, our brothers and sisters, sing your praise for ever. Their glory fills us with joy, and their communion with us in your Church gives us inspiration and strength as we hasten on our pilgrimage of faith, eager to meet them." (Cited in A. Adam, *The Liturgical Year* [New York: Pueblo, 1981], 229.)

Psalm 24:1-6

This psalm has been previously discussed in this volume (see Proper 8, pages 63-65). Its connection with All Saints

Day is made possible by a certain spiritualizing and Christianizing of the text.

Verses 1-6 of the psalm were part of an entrance liturgy used when the doors to the temple precincts were opened to allow entry of pilgrims who had come to Jerusalem to celebrate a festival. The employment of this text on All Saints Day can be seen in the following associations: (1) The object of entry, the temple precincts, referred to in the psalm as the "hill of the Lord" and "his holy place" (verse 3), is understood as the abode of God or the other world, the heavenly destiny, (2) those entering are understood to be the deceased, the dead who were entering the other world, and (3) the ethical requirements for entering the temple (in verse 4) are interpreted as the ethical standards by which the dead are judged.

As we noted earlier in discussing this text at Proper 8, Psalm 24 was used in the early church for understanding Jesus' descent into Hades. In addition, the psalm was also utilized as an interpretive text for expounding his ascent into heaven. It may have been this latter usage that was then adopted to the "entry" of the saints into the heavenly world of glory.

Colossians 1:9-14

In the context of All Saints Day, our attention naturally focuses on that part of today's epistolary lection that mentions "the inheritance of the saints" (verse 12). Before looking at this intriguing phrase, we should first notice that our passage is a continuation of the prayer of thanksgiving begun in verse 3. As he frequently does in his other letters, Paul mentions his unceasing prayers in behalf of his readers (verse 9; cf. Phil. 1:4; I Cor. 1:4; I Thess. 1:2; 2:13; II Thess. 1:3; Eph. 5:20; Philem. 4). Even though the church at Colossae was not established by Paul himself, but by Epaphras, one of his fellow workers (1:7; 4:12), Paul loved it no less than one of his own churches. Thus the tone of the entire prayer is one of genuine pastoral concern. In fact, it should be read as a pastoral prayer in which the beloved apostle thanks God for

287

the faith, love, and hope of the Colossians (1:4-5) and makes specific requests to God for their spiritual welfare.

So applicable are these requests to our own needs that they are worth noting.

1. He requests that they be filled with knowledge of the divine will (verse 9; cf. Luke 12:47; Acts 22:14; Rom. 2:18; James 4:17).

2. He asks that the knowledge they receive surpass that of the Gnostic heretics against whom the letter is addressed by being grounded in "all spiritual wisdom and understanding" (verse 9; Eph. 1:9). This distinction between knowledge and wisdom/understanding should be noted. It is one thing to know, quite another to be wise in understanding. But what is especially called for here is spiritual discernment.

3. His hope is that they will "lead a life worthy of the Lord" (verse 10). Literally, the Greek reads "to walk worthily of the Lord." Of course, the term "walk" is metaphorical and designates one's way of life. But what is important here is that the direction of one's walk is determined not by oneself, but by the Lord (cf. I Thess. 2:12; Eph. 4:1; Phil. 1:27). It is the Lord, both the Lord's will and holy character, that provides the standard by which we lead our lives. Our aim, simply put, is to be "fully pleasing to him," or to lead "a life acceptable to him in all its aspects" (JB).

The direction and shape of this way of life is made clear. It involves "bearing fruit in every good work," which suggests that the spiritual wisdom and understanding mentioned earlier are not merely intellectual attributes but passions of the heart that lead us to act in behalf of others (cf. II Cor. 9:8; Eph. 2:10; II Thess. 2:17; II Tim. 3:17; Tit. 2:14). But, the "life worthy of the Lord" also has its intellectual side. It is not merely Christian praxis, for Paul wants the Colossians to be "increasing in the knowledge of God" (verse 10). "Knowledge," as used here, is not the acquiring of factual information, although this is not excluded. Its object is God, whom we both know and experience. What is clear from this prayer is that the Christian "walk" is a lifelong education in coming to know God (cf. II Pet. 1:2, 8; 2:2; 3:18).

4. He asks that they "be strengthened with all power" (verse 11; cf. Eph. 1:18-19; 3:16). He requests this, knowing

that such a life will require "endurance and patience" (verse 11; cf. Rom. 5:1-5). The temptation will be to become weakened in our resolve, and even to despair (cf. Gal. 6:9). This particular request is well worth remembering on All Saints Day as we recall the host of faithful servants of God who have preceded us in the life of faith, and especially those who have endured uncommonly difficult circumstances. We think first perhaps of the early Christian martyrs, beginning with Stephen (Acts 7) and including many others, such as Polycarp who died a noble death in the second century.

5. He asks that they joyfully give thanks to God (verse 12). Here, he is asking them to adopt the same disposition of thanksgiving and gratitude as he has done in their behalf (verse 3). But it is the reason for which they are asked to give thanks that we should note: because God has "qualified us to share in the inheritance of the saints in light" (verse 12). Since this phrase makes today's passage particularly appropriate for All Saints Day, we should examine it with some care.

One question the interpreter will need to decide is whether the "inheritance" that is mentioned is present or future. Read one way, the passage seems to say that God has made it possible for us, who have embodied the qualities mentioned earlier in the prayer, to have a share in the heavenly inheritance that is still future for us, but already realized by the faithful people of God who have preceded us in death. Read another way, it looks as if Paul is speaking of something that we already enjoy, here and now. This seems to be reflected more clearly in other translations: "Thanking the Father who has made it possible for you to join the saints and with them to inherit the light" (JB), or, "And to give thanks to the Father who has made you fit to share the heritage of God's people in the realm of light" (NEB). Another rendering is provided by C. F. D. Moule, "Giving thanks to the Father who has qualified you to take your share in the territory allotted to God's people—that realm of light."

We should remember that "saints" is a common New Testament designation for Christians, calling attention to their special status as "dedicated ones" (I Cor. 1:2; Rom. 1:7; Acts 2:21). And it is just that: a statement about status rather than character. It is a status that we have been given, not one that we deserve. Thus, what Paul seems to be saying is that the Colossians should be grateful that they were enabled to become full-fledged members of the people of God (cf. Eph. 2:11-13). As the following verses make clear, our transfer from "the power of darkness" into light where we participate fully in "the kingdom of his beloved Son" (verse 13) has already occurred.

Even if the text is fundamentally a statement about our participation with the saints now rather than later, it is no less suitable for reflection on All Saints Day. For one thing, the text as a whole lays out a virtual profile of behavior for those saints, canonized or non-canonized, who have distinguished themselves for "walking worthily of the Lord." In addition, the text still holds out the possibility that much lies ahead of us, both in terms of growth in the knowledge of God and endurance in the face of resistance. This should caution us against a false confidence that the kingdom of God is fully ours here and now. It is both a life and a legacy. We live in it but still look forward to it.

John 11:32-44

The celebration of All Saints Day reminds us that God is a God of the living and not of the dead. Texts appropriate to that affirmation announce resurrection, life eternal, and the inheritance of the faithful among the saints in light. For this reason, we return to the Gospel that proclaims Jesus as the resurrection and the life and to the chapter of that Gospel which says this most dramatically.

John 11:32-44 is the story of the raising of Lazarus, but the story begins in 11:1, and so a review of the entire account is necessary for understanding today's text. Even in the sermon proper the preacher would do well to move the listener through the entire drama. Sometimes we assume that people recall more of a biblical story than they in fact do. But even so, those familiar with a text appreciate being confirmed in what they know. Such a recital would be especially appropriate to John 11:1-44 because, even though this is one of the many sign stories, this one is unique in a literary sense. In the preceding sign stories the pattern is fairly consistent: the sign is performed, followed by a discourse or dispute. Here, however, the sign comes at the end after the gradual heightening of dramatic tension.

To say that John 11:32-44 is part of a sign story is to say that Jesus will act according to "his time" and not in response to requests or pressure ("he stayed two days longer in the place where he was" verse 6) (Recall Jesus' response to his mother at Cana, 2:4). Being a sign also means that what Jesus does will be a revelatory act, an act making God known. In this case, we are told that what is to transpire will be for the glory of God (verse 4). But the reader is also told that the event that follows will result in the glorifying of the Son of God (verse 4). This is Johannine language for the elevation of Jesus upon the cross and his exaltation to the presence of God (12:23-26, 32). In other words, Jesus' act in relation to Lazarus will effect Jesus' own death which, in fact, was the case according to 11:45-57. Neither Mary (verse 32) nor Martha (verse 21) could, of course, know the price that Jesus would pay for raising their brother. They could not know that this act would set in motion the political machinery for Jesus' death (verses 47-48; 12:9-11), that Lazarus' release from the tomb would mean Jesus had to enter it.

But the reader knows, being given clues all along, not only in verse 4 but in the story itself: a tomb near Jerusalem; the tomb a cave covered by a large stone; the stone rolled away; Jesus troubled; Jesus cried out; the grave cloth. In fact, the descriptions of Jesus as "deeply moved and troubled" (verse 33), weeping (verse 35), and "deeply moved again" (verse 38) may be understood as a Johannine Gethsemane, all evidences of agony or grief being absent in John's account of the garden scene itself. Because this is a sign narrative, therefore, the reader knows that the text is not dealing only with a family crisis in Bethany but with the crisis of the world, not only with the death and resurrection of Lazarus but with the death and resurrection of Jesus, not only with what two sisters want but with what the world needs. Jesus will give life not to Lazarus alone but to all who believe.

The key to the entire narrative was stated in the words of Jesus to Martha: "I am the resurrection and the life; he who believes in me, though he die, yet shall he live, and whoever lives and believes in me shall never die" (verses 25-26). Martha expressed faith in a resurrection at the end time (verse 24), but obviously thinking of eternal life only in terms of the hereafter was small comfort to her in a time of grief. Jesus not only corrects her faith but enlarges her hope by moving eternal life from the end time alone to the time of faith in Christ. Christ is the eschatological event, he is the point where death ends and life begins, he provides life on both sides of the grave, here and hereafter. But the story does not have its fulfillment when the sign is understood. Jesus did not ask Martha, "Do you understand this?" Rather he asked her what the entire Gospel asks the reader (20:31): "Do you *believe* this?"

Thanksgiving Day

Joel 2:21-27; Psalm 126; I Timothy 2:1-7; Matthew 6:25-33

Joel 2:21-27

All the texts for this day can help the worshiping community express its thanks to God. Joel 2:21-27 calls for rejoicing and celebration in view of God's promises, including material blessings such as food to eat. Moreover, the Lord promises to be present with the people. The psalm, though not one of thanksgiving, contains harvest motifs. It is a prayer that those who sow in tears shall reap in joy, "bringing his sheaves with him" (verse 6). First Timothy 2:1-7 exhorts the faithful to offer prayers, including ones of thanksgiving, for kings and others in high places, in order "that we may lead a quiet and peaceful life" (verse 2). The Gospel lection contains the teaching of Jesus about anxiety for food and clothing.

The Book of Joel is a liturgical work in two parts. In the first part (Joel 1:2–2:17) the prophet directs the community to convene a service of complaint and petition to God, initially because of the threat of a plague of locusts (1:4-20) and then because of the terrifying prospect of the Day of the Lord. In the second part (Joel 2:18–3:21) the mood changes dramatically because the people have repented. God promises salvation and over and over again assures the people that their prayers have been heard. The Day of the Lord has become a day of salvation because the people trust in their God.

While there is no superscription that dates the book, the political and religious references fit the Persian period, probably about 400 B.C. Joel is an example of a prophet who participated directly, and probably in an officially recognized

293

fashion, in the services of worship in the second temple. We hear him giving the call to prayer and fasting, ordering the priests to gather the people, giving instructions in proper prayer, and then proclaiming the divine response to the people's genuine contrition.

In terms of form, the passage before us is a series of announcements of salvation. In verses 21-23 the prophet is the speaker, proclaiming words of assurance to nature. The land itself is called to rejoice. Then (verse 24) similar calls to celebrate are spoken to the people because God has given the rain. Verses 24-25 amount to a reversal of the bad fortune described in the first part of the book. The Lord promises that there will be plenty of grain, wine, and oil, and that he will restore the losses caused by the locusts. In a final announcement of salvation (verses 26-27) the bounty of nature is related to the joy of worship and the continuing presence of God among the people. When all these things happen, the people will be assured that there is no other God but Yahweh.

On the occasion of Thanksgiving, this reading calls attention to the bounty of nature—the land, animals, pastures, trees, vines, rain—and provides the language for celebration in humble thanks. Experience confirms that there are countless reasons for thanks. But even more, it calls attention to the God from whom we receive all things necessary for life. With the material gifts comes the presence of the Giver, the very one who made and sustains all those things. In that way it coincides with the reading from Matthew: "Seek first his kingdom and his righteousness . . ." (Matt. 6:33).

Psalm 126

This psalm has been previously discussed in the present volume (see Proper 25, pages 226-27). A few comments at this point will be made about the possible use of this psalm in connection with Thanksgiving. The selection of this psalm for this season of the year is based on the psalm's employment of harvest imagery.

The polarities found in the psalm—weeping-shouting, tears-joy, going forth-coming home, sowing-reaping—might be the departure point for developing a sermon. Thanksgiving, of course, embodies one of the poles of human existence, namely joy and extravagance. In a way, all festival times should be periods when normal sentiments and feelings are heightened, intensified, and celebrated to the breaking point. For example, the two dominant characteristics of the Thanksgiving Season are a thankful spirit and a gluttonous indulgence. At this season, we intensify our sense of being dependent and therefore thankful for life's gifts and we gorge our appetites and stuff our stomachs. Both activities are quite appropriate—they are the way in which we interrupt the ordinary flow of life with the insertion of the extraordinary. Tears, sowing, going forth, weeping are pushed into the background and we give full vent to the other pole of human existence. In preaching from this text, the minister should find ways to affirm both the thanksgiving and the extravagance of the season.

I Timothy 2:1-7

This epistolary lection has been chosen as a text for Thanksgiving Day because it urges "thanksgivings" as one form of prayer to be offered on behalf of "all men" (verse 1). Actually, this passage is part of a larger set of instructions concerning the protocol of Christian worship, and it should be read beside other passages urging us to be vigilant and constant in prayer (Acts 2:42; Rom. 12:12; Eph. 6:18; Phil. 4:6; Col. 4:2; I Thess. 5:17). By including "thanksgivings" with "supplications, prayers, [and] intercessions," today's text teaches us that in prayer, we must learn not only to ask but also to acknowledge.

What is striking about these instructions is that they urge us to cast our net widely as we pray. We are instructed to pray "for all men" (verse 1), or put more felicitously, "for everyone" (JB). In its insistence that we pray for all of humanity, our text recognizes that we tend to pray for our own kind and thus urges that we break through such narrowness. And why should Christian prayers be concerned for all humanity? Because this is the scope of God's concern. God, after all, "wants everyone to be saved and reach full knowledge of the truth" (verse 4 JB). As the prophet Ezekiel put it, God takes no pleasure in the death of the wicked (Ezek. 18:23, 32; 33:11; cf. Wisd. 11:26). Or, in the words of Second Peter, God wants no one to perish (II Pet. 3:9; cf. Rom. 11:32).

To clinch his point, it looks as if the author cites part of a primitive Christian confession in verses 5-6 (cf. Nestle, 26th ed., although not printed strophically in RSV, NEB, JB). If these words are creedal, we are reminded that what we confess in worship bears this out, namely that "there is only one God, and . . . only one mediator between God and humankind, himself a man, Jesus Christ, who sacrificed himself as a ransom for them all. He is the evidence of this, sent at the appointed time" (verses 5-6 JB). At the heart of our faith are exclusive claims: one God (I Cor. 8:4, 6; 12:5-16; Rom. 3:30; Eph. 4:5-6; Mal. 2:10), and one mediator, Christ Jesus (Heb. 8:6; 9:15; 12:24). Yet their saving grace is all-embracing, for God through Christ intended to ransom all (Matt. 20:28 and parallels; II Cor. 5:5; Gal. 1:4; 2:20; Eph. 5:2, 25; Tit. 2:14; cf. Ps. 49:8). Just as their salvation was universal in scope, so should our prayers reach beyond ourselves to all humanity.

One might notice the similarity between the sentiments of our text and the teaching of Jesus in Matthew 5:43-48. There, the point is put more sharply as Jesus challenges his disciples to love their enemies and pray for their persecutors. And why? Because God has the capacity to send sunshine and rain on the good and the bad, the just and the unjust. Like our text, Matthew insists that in deciding whom to pray for, Christians should take their cue from God.

But our text goes further in urging us to pray for "kings and all who are in high positions" (verse 2). As before, it seems to recognize that this too will be difficult for us at times because of apathy or because of passionate disagreement. In this respect, our text echoes other New Testament passages that urge us to be prayerful for civil authorities (Rom. 13:1-7; Tit. 3:1; I Pet. 2:13-15; cf. Ezra 6:10; Bar. 1:11-12; Jer. 29:7). Nor are the reasons selfless, for our text quite frankly urges this on the grounds that stable governments make it possible to "lead a quiet and peaceable life" (verse 2; cf. I Thess. 4:11; II Thess. 3:12). Obviously, we should not allow this text to blind us to the realities of corrupt governments, and we do well to balance this picture with the one in the book of Revelation where oppressive rulers are depicted as beasts to be resisted rather than gods to be obeyed.

Our text, then, opens on a note of thanksgiving, but quickly introduces to us dilemmas of our faith. We confess the one God and the one mediator Jesus Christ, and in doing so separate ourselves from those who cannot and will not confess likewise. Yet, our text will not allow us to become a Christian ghetto where we only pray to ourselves and for ourselves. As squarely as we stand within our confession, we nonetheless are bound to see beyond it. To the degree that we are able to do this, we become like God. And to this extent, we can learn to say prayers of thanksgiving.

Matthew 6:25-33

Matthew 6:25-33 is one of several units of teachings of Jesus common to Matthew and Luke but absent from Mark. Scholars have come to assume a sayings-source back of these two Gospels which is, for lack of a better term, called Q from the German *Quelle,* source. But even with a common source, each Evangelist determined the location of the sayings within his own narrative. Luke places the teachings in today's lesson at 12:22-34, immediately after the parable of the rich fool. Matthew sets them within the Sermon on the Mount immediately after sayings on earthly treasures and service to God and mammon.

This lection from Matthew consists of sayings, maxims, and proverbs and, therefore, presents Jesus as the sage, the teacher of wisdom. If the source common to Matthew and Luke portrayed Jesus primarily in the wisdom tradition, that image has been preserved more by Matthew than by Luke. That the form and to a large extent the content of this material were found among the rabbis' instructions to the faith community does not argue convincingly that these are not authentic sayings of Jesus. Matthew says that Jesus, after teaching in parables, told his disciples, "Therefore every scribe who has been trained for the kingdom of heaven is like a householder who brings out of his treasure what is new and what is old" (13:52).

Matthew provides no description of those to whom Jesus addressed these teachings about anxiety. History has proven them equally appropriate for the wealthy and the poor since anxiety about money seems to afflict both those who have it and those who do not. Since, however, the concerns here are as elementary as food and clothing, and given the general socio-economic status of Jesus' listeners, very likely he was speaking to the poor.

The subject matter is anxiety, obsessive and debilitating worry, over material things. Jesus' instruction is not overspiritualized and unrealistic. As to food, clothing, and shelter, Jesus states clearly "your heavenly Father knows that you need them all" (verse 32). What he does say, however, is that anxiety is totally futile (verse 27). Excessive worry does not solve problems, reach goals, overcome difficulties. No one by means of anxiety has added one cubit (yard) to one's life span (stature?). A more fruitful alternative is to take one's mind off oneself and look around at the bounty of God's providence. Studying the face of nature and drawing lessons from observing animals, plants, earth, and sky were characteristics common to sages and teachers of wisdom. In this case, Jesus points to birds of the air and lilies of the field, all of them free of the burdens of laboring men (toil) and women (spin) and yet fed and clothed by a God who cares for every creature. If then, argues Jesus from the lesser to the greater, God cares for birds and flowers, is it not reasonable to trust that no less care will be shown to us?

The words of Jesus on the subject of anxiety about things are of a piece with all his teaching about the kingdom. The call is for radical trust and single-minded service. That which is uncompromisingly primary is orienting one's life to the approaching reign of God (verse 33). After all, life is qualified by what one seeks. If relative, created values are made absolute, there is no release from anxiety with their attainment. The promise is impoverished in its fulfillment, and anxiety returns. But when absolute values (God's kingdom and righteousness) are made absolute, the relative values and creature needs will take their proper place, and with satisfaction. And lest seeking God's kingdom become in itself a new cause of anxiety, Luke concludes this section with, "Fear not, little flock, for it is your Father's good pleasure to give you the kingdom" (12:32).

Scripture Reading Index